Public-Private Partnerships
for Public Health

PUBLIC-PRIVATE
Partnerships for Public Health

Edited by Michael R. Reich

HARVARD SERIES ON POPULATION
AND INTERNATIONAL HEALTH

Harvard Center for
Population and Development Studies
9 Bow Street
Cambridge, Massachusetts 02138
USA

April 2002

Distributed by Harvard University Press

Library of Congress Cataloging in Publication Data

Public-private partnerships for public health / edited by Michael R. Reich.
    p.cm.-- (Harvard series on population and international health)
    Includes bibliographical references and index.
    ISBN 0-674-00865-0 (paperback)
    1. Public health. 2. Public health–Miscellanea. 3. Public-private sector cooperation I.
Reich, Michael R., 1950- II. Series.

RA427. P834 2002
362.1--dc21

                                                                    2001051916

Published by:
Harvard Center for Population and Development Studies
9 Bow Street
Cambridge, Massachusetts 02138
USA

cpds@hsph.harvard.edu

Cover and Interior design by Carol Maglitta Design

Books in the Harvard Series on Population and International Health

Public-Private Partnerships for Public Health
Edited by Michael R. Reich

Population Policies Reconsidered: Health, Empowerment, and Rights
Edited by Gita Sen, Adrienne Germain and Lincoln C. Chen

Power & Decision: The Social Control of Reproduction
Edited by Gita Sen and Rachel Snow

Health and Social Change in International Perspective
Edited by Lincoln C. Chen, Arthur Kleinman and Norma C. Ware

Assessing Child Survival Programs in Developing Countries
By Joseph J. Valadez

Contents

Preface

As we move into the twenty-first century, the face of public health is changing. Governments, international health organizations, and non-governmental organizations, once the central actors in public health initiatives, are looking to the private sector for help. At the same time, private for-profit organizations have come to realize the importance of public health goals for their immediate and long-term objectives, and to accept a broader view of social responsibility as part of the corporate mandate. Public-private partnerships are becoming a popular mode of tackling large, complicated, and expensive public health problems. The idea of partnerships for public health has emerged in national as well as international policy discussions, in both rich and poor countries. Yet the new partners in these initiatives are strangers to each other in many ways. And we are still learning about how best to manage these new partnerships. We know little about the conditions when partnerships succeed, about the strategies for structuring partnerships, or about the ethical underpinnings of partnerships.

In April 2000, the Harvard School of Public Health and the Global Health Council organized a small workshop outside Boston to examine questions about public-private partnerships in international public health. The two-day meeting brought together 50 people from diverse organizations and contrasting perspectives—international agencies, private corporations, development banks, consumer advocacy groups, private foundations, non-governmental organizations, developing country government officials, and academics of various stripes—to explore the issues raised by such partnerships, examine their problems and benefits, and address some of the critical questions being raised. The workshop was just one in a series of meetings on public-private partnerships organized by many different groups around the world in recent years. This flurry of meetings has created an international dialogue on the role of partnerships in health and development initiatives, seeking to understand how to evaluate, develop, and execute public health initiatives that involve both public and private partners.

The examples presented at our workshop all involved at least one private corporation from the pharmaceutical industry and at least one public or non-profit organization, all engaged in international public health. We focused on public-private partnerships seeking to expand the use of specific products with the potential to improve health conditions in poor countries. For the meeting, we expressly selected papers and participants to represent different views on public-private partnerships—both critics and supporters—hoping that the formal and informal conversations would advance our collective and individual thinking. The workshop thus sought to provide:

• Relevant and insightful scholarship on the issues of public-private partnerships

• An open environment to discuss critical questions about public-private partnerships

• An understanding of both the practical and theoretical dimensions of creating effective partnerships

• The creation of a shared ethical vocabulary to serve as the basis for successful partnerships in the future

This book presents the results of the workshop. The essays in this volume offer some fresh perspectives on partnerships, probe some troubling questions, and provide empirical evidence of both benefits and challenges of public-private partnerships. The participants in the meeting also achieved some progress in creating a shared vocabulary, or at least shared understanding, on points of contention, suggesting that dialogue among partisans in public health can help move debates about critical issues forward.

This volume depended on the contributions of many individuals. A. G. Breitenstein helped organize the workshop with unfailing commitment and good nature. Professor Marc Roberts, my friend and colleague for the past two decades, provided intellectual support and camaraderie at critical junctures throughout the entire project. Scott Gordon and Shoshanah Falek assisted at the workshop, ensuring that the meeting would unfold without major problems. Several colleagues reviewed chapters (some read all of them) and provided comments for authors: Marc Mitchell, Scott Gordon, Beatrice Bezmalinovic, and Diana Weil. Sarah Madsen Hardy edited the entire volume with great care and sensitivity, clarifying ideas without imposing unduly. The Global Health Council agreed to co-organize the workshop, and I appreciate the participation and support provided by the GHC's president, Nils Daulaire. Christopher Cahill, responsible for publications at the Harvard Center for Population and Development Studies, expertly guided the manuscript through its final journey to appear as a book. Finally, the authors graciously responded to my comments and queries and respected the timetables and deadlines. Reflecting on this process reminds me that the production of an edited volume is itself a partnership. While producing the book required more time than I had hoped (the nature of partnerships), the volume improved from the contributions of others and truly represents a joint product.

Finally, I express appreciation for the financial support for the workshop and the book provided by four organizations: the Edna McConnell Clark Foundation, Merck & Co., Pfizer Inc, and SmithKline Beecham (now GlaxoSmithKline). While these organizations provided funding for the meeting and are all engaged in public-private partnerships, they did not influence the selection of paper writers or topics, the content of the papers, or the agenda for the workshop. They granted us independence in organizing the meeting and stood behind our approach of inviting people with a broad range of perspectives on public-private partnerships—including people of skeptical and critical views—supporting our guarantee of an open discussion from all perspectives.

Michael R. Reich
Harvard Center for Population and Development Studies
August 2001

1

Public-Private Partnerships for Public Health

Michael R. Reich

PUBLIC-PRIVATE PARTNERSHIPS ARE AT THE TOP OF MANY AGENDAS in international public health these days. When the market fails to distribute health benefits to people who need them—especially to poor people in developing countries—partnerships between public and private organizations are often seen as offering an innovative method with a good chance of producing the desired outcomes. But these partnerships also bring their own problems and controversies. Health activists and researchers have criticized partnerships for diverting resources from public actions and distorting public agendas in ways that favor private companies. This book addresses the organizational and ethical challenges of such public-private partnerships.

Recently, many organizations in public health have established partnerships with private-sector organizations. Academic institutions have created partnerships with private companies for specific research activities, such as the development of new therapies (Blumenthal et al., 1996). The World Bank has announced that it will encourage partnerships as part of its comprehensive development framework. The director-general of the World Health Organization (WHO) called for "open and constructive relations with the private sector and industry" in her first speech after her 1998 election (WHO, 1998). Non-governmental organizations have established new relationships with private for-profit firms and with international agencies. Similar trends are apparent in other international health organizations, particularly in efforts to expand access to drugs and vaccines in poor countries ("The need for public-private partnerships," 2000; Harrison, 1999; Reich, 2000; Smith, 2000). In the United States, "hundreds of millions of dollars" have been invested to promote partnerships around health issues, creating "thousands of alliances, coalitions, consortia and other health partnerships" (Lasker, Weiss & Miller, 2001, p. 179).

But why have public-private partnerships become so prominent at this time? One reason is that public health problems are being pushed onto the international policy agenda, with a rise in advocacy by non-governmental organizations that have gained increasing influence over the past two decades. Globalization processes have promoted the growth and influence of non-governmental organizations in international health (Brown et al., 2000). An example is the campaign by Médecins Sans Frontières to expand access to essential drugs. At the same time, private foundations in the United States have assumed an increasingly active role in creating and supporting public-private partnerships, exemplified by the grants from the Bill and Melinda Gates Foundation, the Rockefeller Foundation, and the Edna McConnell Clark Foundation. The problems addressed by partnerships often involve issues of health equity between the rich and the poor of the world. With globalization, new technologies come quickly to market and spread across rich countries, while the persistent lack of access in poor countries creates a stark and tragic contrast. This gap in access can create dramatic differences in morbidity and mortality, as shown by the unequal access to anti-AIDS drugs in the 1990s.

Yet neither public nor private organizations are capable of resolving such problems on their own. Traditional public health groups are confronted by limited financial resources, complex social and behavioral problems, rapid disease transmission across national boundaries, and reduced state capabilities. At the same time, private for-profit organizations have come to recognize the importance of public health goals for their immediate and long-term objectives, and to accept a broader view of social responsibility as part of the corporate mandate. Pharmaceutical companies, for example, have become involved in a number of high-visibility drug donation programs based on partnerships (see table 2.1). In short, both public and private actors are being driven towards each other, with some amount of uneasiness, in order to accomplish common or overlapping objectives. In the United States, public and private funding agencies have promoted partnerships in public health on the assumption that they would "enable different people and organizations to support each other by leveraging, combining, and capitalizing on their complementary strengths and capabilities" (Lasker, Weiss & Miller, 2001, p. 180).

Yet we know little about the conditions when partnerships succeed. Partnerships can produce innovative strategies and positive consequences for well-defined public health goals, and they can create powerful mechanisms for addressing difficult problems by leveraging the ideas, resources, and expertise of different partners. At the same time, the rules of the game for public-private partnerships are fluid and ambiguous. Since no single formula exists, constructing an effective partnership requires substantial effort and risk. How then do organizations with different values, interests, and worldviews come together to address and resolve essential public health issues? What are the criteria for evaluating the success of public-private partnerships? Who sets these criteria, and with what kinds of accountability and transparency?

This book is organized to address these questions as follows: This introductory chapter summarizes the major issues reflected in the papers presented and ensuing discussion at the workshop held in April 2000 (organized by the Harvard School of Public Health and the Global Health Council). Chapter 2 provides two illustrative examples of public-private partnerships. Chapters 3 and 4 examine successful partnerships, and chapter 5 looks at a troubled partnership and the lessons learned. The final two chapters present differing perspectives on the role of private corporations in partnerships. Chapter 6 argues that private corporations have an ethical obligation to engage in partnerships for health improvement in poor countries, while chapter 7 argues that such partnerships are likely to have a negative impact on United Nations organizations and, therefore, should be strictly regulated and monitored.

Defining Partnerships

What is a public-private partnership? A good working definition would include three points. First, these partnerships involve at least one private for-profit organization and at least one not-for-profit or public organization. Second, the partners have some shared objectives for the creation of social value, often for disadvantaged populations. Finally, the core partners agree to share both efforts and benefits.

But this working definition contains many ambiguities, raising important questions and issues. One set of questions focuses on the nature of public and private. What is public? What is private? The public sector category certainly includes national governments and international agencies (such as WHO and the World Bank). And the private sector category certainly includes for-profit corporations. But where do international non-governmental organizations (NGOs) fit? Organizations such as Médecins Sans Frontières and Helen Keller International are private in the sense that they do not belong to a governmental structure, yet they seek to promote public interests. These non-governmental organizations belong to civil society, a third sector (in addition to the public and private sectors), and are sometimes called civil society organizations. Brown et al. (2000) define civil society as "an area of association and action independent of the state and the market in which citizens can organize to pursue social values and public purposes which are important to them, both individually and collectively" (p. 7). We can view such organizations as belonging to the public side of the equation of public-private partnerships, while recognizing that NGOs are often considered as a third sector on their own, reflecting different values, purposes, interests, and resource mobilization strategies. Private foundations are similar to NGOs, as civil society organizations seeking to promote public interests. We can also consider these foundations on the public side of public-private partnerships, although they lack the formal institutions of public accountability found in governments and inter-governmental agencies. (Indeed, some argue that private foundations have too much power to set public agendas, without sufficient public oversight and input.) As the case studies show, many different kinds of organizations are joining public-private partnerships, and they bring with them different cultures, governance structures, and financial resources. These differences create challenges in the partners' efforts to collaborate effectively and achieve their objectives.

A second set of questions addresses the nature of partners. Who is a partner, and who should decide? For example, should the recipients of a public-private drug donation program be considered partners? Should these recipients participate in the design, implementation, and oversight of a public-private partnership? If so, in what ways? What kind of governance structure could allow the participation of recipients and promote accountability while assuring effectiveness?

Partnerships can involve a range of partners with different rights and responsibilities, including core partners, who assume key responsibilities for the joint enterprise, and in-country partners, whose participation is necessary for successful implementation. Some partnerships give prominent roles in governing structures to recipients, while others do not. Specific cases demonstrate the diversity of organizations within a single partnership. For example, the International Trachoma Initiative involves two core partners—Pfizer (a private for-profit pharmaceutical company) and the Edna McConnell Clark Foundation (a private foundation)—plus many additional partners, including national governments, other private foundations and non-governmental organizations (such as Helen

Keller International), and the World Health Organization (see chapter 3). The chapters in this book discuss a number of important issues related to partnership structures, including the processes through which partnerships are formed, the ways in which different organizations relate to each other, and the broader policy implications of public-private partnerships.

Diversity of Partnerships

Many kinds of public-private partnerships for health have emerged in recent years. The Initiative on Public-Private Partnerships for Health (located in Geneva, with the Global Forum on Health Research) is creating an inventory of partnerships, using ten different categories (table 1.1). Its list included over sixty different public-private partnerships for health as of October 2000. These partnerships include at least 16 major efforts that involve WHO in significant ways (table 1.2). Several prominent examples are worth noting briefly here.

One example is the Accelerating Access Initiative, an effort by five pharmaceutical companies, announced in May 2000, to collaborate with five international agencies in finding mechanisms to provide access to HIV/AIDS-related care and treatment in poor countries, including significant price discounts for anti-AIDS drugs (UNAIDS, 2000). One year later, agreements had been reached in only three countries—Senegal, Rwanda, and Uganda. This reflects the difficulties in moving from dialogue to action (Schoofs & Waldholz, 2001).

Table 1.1

CATEGORIES OF PUBLIC-PRIVATE PARTNERSHIPS FOR HEALTH

1. Partnerships for disease control—product development
2. Partnerships for disease control—product distribution
3. Partnerships for strengthening health services
4. Partnerships to commercialize traditional medicines
5. Partnerships for health program coordination
6. Other international health partnerships
7. Country level partnerships
8. Private sector coalitions for health
9. Partnerships for product donations
10. Partnerships for health service delivery

Source: Widdus et al., 2001.

Table 1.2

LIST OF WHO PUBLIC-PRIVATE PARTNERSHIPS

European Partnership Project on Tobacco Dependence

Global Alliance for TB Drug Development

Global Alliance to Eliminate Lymphatic Filariasis

Global Alliance to Eliminate Leprosy

Global Alliance for Vaccines and Immunization

Global Elimination of Blinding Trachoma

Global Fire Fighting Partnership

Global Partnerships for Healthy Aging

Global Polio Eradication Initiative

Global School Health Initiative

Multilateral Initiative on Malaria

Medicines for Malaria Venture

Partnership for Parasite Control

Roll Back Malaria

Stop TB Initiative

UNAIDS/Industry Drug Access Initiative

Source: World Health Organization website (www.who.int) search on 'partnership' and 'global alliance'.

The conflicts over expanding access to anti-retrovirals provide a striking counterpoint, along several dimensions, to the partnership that arose to provide access to ivermectin for onchocerciasis. The nature of the disease and the treatment, the markets and profits of the products, the political context, the positions of governments, the economic and social costs—all make a difference in the capacity of public-private partnerships to achieve results.

A second example is the Global Alliance for Vaccines and Immunizations (GAVI), whose origins are described by William Muraskin in chapter 6 of this volume. This partnership was galvanized by a five-year commitment of $750 million from the Gates Foundation in November 1999, and has subsequently received contributions from the governments of Norway, the Netherlands, the United Kingdom, and the United States, for a total fund of over a billion dollars. The partners for GAVI include: national governments, the Gates Children's Vaccine Program at PATH, the International Federation of Pharmaceutical Manufacturers Associations (IFPMA), research and public health institutions, the Bill and Melinda Gates Foundation, the Rockefeller Foundation, the United Nations Children's Fund (UNICEF), the World Bank Group, and the World Health Organization. GAVI has made a number of grants to developing countries to support immunization programs and may also provide financial support for the development of new vaccines (GAVI, 2000).

A third example of a recently formed partnership is the Medicines for Malaria Venture (MMV). This entity has been established as an independent foundation under Swiss law, and operates as a non-profit business to spur development of new antimalarial drugs, using a public venture capital fund and a small management team (Ridley & Gutteridge, 1999). The MMV partners include: the World Health Organization, the International Federation of Pharmaceutical Manufacturers Associations, the World Bank, the government of the Netherlands, the UK Department for International Development, the Swiss Agency for Development and Cooperation, the Global Forum for Health Research, the Rockefeller Foundation, and the global Roll Back Malaria Partnership. The president of the IFPMA stated that the MMV symbolizes "the start of a new era of partnership between the research-based pharmaceutical industry and the WHO to bring about real improvements in world health" (MMV, 1999).

A fourth example is the partnership to assure continued availability of a life-saving drug, eflornithine, to treat human African trypanosomiasis. This partnership involves private companies, non-governmental organizations, and the WHO in an unusual collaboration. In December 1999, the manufacturer for eflornithine, Hoechst Marion Roussel (now Aventis), donated the patent rights and manufacturing know-how to WHO. Then WHO and Médecins Sans Frontières (MSF) sought to find a third party manufacturer willing to produce the drug, which MSF would distribute in sleeping-sickness treatment programs in affected countries (Pecoul & Gastellu, 1999). In the fall of 2000, Bristol-Myers Squibb (along with several other companies) introduced an eflornithine cream for removing facial hair in women—a lifestyle drug for sale in rich-country markets—perhaps without full understanding of the implications of producing a drug that has other applications in tropical medicine. These companies, including Aventis, subsequently agreed in February 2001 to provide WHO and MSF with sixty thousand doses of eflornithine—enough to last three years ("New lease on life," 2001). And in May 2001, Aventis reached an agreement with WHO to donate three drugs for treating sleeping sickness for five years (valued at $5 million per year) plus funding to support WHO's research programs (MSF, 2001). This partnership emerged from the campaign for drug access carried out by Médecins Sans Frontières, and was based in part on twenty years of collaborative research between Hoechst Marion Roussel and the United Nations Development Program/World Bank/WHO Special Program for Research and Training in Tropical Diseases (TDR) to support the discovery and development of eflornithine.

These examples show that public-private partnerships for health (even considering only five involving WHO) are diverse in many respects: the number of partners involved, the kinds of organizations involved, the funding levels and funding sources, the objectives for the partnerships, and the organizational structures of the partnerships. What factors have motivated these disparate organizations to come together in partnerships?

Motives for Initiating Partnerships

Until recently, the public and for-profit private sectors working in the health arena often viewed each other with "antagonism, suspicion, and confrontation," as reported by Adetokunbo Lucas (see chapter 2). These tensions are now being supplanted by increasing rapprochement and positive encouragement for public-private partnerships in health. According to Lucas, a chief factor encouraging these partnerships is that neither side alone can achieve its specific goals; collaboration is unavoidable to solve certain problems. Multi-member partnerships, which have recently become popular, reflect a recognition that some problems require many partners and complex organizational mechanisms to address all the different aspects.

The chapter by Lucas discusses partnerships initiated by the UNDP/World Bank/WHO Special Program for Research and Training in Tropical Diseases (TDR). Lucas served as TDR director from 1976 to 1986, and understood that public-private partnerships were essential for progress on TDR's mandate of discovering and developing new and improved technologies for the control of tropical diseases affecting the poor in developing countries. This goal could not be achieved through efforts by either the public sector or the private sector working alone. The case of TDR shows persuasively that the public sector can work with the private sector in ways that advance public interest.

Lucas also presents four cases of philanthropic drug donation programs (table 2.1). These efforts by pharmaceutical companies require clearly defined public health goals, involve several components (beyond the product) in a strategic plan for addressing the problem, and depend on the collaborative efforts of several partners. These partnerships were pursued, according to Lucas, because there were no viable alternatives to solve the problems of drug development and distribution. Moreover, in cases where partnerships have not developed, potential health gains have not been achieved in developing countries. One example is the drug praziquantel, which was developed for schistosomiasis (Reich & Govindaraj, 1998). While public-private collaboration occurred during the development phase of praziquantel (with WHO involved in helping arrange clinical trials for the drug), an effective partnership for its distribution did not emerge, substantially limiting the number of people in developing countries who could benefit from this pharmaceutical product.

But considerable skepticism exists about the motives of private firms that engage in partnerships, even when the efforts have major public health benefits. Private firms are often assumed to be solely seeking future profits and markets through partnerships, or to be seeking control over the agendas of international organizations, or to be using donations in order to claim tax deductions for financial reasons, or to be seeking new products, subsidized by public funds, to be used for private sale and profits. There is no doubt that private firms are primarily profit-seeking organizations; the question is whether they can participate effectively in partnerships that address global health inequities or health problems of poor countries. The strength of these assumptions in the public sector reflects a cultural gap between the private and public sectors, as well as real problems that require serious ethical consideration, as discussed below.

Processes for Creating Partnerships

Constructing an effective partnership among diverse organizations is hard work. In chapter 3, Diana Barrett, James Austin, and Sheila McCarthy introduce a general framework for the processes of creating partnerships, illustrated through an analysis of the International Trachoma Initiative (ITI). Establishing the ITI involved the two core partners in "a highly integrative relationship of strategic importance to both organizations with high levels of engagement and managerial complexity." In this case, as in others, creating an effective partnership was more complicated than initially anticipated because of the challenges of bringing together the core partners and of structuring relationships with other groups involved.

Partnerships confront seven organizational challenges—what Austin (2000) calls "the seven C's of strategic collaboration" (table 1.3). Navigating these "seven C's" is not easy. Of particular importance is the challenge of creating value. To assure a sustainable collaboration, the value created must be useful to society, and value must flow to all core partners. In addition, creating a partnership is a continual learning process, with the potential for unexpected lessons. For example, participating in the ITI the partnership on trachoma led the Clark Foundation to rethink its core work in philanthropy—to view its activities more in the form of long-term investments than short-term grants. And for Pfizer, the experience with ITI led the company to embrace the idea of public-private partnerships as "a new mode of cooperation" that offers hope for health improvement in sub-Saharan Africa. Subsequently, after enormous pressure from advocacy groups, the company initiated a donation program for an anti-AIDS drug (Diflucan, or fluconazole) in South Africa (McKinnell, 2001).

The Mectizan Donation Program is often considered one of the most successful partnerships so far—a partnership created by Merck and the Task Force for Child Survival and Development, a non-governmental organization. Chapter 5, by Laura Frost, Michael R. Reich, and Tomoko Fujisaki, reviews the history of Merck's decision to develop and donate ivermectin for treatment of onchocerciasis and the processes for initiating this partnership. While Merck and the WHO collaborated on the development of this drug, they did not create a formal partnership for its distribution. Instead, Merck worked with the Task Force to establish a new entity. Merck and the WHO were unable to agree on a joint organizational mechanism (suggesting that the two could not build a relationship

Table 1.3

THE SEVEN C'S OF STRATEGIC COLLABORATION
Clarity of purpose
Congruency of mission, strategy, and values
Creation of value
Connection with purpose and people
Communication between partners
Continual learning
Commitment to the partnership

Source: Austin, 2000.

of trust necessary for a partnership), although the WHO subsequently provided continuing technical advice to the partnership's expert committee. The problems in this case reflect broader difficulties that the WHO has experienced in creating partnerships. These difficulties are attributed to the WHO's organizational culture, resistance to information sharing, and obstacles to network building (Kickbusch & Quick, 1998; Birmingham, 2000). The WHO is now seeking to address these problems, and the WHO leadership is more open to partnerships with the private sector, as reflected in the recent proliferation of partnerships involving WHO (shown in table 1.2).

Merck and the Task Force managed to construct a successful partnership through their use of common objects, people, and ideas (called "boundary objects" in chapter 5), which allowed them to span their diverse social worlds, decide on shared goals, and create a relationship of trust. This partnership has been successful in the benefits provided to recipients (a total of 132 million treatments approved between 1988 and 1999), the support provided to the partnership by the international community for onchocerciasis control, the enhanced public images of both partners, the reduced human suffering among persons affected by onchocerciasis, and the persistence of the partnership for more than a decade. In particular, this partnership is successfully reducing the level of infection below that at which the disease causes blindness, thereby making it possible to eliminate onchocerciasis as a public health problem. TDR and others continue the search for a safe and effective macrofilaricide, which in conjunction with ivermectin could make eradication of onchocerciasis a feasible goal.

Unfortunately, the history of efforts to collaborate on new vaccine development shows how problems in the processes of creating partnerships can lead to organizational demise. William Muraskin examines the history of the Children's Vaccine Initiative (CVI) in chapter 6. The problems in this case involved high levels of distrust between the public and private sectors, and corrosive competition among international agencies. Muraskin shows how individuals, international agencies, and private firms interacted first to design the CVI and then to demolish it. He also demonstrates how technical analysis of the international vaccine market, performed for UNICEF by a private consulting firm, changed the terms of the debate and enhanced understanding across the public-private divide.

In reflecting on the birth and death of the CVI, Muraskin emphasizes the public sector's need to gain a better understanding of the private sector. "For the private sector to successfully cooperate with the public sector it is necessary for the latter to understand and accept the basic legitimacy of private enterprise and the profit motive that drives it; that is very hard for many public health officials to do when children are sick and dying from the lack of money to buy vaccines." He also stresses the need for industry to meet the public sector halfway and recognize the public interest in vaccines. "If there are no industry leaders visionary enough to balance public and private concerns, then bridges cannot be built."

These lessons will be important for the new partnership on vaccines, known as the Global Alliance for Vaccines and Immunization (GAVI), to consider and learn from, as well as for ongoing discussions about the idea of creating a purchase fund for an HIV-vaccine. Proponents of a purchase fund argue that it would provide financial incentives to persuade the pharmaceutical industry to expand its research efforts and would also enable greater and faster access to new vaccines (once developed) for distribution to the world's poor (Glennerster & Kremer, 2000). Whether this would happen remains unproven.

Ethics of Partnerships

Underlying the discussion of partnerships (and debates over definitions, motives, and processes) are basic questions of ethics. Which partnerships are good ones, and how do you know? Who has what kind of social responsibility and why? How do you assure accountability of partnerships and to whom? How should partnerships relate to international health agencies, such as the WHO?

There is growing agreement that partnerships can play a pivotal role in fulfilling our moral obligations to improve the health status of people in poor countries, as argued in chapter 4 by Marc J. Roberts, A. G. Breitenstein, and Clement S. Roberts. They maintain that people in rich countries have a moral obligation to help people in poor countries. They further contend that private corporations have social responsibilities and that managers within firms have moral obligations. In their view, global health companies have a special obligation to help because of their competence, resources, and expertise—their capacity to make a significant contribution to the health of poor people. Finally, they believe that partnerships can play an important role precisely because they can bring the creative potential of multiple perspectives to bear on critical problems.

An ethical assessment of public-private partnerships depends partly on their consequences. Chapter 4 also provides a hopeful view, drawing on the notion of social capital, which explains the capacity of some societies to solve collective problems by the greater accumulation of trust and connection among their members (Putnam, 1993). Public-private partnerships—new problem-solving institutions that can work creatively and flexibly outside the existing bureaucratic framework—may thus represent a form of international social capital.

Others are less sanguine about the ethical basis of partnerships. In chapter 2, Lucas suggests that the WHO should develop guidelines for philanthropic single-disease drug donation programs in addition to the current guidelines for drug donations (WHO, 1996). The new guidelines would seek to assure companies' long-term commitment, promote effective management of the program and collaboration with partners, and guard against real and apparent conflicts of interest. WHO is currently addressing the ethical issues of its own role in partnerships through its *Guidelines on Interaction with Commercial Enterprises* (WHO, 1999). This document, however, has generated criticism from some activist groups for not providing sufficient oversight to reduce conflicts of interest (Health Action International, 1999). But in late 2000, the Interagency Pharmaceutical Coordination Group did develop draft guidelines on single-source drug donation programs, seeking to address some of the questions raised by Lucas and others. The document starts with the statement, "Drug donations and preferential pricing arrangements, when carefully planned and properly managed, can make an important contribution towards reducing the cost of health care, and help reduce unnecessary suffering and save lives" (IPCG, 2000).

In part, the ethical assessment depends on the capacity of partnerships to produce results (from a consequentialist perspective). Experience to date shows that some single-disease donation programs have successfully implemented their agendas and achieved positive results, while others have encountered difficulties. Two successful implementers are described in this volume: the Mectizan Donation Program and the International Trachoma Initiative. On the other hand, the Malarone Donation Program, created by Glaxo-Wellcome for its new malaria drug, encountered problems in implementation, and ended in September 2001 on completion of the pilot phase, which showed that the donation program was "not an efficient and effective use of resources to achieve the objective of reducing suffering and death from malaria" (Malarone Donation Program, 2001).

Kent Buse and Gill Walt, in their provocative analysis in chapter 7, express serious concerns about the actual and potential impacts of partnerships on the United Nations (UN) system. They are concerned that partnerships "will further fragment international cooperation in health and undermine UN aims for cooperation and equity among states." In particular, they are worried about the accountability of partnerships, their impact on critical functions of UN agencies (such as setting global standards and norms), and the potential negative impact on global inequities caused by focusing on "relatively narrow" issues rather than more difficult problems. To address these points, they recommend a debate on a regulatory framework and "legitimate oversight body" that could "differentiate between acceptable and unacceptable" partnerships. Similar views are expressed in an article on the Global Alliance for Vaccines and Immunization, by Anita Hardon, who views GAVI as emphasizing the introduction of new, underused vaccines (such as hepatitis B)—to serve private industry's interests—rather than assuring the use of existing, standard vaccines—to serve public health objectives (Hardon, 2001). This presentation, however, underestimates the way that GAVI is providing funds to assure sustained coverage to basic vaccines *and* to expand access to newer vaccines, as well as using access to newer vaccines as an incentive for countries to build a solid foundation for meeting basic needs of standard vaccines.

Buse and Walt view the UN system as accomplishing critical functions of global governance in health and call for efforts to strengthen the coordination and protection of these functions. This perspective seeks to assure that partnerships comply with the UN system, by creating regulatory mechanisms that would enhance UN control of partnerships and the international health agenda. A contrasting viewpoint, expressed at the workshop, considers the UN system inherently fragmented and competitive among its different agencies (as shown in Muraskin's chapter on the Children's Vaccine Initiative), and calls for public-private partnerships to fill in gaps not covered by the UN system and undertake projects difficult for the UN system to pursue effectively. This perspective deems it counterproductive to seek a UN system that would try to do everything, and criticizes Buse and Walt's proposal as being too centralized, controlling, and ineffective.

This debate over the relationship between new partnerships and the UN system reflects fundamental questions about the kinds of global health governance that are most desirable for international health: centralized versus decentralized control, international regulation versus other forms of intervention, mechanisms to assure the accountability of corporations and international agencies, and the compatibility of the core values of public and private sectors.

Conclusions

For now, it seems certain that the number of public-private partnerships will continue to grow in international health, and that the kinds of partnerships and partners will continue to diversify. Partnerships offer the potential to combine the different strengths of public and private organizations, along with civil society groups, in addressing health problems in poor countries. A fundamental dilemma of such partnerships is how to achieve their potential while assuring their accountability—without suppressing their creative influence, entrepreneurial spirit, or organizational capacity to improve the health of poor people in developing countries. In addition, public-private partnerships need to specify what accountability means (to whom? governments? shareholders? intended beneficiaries?) and how that accountability can be implemented and assured with adequate transparency. Resolving this dilemma will require the participation of all groups, including the intended beneficiaries, in order to expand mutual understanding and establish effective institutions that span the public-private divide. For example, a major debate is now unfolding over how to design the Global Health Fund (for AIDS, malaria, and tuberculosis) so that it is both effective and accountable (Brugha & Walt, 2001).

Achieving the potential benefits of public-private partnerships thus requires not only the good will to make an input such as a drug or vaccine available, but also the capacity to manage effective organizational integration along the entire route from producer to consumer. How many of the recently created partnerships will persist and successfully implement their programs in multiple countries? Will they be able to create sustainable approaches that countries are willing to incorporate into public bureaucracies, supported by government funds? How many initiatives can a single recipient country handle at the same time? And will donors develop "initiative fatigue" and eventually move on to the next popular solution? The experience to date demonstrates that partnerships can play a critical role in addressing global health inequities and producing tangible benefits for enhanced social welfare (although more evidence is needed on the long-term consequences), but they also require careful steering to avoid the pitfalls that abound.

This chapter is a revised and expanded version of a paper first published in *Nature Medicine*, 6(6), 617–620, 2000.

References

Austin, J. (2000). *The Collaboration Challenge: How Nonprofits and Businesses Succeed Through Strategic Alliances*. San Francisco: Jossey-Bass Publishers.

Birmingham, K. (2000). Ministers pledge to stop TB. *Nature Medicine, 6*(5), 491–492.

Blumenthal, D., Causino, N., Campbell, E., & Louis, K. S. (1996). Relationships between academic institutions and industry in the life sciences: An industry survey. *New England Journal of Medicine, 334*(6), 368–373.

Brown, L. D., Khagram, S., Moore, M. H., & Frumkin, P. (July 2000). Globalization, NGOs, and multi-sectoral relations. Working Paper #1, The Hauser Center for Nonprofit Organizations, Harvard University.

Brugha, R., &Walt, G. (2001). A global health fund: A leap of faith? *British Medical Journal, 323,* 152–154.

Glennerster, R., & Kremer, M. (2000). A better way to spur medical research and development. *Regulation, 23*(2), 34–39.

Global Alliance for Vaccines and Immunization. (2000, November 20). Global fund for children's vaccines approves support to eight more countries; five year commitment now exceeds $250 million [GAVI press release].

Hardon, A. (2001). Immunization for all? A critical look at the first GAVI partners meeting, *HAI Europe, 6*(1), 2–9.

Harrison, P. H. (1999). A new model for collaboration: The alliance for microbicide development. *International Journal of Gynecology & Obstetrics, 67,* S39–S53.

Health Action International. (1999, December 22). Comments on WHO *Guidelines on Interaction with Commercial Enterprises* (preliminary version, July 1999), Amsterdam. (*www.haiweb.org/news/HAI _comment_WHO_Guidelines.html*).

Interagency Pharmaceutical Coordination Group. (2000, December 5). *Guidelines for accepting or endorsing preferential prices or donations of single-source pharmaceuticals.* Draft. Geneva: WHO Department of Essential Drugs and Medicines Policy.

Kickbusch, I, & Quick, J. (1998). Partnerships for health in the twenty-first century. *World Health Statistics Quarterly, 51,* 68–74.

Lasker, R. D., Weiss, E. S., & Miller, R. (2001). Partnership synergy: A practical framework for studying and strengthening the collaborative advantage. *The Milbank Quarterly, 79*(2), 179–205.

Malarone Donation Program. (2001, July). Malarone Donation Program to end on completion of the pilot phase. (*www.malaronedonation.org/malarone_text.html*).

McKinnell, H. A. (2001, March 31). Partnerships offer hope in sub-Saharan Africa. *The Economist*, p. 44.

Medicines for Malaria Venture. (1999, November 3). WHO, partner agencies and industry launch unique venture to develop malaria drugs [Press release]. Geneva: World Health Organization/67.

Médecins Sans Frontières. (2001, May 3). Supply of sleeping sickness drugs secured [Press release]. Geneva:Author.

The need for public-private partnerships (2000) [Editorial]. *Nature Medicine, 6*(5), 481.

New lease on life for resurrection drug (2001). *TDRnews*, No. 64.

Pecoul, B., & Gastellu, M. (1999). Production of sleeping-sickness treatment. *The Lancet, 354*(9182), 955–956.

Putnam, R. D. (1993). *Making democracy work: Civic traditions in modern Italy.* Princeton: Princeton University Press.

Reich, M. R. (2000). The global drug gap. *Science, 287*(5460), 1979–1981.

Reich, M. R., & Govindaraj, R. (1998). Dilemmas in drug development for tropical diseases: Experiences with praziquantel. *Health Policy, 44*(1), 1–18.

Ridley, R. G., & Gutteridge, W. E. (1999, October 15). Paper presented at the Médecins Sans Frontières Symposium: Drugs for Communicable Diseases, Stimulating Development and Availability, Paris.

Schoofs, M., & Waldholz, M. (2001, March 7). Price war breaks out over AIDS drugs in Africa as generics present challenge. *Wall Street Journal*.

Smith, R. (2000). Vaccines and medicines for the world's poorest: Public-private partnerships seem to be essential. *British Medical Journal, 320*, 952–953.

United Nations Program on HIV/AIDS. (2000, May 11). New public/private sector effort initiated to accelerate access to HIV/AIDS care and treatment in developing countries [Press release]. Geneva: Author.

Widdus, R., Holm, K., Chacko, S., & Currat, L. (2001). Towards better defining 'public-private partnerships' for health. *Geneva: Inititiative on Public-Private Partnerships for Health, Global Forum for Health Research.*

World Health Organization. (1996, 1999). *Guidelines for drug donations.* Geneva:Author.

World Health Organization. (1998, September 30). WHO/Private sector talks [Press release 64] Geneva:Author.

World Health Organization. (1999). *Guidelines on interaction with commercial enterprises.* Draft. Geneva:Author.

2

Public-Private Partnerships: Illustrative Examples

Adetokunbo O. Lucas

MANY COUNTRIES HAVE ACCUMULATED experience of successful collaboration between the public sector and non-governmental organizations and other private-sector, non-profit institutions in the delivery of health care (Cross, 1998). On the other hand, until recently, the relationship between the public and the for-profit private sectors has been more tentative. On occasion it has even been characterized by antagonism, suspicion, and confrontation. For example, the World Health Organization's (WHO) promotion of the Essential Drug Program initially provoked strong reactions from the pharmaceutical industry. Concern about the inappropriate marketing of baby foods in developing countries prompted some non-governmental organizations and other activists to mount pressure on manufacturers of baby foods. This negative reaction also influenced attitudes toward the pharmaceutical industry. However, in recent years, increasing rapprochement between public and private organizations is giving rise to positive encouragement of public-private partnerships in the health sector. These relationships have developed slowly and cautiously. The main objective is to achieve the maximum benefit from public-private partnerships without compromising public interest.

In this chapter, the term public-private partnership is used to refer specifically to the collaborative programs between the public sector and the for-profit section of the private sector. In the rest of the chapter, the term private sector will be used to refer to the for-profit, commercial private sector, excluding not-for-profit non-governmental organizations and institutions within civil society.

The chapter describes two illustrative examples of public-private partnerships: first, the UNDP/World Bank/WHO Special Program for Research and Training in Tropical Diseases (TDR) and then philanthropic drug donation programs. These cases are presented as illustrative examples of public-private partnerships from which one can learn some useful lessons that could guide future policies and programs.

Highlights of TDR: An Example of Public-Private Collaboration

In the mid-1970s, from the analysis of the health situation in developing countries of the tropics, the World Health Organization and other international organizations made the following observations:

- Malaria and other parasitic and infectious diseases remain major causes of disease, disability, and death in many developing countries
- The available technologies for the prevention and treatment of these conditions are inadequate to bring them under control, and the efficacy of existing tools is being eroded by the emergence of drug resistant strains of the parasites and insecticide resistant strains of the vectors
- The rapid advances in the biomedical sciences, notably in biochemistry, immunology, molecular biology, and genetic engineering, if suitably exploited, could lead to the development of new generations of effective tools for the control of these diseases
- Market analyses dissuade the pharmaceutical industry from investing resources for research and development on these problems that mainly affected poor people in poor countries
- The countries where these diseases are endemic lack the capacity to undertake the research and development effort that is required to solve these problems

WHO, in collaboration with two other international organizations, UNDP and the World Bank, responded to this situation by establishing TDR. The program has two interrelated objectives (Godal et al., 1998; TDR, 1998):

Research & Development: to develop safe, acceptable, and affordable methods of prevention, diagnosis, treatment, and control of TDR's target diseases

Training & Strengthening: to strengthen the capability of developing disease-endemic countries to undertake the research required to develop new technologies for the control of these diseases

Initially, six groups of diseases were included in the program: malaria, schistosomiasis, the trypanosomiases (African trypanosomiasis and Chagas disease), leishmaniasis, the filariases (onchocerciasis and lymphatic filariasis), and leprosy. The program used three criteria in selecting these diseases:

- The public health significance of the disease as a major cause of morbidity and mortality
- Existing technologies judged inadequate to bring the disease under control

- The existence of promising leads indicating that biomedical research could generate new and improved technologies for preventing or treating the disease

More recently, dengue and tuberculosis were added to the list of diseases in the TDR portfolio. Cosponsored by the United Nations Development Program, the World Bank, and WHO, TDR was clearly a public-sector initiative, but it collaborated with the private sector on aspects of its program. It was clear that TDR could not achieve some of its specific goals, especially the development of new drugs, without the collaboration of industry. Table 2.1 gives an illustrative list of private institutions that were involved with TDR during the first two decades of its operation. Because of the acrimonious controversies between the public and the private sectors, TDR's interactions with the pharmaceutical industry were

Table 2.1.TDR's Collaborations with the Pharmaceutical Industry

1. ACF Beheer, B.V., Maarssen, Netherlands
2. Bayer A.G., Leverkusen, Germany
3. Biobras-Bioquimica do Brasil, Montes Claros, Brazil
4. Burroughs Wellcome Company, Research Triangle Park, North Carolina, USA
5. Ciba Geigy, Ltd., Basle, Switzerland
6. Daiichi Pharmaceutical Co. Ltd., Tokyo, Japan
7. Eli Lilly and Company, Greenfield, Indiana, USA
8. Genetic Institutes, Boston, Maryland, USA Glaxo Group Research Ltd., Greenford, UK
9. IHARABRAS S.A., Industrias Quimicas, Sao Paulo, Brazil
10. International Federation of Pharmaceutical Manufacturers Associations, Geneva, Switzerland
11. Janssen Research Foundation, Beerse, Belgium
12. Laboratorios Gador, Buenos Aires, Argentina
13. Merck and Co., Inc., Rahway, New Jersey, USA
14. E. Merck Pharma, Darmstadt, Germany
15. Novo Nordisk A/S, Bagsvaerd, Denmark
16. Pasteur-Mérieux-Connaught, Swiftwater, Pennsylvania, USA
17. Pharmacia Farmitalia Carlo Elba, Milan, Italy
18. Rhône-Poulenc Rorer Doma, Antony, France
19. SmithKline Beecham Pharmaceuticals, London, UK
20. Vestar, Inc., San Dimas, California, USA
21. Zeneca Pharmaceuticals, Macclesfield, UK

initially cautious, guarded, and closely monitored by the Joint Coordinating Board (JCB), the program's governing body.[1] JCB kept a watchful eye on TDR's links with industry, assuring the sponsors and other interested parties that in all the contracts and joint activities, the public interest was well protected.

TDR interactions with the private sector have included:

- contributions of scientists from the pharmaceutical industry to TDR;
- specific services to TDR from industry; and
- joint programs.

Contributions of scientists from pharmaceutical companies to TDR

TDR used a global network of scientists to develop, implement, and review its research and development projects. The scientists, drawn from academic and research institutes as well as from industry, were selected strictly on the basis of individual merit and relevance to the needs of the program. The scientists from drug companies contributed to TDR's task forces, working groups, and steering committees in their special areas of expertise, but they were not appointed as representatives of their companies. These outstanding scientists from industry (including two Nobel Prize winners) gave service to TDR on a pro bono basis; they received no fees or honoraria beyond their travel and subsistence expenses.

An integrated network served each component of the TDR program. For example, the search for new drugs for the treatment of onchocerciasis involved interrelated processes ranging from basic biochemistry, synthesis of chemical compounds, compounds, screening of candidate compounds for biological activity, and clinical evaluation in human subjects (fig. 2.1).

Comparative biochemistry: Scientists, mainly based in academia, studied the biochemical processes in onchocercal and related worms in the hope of finding suitable targets for chemotherapeutic attack.

Synthesis of chemical compounds: Chemists synthesized candidate compounds on the basis of clues derived from comparative biochemistry. They also synthesized analogues of known drugs in the hope of finding compounds with enhanced efficacy and reduced toxicity.

Biological screening: The program established a screening system that examined candidate compounds for their biological activity. The compounds progressed from tests in small animals to more definitive screens that were more accurately predictive of their effect on human onchocerciasis. The most promising

Figure 2.1. New Drugs for Onchocerciasis

compounds were tested in Australia using cattle that are naturally infected with a related onchocercal worm. This cattle screen gave the best prediction of what a compound would do in human cases of onchocerciasis. Some of the compounds came from the synthesis program. TDR also offered the screening service to industry and protected their intellectual property by accepting coded compounds, thereby keeping the chemical structure confidential.

Clinical evaluation: Compounds that showed efficacy in the cattle screen and passed relevant toxicity tests were evaluated in humans at a clinical research center in Tamale, Ghana (Awadzi, 1997), and for the effects on eyes in Nigeria (Abiose, 1998).

Ivermectin (under the brand name Mectizan) was one of the compounds that Merck submitted for evaluation in the cattle screen. The company developed the drug and evaluated it in collaboration with TDR.

Specific services to TDR from industry
TDR requested and obtained a variety of specific services from pharmaceutical companies including:

- **Special reagents required by research scientists**, e.g., radio-labeled chemicals
- **Good Manufacturing Practice (GMP) facilities** for biological reagents that will be tested in humans

GMP facilities are required by law for preparing reagents to be tested on humans. Lacking GMP facilities, scientists in university departments and research institutes are therefore dependent on the resources of the pharmaceutical industry for this essential stage in the development of candidate agents. For example, armadillo-derived leprosy bacilli, subsequently used for producing test vaccines, were processed and stored on behalf of TDR by a pharmaceutical company, the Wellcome Research Laboratories.

Joint activities of TDR and industry

Drug companies participated with TDR in exploring some promising leads and ideas:

TDR's screening facilities: The program made available to industry its drug screening facilities. For example, over 10 thousand compounds passed through the network of biological screens for testing candidate drugs for the treatment of onchocerciasis. One of the compounds tested was ivermectin, which eventually proved to be an outstanding product.

Clinical evaluation: TDR worked with industry in the clinical evaluation of new drugs, e.g. mefloquine (Hoffman la Roche), ivermectin (Merck), and elfornithine (Hoechst Marion Roussel, Inc.).

Since its inception in 1975, TDR has funded over eight thousand projects involving 6,500 scientists including:

- U.S.$300 million in grants for 5,300 research and development projects in 127 countries
- U.S.$117 million for 2,700 Research Capability Strengthening projects in 80 countries, with 1,100 scientists from developing countries completing research training

TDR's research and development effort has been credited with the successful introduction of effective new technologies; 67 disease control tools have been developed, of which 38 are in use for disease control. Using tools and strategies generated with TDR support, there is now the prospect that onchocerciasis, lymphatic filariasis, leprosy and Chagas disease can be eliminated.

Features of TDR's partnerships with the private sector

Characteristic features of TDR's involvement with industry include the following elements:

Mutual respect: In some international multilateral agencies, political considerations influence the selection of technical advisers to a degree that compromises the quality of their expert panels. Distinguished scientists find it difficult to work comfortably in such teams. TDR's working groups include distinguished scientists from all over the world—from developed and developing countries, from both sides of the iron curtain, and from academia, research institutes, and health departments, as well as from industry. The realization that they have been selected on the basis of their personal expertise facilitates peer-level relationships among the scientists and generates mutual respect for each other, as well as for the program.

Clear goal orientation: Although TDR supports a wide range of research activities, each group works toward the achievement of clearly defined goals. The strategic work plans include benchmarks for monitoring progress. Scientists from industry are well adapted to this approach but scientists from academia, more used to open-ended type of research plans, also become engaged with the TDR industrial production approach.

Sensitivity to each other's requirements: As a publicly funded program, TDR's activities have to be transparent for the purpose of accountability to the sponsoring agencies, as well as to the public at large. On the other hand, some of the collaborative research involves information and intellectual property of commercial value. TDR is able to accommodate both requirements by providing full disclosure of its operations but arranging for confidentiality on specific matters where indicated. For example, in screening chemical compounds for industry, TDR agreed to handle coded samples without requiring the company to disclose the structure of the molecules.

Protecting the public interest: The essence of partnership is joint investment of effort and fair sharing of rewards. In drawing up contracts with the private sector, TDR pays close attention to the rights of the public sector to intellectual property that is produced through joint efforts. It has been possible to obtain various concessions in the public interest such as tiered pricing for sales to the public sector (as in the case of mefloquine) and sublicensing of patents (as in the case of eflornithine). As described at the WHO website:

> *Public/private partners in sleeping sickness: WHO and Hoechst Marion Roussel, Inc. sign a License Agreement allowing WHO to arrange for the production of eflornithine—the 'resurrection drug' for African trypanosomiasis.*
>
> *The initiative involves the drug eflornithine, on which WHO and Hoechst Marion Roussel have collaborated for a number of years. This drug has been*

nicknamed the 'resurrection drug' because of its spectacular effect on patients in the late stages of the disease, when the patient is comatose. However, although first registered for use in sleeping sickness in 1990, the drug is not in commercial production, partly because of the limited market, which makes it not at all attractive to the private sector, and partly due to its expense and hence non-affordability by endemic countries. On 6 December 1999, the World Health Organization and Hoechst Marion Roussel, Inc., signed a License Agreement in Geneva granting WHO reference right to the license to produce eflornithine. The agreement will allow technology for production of the drug to be transferred from Hoechst Marion Roussel to a third party, in the private sector, which will manufacture eflornithine.

Present at the signing was Dr. C. Bacchi, who discovered that eflornithine cured trypanosome infection experimentally while working under support from TDR and drew attention to the parasite's unique polyamine metabolism. The drug was originally developed for use in cancer but did not meet expectations; it is now licensed for use in sleeping sickness in the U.S., Europe, and 12 African countries. The arrival of eflornithine provided an alternative drug for the treatment of gambiense sleeping sickness, the form of sleeping sickness that occurs in west and central Africa; but for the rhodesiense form of sleeping sickness that occurs in central and eastern Africa, there is no alternative treatment. (WHO, 2000)

Comments on the TDR experience

TDR's experience with industry shows what can be achieved by carefully designed public-private partnerships. The relationships have been cordial and productive. TDR's mandate was to discover and develop new and improved technologies for the control of tropical diseases affecting the poor in developing countries. Neither the public sector nor the private sector working alone was able to achieve this goal. Through public-private partnerships, TDR assembled a critical mass of expertise and resources that has produced a steady stream of new knowledge and effective technologies. Not only have new products emerged, but there is now evidence that several of the target diseases are now in the process of being eliminated: Chagas disease, leprosy, lymphatic filariasis, and onchocerciasis (UNDP/World Bank/WHO Special Program for Research & Training in Tropical Diseases, 1997; Blanks et al., 1998)

Promoting Public-Private Partnerships for Health Research

Only 10 percent of the $50 to $60 billion that is spent every year for health research is used for research on the health problems of 90 percent of the world's people. A new entity, the Global Forum for Health Research (1999) has drawn attention to this 10/90 disequilibrium. It is seeking solutions to the problem in collaboration with the World Health Organization, the World Bank, private foundations, the pharmaceutical industry, NGOs, and other stakeholders. The central objective of the Global Forum is to help correct the 10/90 gap and focus research efforts on diseases representing the heaviest burden on the world's health by improving the allocation of research funds and by facilitating the collaboration among partners in both public and private sectors. It played an important role in the negotiations that led to the creation of the Medicines for Malaria Venture. The Global Forum has begun a project to identify all significant public-private partnerships and to map their origins, participants, aims, governance structures, degree of success, constraints, and difficulties. It hopes that by facilitating the exchange of information among potential partners, this database will promote and guide the development of new public-private partnerships.

Philanthropic Drug Donation Programs

Donation of drugs is a well-established charitable activity of private drug companies. Such gifts provide relief in times of disasters and other emergencies, as well as supporting poor countries and their communities. A more recent phenomenon is the donation of specific drugs with explicit major public health goals. Through its donation of ivermectin (Mectizan), Merck and Co., Inc., became the pioneer of this new type of giving (Dull & Meredith, 1998; Fettig, 1998).

The basis of the Merck donation is summarized by a telex sent on June 20, 1986, from Robert D. Fluss of Merck's Division of International Public Affairs to the director of TDR, Adetokunbo O. Lucas:

> Merck and the WHO have collaborated extensively on the development of ivermectin for onchocerciasis. We are very encouraged by the prospects that this drug will be the first new agent available in several decades, which will allow for the safe and effective treatment of patients on a mass scale. Merck intends to continue to cooperate with the WHO, the Onchocerciasis Control Program and endemic country governments, in their efforts to develop and implement programs so that the drug, when approved for use, can be distributed efficiently.

> *The special circumstances associated with this disease and the interest of several organizations and governments have caused Merck from the outset to consider ways of accommodating a variety of objectives. First and foremost is ensuring that the drug will be put to optimum use for the benefit of onchocerciasis patients and others who may be at risk of developing this disease. The company concluded that, in this case, the best way to achieve the full potential of ivermectin was to ensure that the economic circumstances of patients and governments in onchocerciasis-endemic areas would not prevent or restrict widespread use of the product once it is approved. Consequently, Merck is undertaking to make appropriate arrangements, if necessary with other interested parties, to make needed quantities of the drug available to these governments and patients at no cost to them for the treatment of onchocerciasis. (UNDP/World Bank/WHO Special Program for Research and Training in Tropical Diseases, 1994)*

Several other companies have now followed Merck's example in initiating philanthropic programs (table 2.2) (Kale, 1999; Wehrwein, 1999).

Charity versus philanthropy

Andrew Carnegie, the well-known philanthropist, made a clear distinction between charity and scientific philanthropy in his speeches and writings, most notably in his famous essay, "The Gospel of Wealth." He presents philanthropy as the mechanism by which "the surplus wealth of the few will become the property of the many. . . . *Administered for the common good . . . this wealth can be made a more potent force . . . than if distributed in small sums to the people themselves*" (author's emphasis). He warns that charity could have a "degrading pampering tendency on the recipients" whereas philanthropy was socially significant and beneficial (Wall, 1970). Charity can be a simple act like giving a handout to a beggar or writing a check to support a worthy cause. Philanthropy can be a more complex venture as, for example, establishing community libraries to support education and thereby empower people and reduce poverty. The first type of drug donation, consisting of random distribution of largesse, can be rightly described as charity. The donation of ivermectin, involving a clearly defined public health goal, can be classed as philanthropy.

Characteristic features of drug philanthropy

The four programs listed in table 2.2 have three important characteristic features:

Table 2.2. Philanthropic Drug Donation Programs

DRUG COMPANY	DRUG TARGET DISEASE(S)	PUBLIC HEALTH GOAL	PROGRAM MANAGER	MAJOR PARTNERS*
Merck	**Mectizan:** Onchocerciasis, lymphatic filariasis**	Elimination of onchocerciasis (and lymphatic filariasis in Africa)	Task Force for Child Survival & Development (Carter Center)	• Merck & Co. • Task Force for Child Survival & Development • WHO • African Program for Onchocerciasis Control
Pfizer	**Zithromax:** Trachoma	Elimination of blinding trachoma	International Trachoma Initiative	• Pfizer Inc. • Edna McConnell Clark Foundation • WHO
SmithKline Beecham	**Albendazole:** Lymphatic filariasis	Elimination of lymphatic filariasis	WHO	• SmithKline Beecham • WHO
Glaxo Wellcome	**Malarone:** Malaria	Control of drug-resistant malaria	Task Force for Child Survival & Development (Carter Center)	• Glaxo Wellcome • Task Force for Child Survival & Development • WHO—Roll Back Malaria

* In each case, many more partners are involved than are shown on these illustrative lists.
** An additional commitment by Merck.

A clearly defined purpose: In each case, the donation aims at a clearly defined public health goal in terms of a measurable and significant impact on the target disease. The objectives are described in somewhat ambitious terms such as, "global elimination of lymphatic filariasis" and "It is possible now that the world can soon end its war against blinding trachoma, a fight that has been waged for at least two hundred years."

Close link to a disease control program: The drug donation is designed as a component of the strategic plan for dealing with the problem. For example, in the donation of azithromycin for the elimination of trachoma, the control program includes four elements, the so-called SAFE strategy: Surgery, Antibiotic therapy, Face washing, and Environmental change (to increase access to clean water and better sanitation, and to increase health education) (Prüss & Mariotti, 2000).

Involving partnership with relevant stakeholders: Implementation of each program requires the collaborative effort of several partners (WHO, 1999a). Apart from the national government, partners usually include the donor company, WHO, institution responsible for program management, and non-governmental organizations that may undertake drug distribution and other interventions.

Brief summaries of selected programs

1. Trachoma, caused by infection with the organism Chlamydia trachomatis, is the commonest cause of preventable blindness. Under the leadership of the World Health Organization, a global strategy for the elimination of the disease has been developed and is being implemented in the most affected countries. Until recently, the application of tetracycline ointment daily for six weeks was the standard treatment. The replacement of the ointment with a single oral treatment with azithromycin greatly simplified the treatment of trachoma. The donation of azithromycin by Pfizer fulfills the main criteria for drug philanthropy. The purpose is to eliminate blinding trachoma. The donation is part of the global program that WHO prescribed consisting of surgery, antibiotic, face washing, and environmental sanitation. In the first five highly endemic countries that the program selected, significant partnerships have been developed including governmental and non-governmental agencies.

2. Lymphatic filariasis is a disfiguring and debilitating disease due to infection with filarial worms. In 1997, the Fiftieth World Health Assembly adopted resolution WHA50.29, calling for the global elimination of lymphatic filariasis as a public health problem. SmithKline Beecham has offered to provide albendazole free of charge to WHO for use by governments and other organizations working in association with these governments. The purpose of the drug philanthropy is the global elimination of lymphatic filariasis as a public health problem. The program is being developed and is expected to involve the treatment of all 'at risk' populations annually for four to six years. Since up to 1.1 billion people may be at risk of infection, the donation could comprise as many as 6 billion doses of albendazole over the lifetime of the program, estimated at 20 to 25 years. The drug will be given in combination with di-ethyl carbamazine to increase its efficacy, but in Africa, because of the danger of untoward reactions in patients who are concurrently infected with onchocerciasis, Merck has offered a free donation of ivermectin to be used

in combination with albendazole. Relevant partnerships are being forged to implement the program.

3. The Malarone Donation Program has proved to be a more complicated enterprise. The donated drug, Malarone, is highly effective against falciparum malaria and is specifically indicated for patients who are infected with drug resistant strains of the parasite. The drug is expensive (about U.S.$40 per course) and needs to be given over a three day period. It is, therefore, not suitable for mass treatment or community based distribution; rather, it is reserved as a second-line drug for patients who have laboratory evidence of failed treatment with standard drugs. It meets criteria for drug philanthropy. The purpose of the drug donation is:

- To reduce suffering and deaths from malaria by appropriate use of donated Malarone in endemic areas with known resistance to standard treatment
- To examine the most effective and responsible method of introducing a new, donated anti-malarial for use in endemic countries
- To explore ways to develop public-private partnerships for improving the health of people at risk from tropical disease

The pilot program in Kenya and Uganda was designed to determine the best way of incorporating the use of Malarone into the national malaria control program. The pilot programs were developed in partnership with the national governments and other agencies involved in malaria control (Oyediran & Heisler, 1999; Malarone Donation Program, 2001).

Experience gained so far

The Mectizan Donation Program (MDP) has operated long enough for one to undertake a meaningful review of its functioning and its achievements (Foege, 1998). Each year, the program approves requests for 30 to 40 million treatments (table 2.3). Most of the endemic areas of onchocerciasis both in Africa and in South America are covered. Several factors have contributed to the success that MDP has achieved so far:

An outstanding drug: Mectizan has a profile of good features that make it ideal for mass distribution: efficacy, safety, simple regime (single dose by mouth once a year), well tolerated (improved sense of well being encourages patients to report for repeat doses). Mectizan is the most potent anti-infective agent in clinical use; the single adult dose of 12 mg. once a year compares favorably with antibiotics

Table 2.3. Number of Mectizan Treatments Approved through Community-based Mass Treatment and Humanitarian Donation Programs, 1988-1999

YEAR	COMMUNITY-BASED	HUMANITARIAN*	TOTAL
1988	255,000	26,000	281,000
1989	239,200	112,200	351,400
1990	1,321,500	342,500	1,664,000
1991	2,779,800	448,300	3,228,100
1992	4,879,500	509,800	5,389,300
1993	9,050,300	324,600	9,374,900
1994	11,801,800	282,200	12,084,000
1995	15,607,700	269,900	15,877,600
1996	19,141,400	159,700	19,301,100
1997	33,725,000	169,500	33,894,500
1998	30,668,500	73,200	30,741,700
1999	29,740,700	110,400	29,851,100
TOTAL	**159,210,400**	**2,828,300**	**162,038,700**

* The Humanitarian program responds to random requests from individual practitioners for use in clinics and in other institutions. The program is managed directly by Merck from their Paris office (adapted from P. Gaxotte, 1998, Onchocerciasis and the Mectizan donation program, Sante, 8(1), 9-11.

like penicillin and tetracycline that require doses of 1000 mg. or more per day. Mectizan does not kill the adult worm and so it must be given annually to eliminate the larvae. Di-ethyl carbamazine (DEC), which was previously used for treatment of onchocerciasis, provoked reactions in infected eyes, often causing further damage; ivermectin does not cause such damaging complications and promotes the healing of early lesions (Abiose, 1998).

Unequivocal commitment by Merck: The donor company's commitment is summarized in the statement: "Providing Mectizan to as many who need it for as long as necessary." Merck recently announced a major expansion of the Mectizan Donation Program. In response to the finding that Mectizan is also effective against lymphatic filariasis, Merck will expand its donation within Africa for the treatment of lymphatic filariasis as well as onchocerciasis.

Effective Management: The Task Force for Child Survival and Development has set up an efficient mechanism for distributing the drug through the health authorities in the endemic countries and their partners. The distribution of ivermectin involves a wide network of organizations and agencies including the

World Heath Organization, ministries of health, national and international non-governmental organizations, and other community-based organizations.

Expert Guidance: The Mectizan Expert Committee, consisting of public health experts and liaisons from Merck and WHO, provides technical guidance to the program. With this arrangement, the donor company keeps in close touch with the program while ensuring that commercial interests do not interfere with operational decisions.

Comments on drug philanthropy

The Mectizan Donation Program has accumulated a decade of experience but the other programs are relatively young and are still largely in their formative period. Even at this early stage, it is valuable to ask critical questions about the concept of drug philanthropy and its implementation. Relevant questions at this stage include:

Priorities: Does the program address a problem of significant public health importance? Or, will it divert attention and resources away from more important national and regional priorities?

Program: Is the program technically sound? Does the drug have an appropriate profile of features to suit the needs of the program—efficacy, safety, tolerance, mode of application, etc.? Does it constitute a significant improvement on the existing package of interventions?

Prospects: Are the stated goals realistic? Can the distribution of the drug together with the other planned inputs deliver the expected outcomes? Is there an appropriate infrastructure in place or can it be developed to support the planned interventions?

These and similar issues need to be addressed in the planning stage of a special donation program.

Guidelines for drug philanthropy

WHO's guidelines for drug donations deal mainly with response to emergencies and some long term bilateral charitable gifts (WHO, 1996; 1999b). The first version was issued in May 1996 and represented the consensus of WHO in consultation with a wide range of organizations.[2] WHO has drawn up guidelines aimed at reducing inappropriate donations and guarding against abuse (WHO, 1999). But these guidelines do not apply to the new philanthropic drug donation programs.

At the very least, the new guidelines should address the three characteristic features of drug philanthropy:

- **Purposeful:** defined public health goal; measurable and significant impact
- **Defined disease control program:** strategic plan including chemotherapy as a component
- **Collaboration with relevant partners:** including those from both public and private sectors

The guidelines should address the issue of how to develop such programs when the donation involves the introduction of a new drug, as in the case of ivermectin and Malarone. The new guidelines should also address some of the issues that have arisen from the experience derived from the operation of the four pioneer programs.

Commitment: The donor company should be willing to make a long-term commitment. The long-term commitment may follow an initial pilot phase.

Management: Competent, effective management is required to deal with the various aspects of the program including mobilization of and collaboration with partners.

Avoidance of conflict of interest: In order to guard against real and apparent conflicts of interest, the system should include an appropriate buffer between the donor company and the operational decisions. Each of the four programs has endeavored to achieve this objective by handing over the management to a third party, supported by an independent expert advisory committee. For the Mectizan Donation Program, Merck devolved decision making to the Mectizan Expert Committee, a group of scientists and public health practitioners. Merck provided the supplies of Mectizan as recommended by the expert committee. In order to provide direct charitable contributions, Merck operates a humanitarian program from its Paris office; it provides gifts of Mectizan in response to requests from individual practitioners unrelated to the main program.

Comments on Public-Private Partnerships

The crisis in the health sector has induced governments in many developing countries to review the relationship between the public and the private sectors. Public-private partnerships will become increasingly more significant in the coming years as policy makers explore options for promoting complementary involvement of the private sector.

Philanthropy from the pharmaceutical industry is not a new phenomenon. The Wellcome Trust, the largest medical philanthropic foundation, with assets of the order of £13 billion pounds sterling (over U.S.$20 billion), is the product of the munificence of Sir Henry Wellcome, the owner of a pharmaceutical company. In spite of these and other philanthropic acts by some pharmaceutical companies, some people remain very skeptical about the motives of drug companies in making drug donations.

WHO now strongly supports the promotion of public-private partnerships with the caveat that such partnerships should be mutually beneficial; the transparent arrangements should be seen to make significant contributions to the health of people especially the populations in developing countries (WHO, 1998). This new policy of developing partnerships with the private sector has not gone unchallenged. Some of the activists who have vigorously campaigned against the private sector have expressed their unhappiness with WHO's new policy, as communicated in this statement appearing on the website of Baby Milk Action:[3]

> The industry agenda to coopt the UN and work in partnership with agencies such as WHO continues to cause alarm amongst NGOs working to protect public health. With the stakes so high, WHO's new draft Guidelines on Interaction with Commercial Enterprises could have an important role to play. The guidelines are, however, very disappointing and seem to be more an attempt to seek public approval for partnerships with corporations than to ensure that WHO stays true to its mandate to improve health. Some good suggestions are made, but the language used is contradictory and confusing, stressing the need for such things as "mutual respect, trust, transparency, and shared benefit." These concepts hold very different meaning for transnational corporations who have entirely different aims and values. Commercial enterprises are called on to abide by WHO policies on medicinal drugs, tobacco, and chemical and food safety, but no mention is made of WHO's infant feeding policies. (Baby Milk Action, 2001)

In spite of these criticisms and reservations, under its new leadership WHO has clearly indicated its commitment to work with the private sector. Dr. Gro Bruntland, the director-general of WHO, has held roundtable consultations with representatives of the pharmaceutical industry. WHO is also engaging industry on research projects aimed at finding new medicines for developing countries, on mechanisms for strengthening the Essential Drug Program, for combating the illegal traffic in fake medicines, etc. Several of WHO's new initiatives involve partnerships with the private sector:

- Roll Back Malaria
- Medicines for Malaria Venture
- Medicine for African Sleeping Sickness

Conclusion

The two examples of TDR and the drug donation philanthropic programs illustrate successful experiments in public-private partnerships. The TDR and donation programs can be seen as operating at different points in a continuum stretching from discovery to development, and finally to distribution of new drugs and other tools for disease control. The case studies illustrate needs and opportunities that can be met through public-private partnerships (Etya'ale, 1998).

Neither the public sector nor the private sector acting alone could have solved the problems that TDR tackled. By mobilizing the resources from both sectors, TDR developed mechanisms that produced new technologies that have been used effectively in controlling the target diseases. The important lesson to be learned from the TDR experience is that public-private partnerships can be used as effective mechanisms for developing new and improved technologies for controlling diseases affecting people in developing countries.

The examples of drug philanthropy need to be interpreted with care. Obviously, drug philanthropy cannot be a universal mechanism for providing drugs for use in developing countries. On careful reflection, one may be led to the conclusion that apart from the monetary value of the donated drug, the greater value of the cases of drug philanthropy is in leveraging well-designed and effectively managed control programs in collaboration with their partners.

Notes

1. The 30 member board includes the cosponsors (3), representatives of governments in developing countries (12), representatives of donors (12), and three other agencies or governments.

2. Churches' Action for Health of the World Council of Churches, the International Committee of the Red Cross, the International Federation of Red Cross and Red Crescent Societies, Médecins Sans Frontières, the Office of the United Nations High Commissioner for Refugees, OXFAM, and the United Nations Children's Fund. In 1999 the number of cosponsors expanded to include Caritas

Internationalis, the International Federation of Pharmaceutical Manufacturers Associations, Pharmaciens Sans Frontières, UNAIDS, the United Nations Development Program, the United Nations Population Fund, and the World Bank.

3. Baby Milk Action describes itself on this website as "a non-profit organization which aims to save lives and to end the avoidable suffering caused by inappropriate infant feeding. Baby Milk Action works within a global network to strengthen independent, transparent and effective controls on the marketing of the baby feeding industry."

References

Abiose, A. (1998, April). Onchocercal eye disease and the impact of Mectizan treatment. *Annals of Tropical Medicine & Parasitology, 92* (Suppl 1), S11–22.

Awadzi, K. (1997, October). Research notes from the Onchocerciasis Chemotherapy Research Centre, Ghana. *Annals of Tropical Medicine & Parasitology, 91*(7), 703–11.

Baby Milk Action (2001). Baby Milk Action homepage. Available from: *http://www.babymilkaction.org/*

Blanks, J., Richards, F., Beltran, F., Collins, R., Alvarez, E., Zea Flores, G., Bauler, B., Cedillos, R., Heisler, M., Brandling-Bennett, D., Baldwin ,W., Bayona, M., Klein, R., & Jacox, M. (1998, June). The Onchocerciasis Elimination Program for the Americas: A history of partnership. *Pan American Journal of Public Health, 3*(6), 367–74.

Cross, C. (1998, April). Partnerships between non-governmental development organizations. *Annals of Tropical Medicine & Parasitology, 92* (Suppl 1), S155–6.

Dull, H. B., & Meredith, S.E. (1998). The Mectizan Donation Program: A 10-year report. *Annals of Tropical Medicine & Parasitology, 92* (Suppl 1), S69–71.

Etya'ale, D. E. (1998, April). Mectizan as a stimulus for development of novel partnerships: the international organization's perspective. *Annals of Tropical Medicine & Parasitology, 92* (Suppl 1), S73–7.

Fettig, C. T. (1998) The donation of Mectizan. *Annals of Tropical Medicine & Parasitology, 92* (Suppl 1), S161–162.

Foege, W. H. (1998, April). 10 years of Mectizan. *Annals of Tropical Medicine & Parasitology, 92* (Suppl 1), S7–10.

Gaxotte, P. (1998). Onchocerciasis and the Mectizan Donation Program. *Santé, 8*(1), 9–11.

Global Forum for Health Research (1999). *The 10/90 Report On Health Research.* Geneva: Author.

Godal, T., Goodman, H. C., & Lucas, A. (1998). Research and training in tropical diseases. *World Health Forum,* 19(4), 377–381.

Kale, O. A. (1999). Review of disease-specific corporate drug donation programs for the control of communicable diseases. Paper presented at a conference jointly sponsored by Medecins Sans Frontieres Foundation (Paris) and WHO on Drugs for Communicable Diseases: Stimulating Development and Securing Availability.

Malarone Donation Programme (2001). Malarone donation program to end completion of the pilot phase [Online]. Available from: *http://www.malaronedonation.org/*

Oyediran, A. B. O. O., & Heisler, M. H. (1999). Malarone Donation Program. *Journal of Travel Medicine,* 6 (Suppl.), S28–S30.

Prüss, A., & Mariotti S. P. (2000). Preventing trachoma through environmental sanitation. *WHO Bulletin,* 78(2), 258.

UNDP/World Bank/WHO Special Program for Research & Training in Tropical Diseases (1994). *Tropical diseases research: Progress 1975–1994.* Geneva: World Health Organization.

UNDP/World Bank/WHO Special Program for Research & Training in Tropical Diseases (1997). *Prospects for elimination: Chagas' disease, leprosy, lymphatic filariasis, onchocerciasis.* (TDR/GEN/97.1). Geneva: World Health Organization.

UNDP/World Bank/WHO Special Program for Research & Training in Tropical Diseases (1998). *Tropical disease research: Progress 1997–98.* Geneva: World Health Organization.

Wall, J. F. (1970). *Andrew Carnegie.* Pittsburgh: University of Pittsburgh Press.

Wehrwein, P. (1999, Summer). Pharmacophilanthropy. *Harvard Public Health Review,* 32–39.

World Health Organization (1996). *Guidelines for drug donations.* WHO/DAP/96.2. Geneva: Author.

World Health Organization (1998). *Health for all in the twenty-first century.* Document A51/5. Geneva: Author.

World Health Organization (1999a). *Building partnerships for lymphatic filariasis.* Geneva: Author.

World Health Organization (1999b). *Guidelines for drug donations* (revised). WHO/EDM/PAR/99.3; 1–23. Geneva: Author.

World Health Organization (2000, February). "Public/private partners in sleeping sickness." *TDR News, 61.* Available from: *http://www.who.int/tdr/publications/tdrnews/news61/eflornithine.htm*

3

Cross-Sector Collaboration: Lessons from the International Trachoma Initiative

Diana Barrett, James Austin, and Sheila McCarthy

IN NOVEMBER 1998 THE EDNA MCCONNELL CLARK FOUNDATION and Pfizer Inc announced the formation of the International Trachoma Initiative (ITI), an organization with the immediate goal of implementing a multifaceted strategy to combat trachoma, a disease that blinds millions in developing countries. The creation of the ITI represented the latest phase of a strategic alliance between the Edna McConnell Clark Foundation (Clark)—a large, private, New York-based philanthropic foundation that in 1998 awarded $28 million in grants—and Pfizer—a global pharmaceutical company that in 1998 generated over $13.5 billion in revenue. An analysis of the partnership's evolution offers lessons of the potential power of this type of collaboration to more effectively leverage philanthropic resources.

In his book *The Collaboration Challenge* (2000) James Austin argues that cross-sector partnerships will increase in frequency and importance in the coming years, given the political, economic, and social forces that are driving more and more for-profit corporations and non-profit organizations to increase the scope and nature of their collaboration. Many are moving from arm's length philanthropic relationships toward collaborative relationships that are more intense, more strategic, and involve joint value creation. The shift represents an opportunity to magnify the social value and the benefits to the partners, but carries with it greater challenges and managerial demands than the traditional model of financial donation. Harvard Business School professor Michael Porter recently argued that philanthropy must focus on the creation of value rather than simply the donation of money, and, furthermore, that this is the social obligation of foundations, given the tax status they enjoy (Porter & Kramer, 1999). He suggests that a way to accomplish this is for foundations to act as catalysts for partnerships.

This chapter aims to deepen our understanding of the process of cross-sector collaboration in the public health arena and the factors contributing to effective

partnering. It examines the evolution of the Clark-Pfizer alliance, with particular reference to research findings from other studies of strategic partnerships
between non-profit organizations and corporations. After a brief description of
trachoma, we provide an overview of the evolution of the Clark-Pfizer relationship and then examine in more detail critical elements of the partnering process:
making the connection, achieving strategic congruency, creating value, and
managing the strategic integration.

Trachoma

According to the World Health Organization (WHO), about one out of every
ten people in the world are at risk of getting trachoma, over 150 million people
have the disease, and approximately 6 million are blind from it (Thylefors,
1995). Caused by the *chlamydia trachomatis* bacterium, the disease produces infections of the upper eyelid. Repeated infections over the course of many years
deform the eyelid, damaging the cornea and eventually leading to blindness.
Trachoma disproportionately affects women and has devastating consequences
for families (ITI, 2000). Importantly, the disease is both treatable and preventable. However, given the economic and development status of the countries
WHO has identified as high priority (table 3.1), resources to combat the disease
are often scarce. Adding to the difficulty of treatment are the different types of
resources needed for effective control of the disease, including surgery, antibiotics, and personal and environmental hygiene. In 1997, WHO formed the
Global Alliance to Eliminate Trachoma by 2020 (GET 2020), a coalition

Table 3.1. WHO-Identified Priority Countries

AFRICA	MIDDLE EAST	ASIA
Chad	Algeria	Myanmar
Ethiopia	Morocco	Nepal
Gambia	Oman	Pakistan
Ghana	Yemen	Vietnam
Guinea-Bissau		
Mali		
Niger		
Tanzania		

Source: World Health Organization Program for the Prevention of Blindness.

involving representatives from the research, governmental, non-profit, and for-profit sectors. According to the report of its first meetings, GET 2020 saw as its challenge "to coordinate activities and to mobilize resources to assist national governments with trachoma control programs as part of primary health care" (GET 2020, 1997, p. 3).

The activities of GET 2020 were centered on a multifaceted approach to control trachoma known by the acronym SAFE, which included:

Surgery to correct advanced stage trachoma
Antibiotics to treat active infection
Face washing to reduce disease transmission
Environmental improvement to increase access to clean water, better sanitation, and health education.

It also encouraged support for a World Health Assembly resolution in May of 1998 describing the SAFE strategy and calling on ministries of health to eliminate trachoma as a cause of blindness.

As part of its Program in Tropical Disease Research, the Clark Foundation had supported many of the studies that had contributed to the understanding of the disease and its control strategies. Beginning in 1985, it had provided grants for studies that formed the scientific basis for the development of the SAFE strategy (Clark Foundation, 1988–1999). The SAFE strategy underscores the complexity of trachoma control and the need for a comprehensive approach.

Evolution of the Clark-Pfizer Relationship

Austin's research on alliances between non-profit organizations and corporations revealed that they sometimes evolve along a "collaboration continuum." This continuum begins with a traditional *philanthropic* relationship of simply granting and receiving financial aid, then moves to a *transactional* stage in which the organizations engage in one or more focused activities, with both sides contributing resources to carry out goals seen as mutually beneficial. This increases the importance and potential benefits of the relationship to both organizations. The third *integrative* stage on the continuum entails a broader and deeper fusion of people, institutional resources, and activities that hold high strategic value for the partners. This organizational integration is more akin to an ongoing joint venture than a specific transaction. Some of the characteristics of the relationships between organizations in the different stages are shown in table 3.2.

Table 3.2 Collaboration Continuum

NATURE OF RELATIONSHIP

Philanthropic >>>> Transactional >>>> Integrative

Level of Engagement

Low >>>>>>>>>>>>>>>>>>>>>>>>>>>>>High

Importance to Mission

Peripheral >>>>>>>>>>>>>>>>>>>>>>>>Central

Magnitude of Resources

Small >>>>>>>>>>>>>>>>>>>>>>>>>>>Big

Scope of Activities

Narrow >>>>>>>>>>>>>>>>>>>>>>>>>Broad

Interaction Level

Infrequent >>>>>>>>>>>>>>>>>>>>>>>Intensive

Managerial Complexity

Simple >>>>>>>>>>>>>>>>>>>>>>>>>Complex

Strategic Value

Modest >>>>>>>>>>>>>>>>>>>>>>>>>Major

Source: Austin, 2000, p. 35.

The Clark-Pfizer relationship can be viewed within the context of Austin's collaboration continuum, although the nature of the interaction is somewhat different because Clark is a resource-granting organization. That is, unlike the non-profit organizations in the Austin study, which were operating non-profit organizations receiving funds, the Clark Foundation grants funds. Nevertheless, the framework is useful for analyzing the evolution of the Clark-Pfizer relationship.

Clark and Pfizer's initial relationship began in the early 1990s when each organization provided support for pilot studies to test the efficacy of Pfizer's antibiotic Zithromax (azithromycin) in children with clinically active trachoma. In 1992 and 1993, a pilot study was conducted by Dr. Julius Schachter and Dr. Chandler R. Dawson in Egypt. Dr. Robin Bailey and Dr. Sheila K. Mabey conducted a separate independent study in Gambia. Both compared Zithromax to the existing treatment of topical tetracycline and found equivalent or greater effectiveness. This led to the Azythromycin in Control of Trachoma (ACT) study carried out in Egypt, Gambia, and Tanzania, which was supported by Pfizer, Clark, and the National Institute of Allergy and Infectious Disease. Pfizer's primary liaison for these scientific studies was the medical director for anti-infectives in the international pharmaceutical group. Data from these studies indicated that Zithromax was an effective one-dose therapy for trachoma. This represented a vast improvement over the existing tetracycline treatment, which required topical application twice a day for six weeks, a regimen much more difficult to comply with.

At this stage, the Pfizer and Clark relationship can be viewed as philanthropic in terms of the characteristics delineated in table 3.2. While the two organizations collaborated at some level on these studies, the scope of activities was narrow and the interaction centered around the research and clinical staff in Pfizer's international pharmaceutical group and the researchers funded by Clark. However, the relationship started to shift as both Pfizer and Clark began to recognize the potential of Zithromax in broader trachoma control efforts and the opportunities that this presented.

In 1994 and again in 1995, Dr. Joe Cook, head of the Program for Tropical Disease Research at the Clark Foundation, briefed Paula Luff, manager of Corporate Philanthropy Programs at Pfizer, on the status of the Zithromax pilot studies. In 1995 they discussed the possibility of piloting a trachoma control program in Morocco. The international pharmaceutical group at Pfizer was also monitoring the progress of the ACT study and had begun thinking about the possibility of donating Zithromax once the ACT study had been completed and the WHO had recommended the use of Zithromax in the treatment of trachoma. In November of 1995 an interdivisional working group was formed at Pfizer to analyze the possibility of such a donation program. Of immediate concern was whether to recommend that Pfizer support a pilot project in Morocco. This project would involve significant collaboration with the Clark Foundation, the ministry of health in Morocco, and Helen Keller International, an operating non-profit involved in blindness prevention with a strong presence in Morocco. The working group met on a regular basis to work through the various issues associated with the project.

The relationship migrated from the philanthropic to the transactional stage with the decision to move forward with the Moroccan pilot. This was a focused activity in which both sides were contributing specific resources. As this trial went forward, the level of engagement between Clark and Pfizer increased, as did the strategic importance of the program for both organizations. Clark, with 25 years of experience in tropical disease research, provided the expertise of its tropical disease staff as well as funding. It also brought good will, which had been built up over many years of working with ministries of health, including their investigators, and non-governmental organizations in the endemic countries.

Pfizer, in addition to donating Zithromax for the pilot project, provided grants for public education to support other components of the SAFE strategy. Moreover, from the outset, the working group began to plan for expansion. The pilot was viewed by Pfizer's working group as an opportunity to understand better both the effectiveness of Zithromax and the challenges associated with its incorporation into a larger public health program.

Over the course of the Morocco Pilot, the interactions between Clark's tropical disease staff and Pfizer's working group intensified. Indeed, the Moroccan Pilot required partnership not only with Clark, but also with a range of organizations within the country. Thus, when the senior leadership at Pfizer and Clark made the decision to expand the trachoma program, the strategic centrality of the activity, the level of engagement, and the magnitude of resources all increased significantly, moving their collaboration into the integrative stage. This culminated in the decision to create a new non-profit organization, the International Trachoma Initiative—a joint venture with shared funding, combined governance, and the fusion of both organizations' core competencies. Let us now turn to the key elements that drove the relationship.

Making the Connection

Cross-sector partnerships do not happen; they are built. An emotional connection with the social purpose is usually the catalyst for forming the relationship. The prospect of a program that prevented blindness from trachoma resonated with leaders at both Clark and Pfizer. The Clark Foundation had spent 25 years funding research to prevent tropical diseases and now had an opportunity to build on this experience and see its research applied in affected communities. Indeed, it had funded the research that was credited by many with moving the scientific field of trachoma control forward and now had the opportunity to "finish the job." That is, it could help to make operational its research in a way that directly improved the lives of disadvantaged people, fulfilling Clark's core mission.

Leaders at Pfizer were also able to connect on an emotional level with this initiative. As one Pfizer manager put it, "One of the reasons people enjoy working at Pfizer is that we conduct medical research that helps with the illnesses that mankind suffers" (personal communication, November 8, 1999). Indeed, this type of initiative fit with Pfizer's stated value of providing care to those in need. Specifically, managers throughout Pfizer, including its marketing and clinical staffs, were motivated to pursue the use of Zithromax in the prevention of trachoma. Indeed, the internal working group that was formed to analyze the issues surrounding a philanthropic program was voluntary and required participants to take on this work over and above their existing responsibilities. Clearly, there was an emotional connection that served as a powerful motivator.

But connecting with the social purpose is not enough. The key staff involved in the collaboration must also be compatible. Bad interpersonal chemistry can quickly kill an alliance. Therefore, a "getting acquainted" period and process is needed to ascertain compatibility and develop a positive relationship. Clark and Pfizer interacted over eight years, beginning with the initial pilot studies in the early 1990s. This interaction intensified through their collaboration on the Morocco Pilot Study. This incremental engagement process also enabled them to undertake a due diligence assessment of each other to assess attitudes, capabilities, and commitment. Internally, Pfizer had considered several options in managing a trachoma initiative. These options included housing the program internally, partnering with other organizations, or partnering with Clark. In the end, the group recommended a partnership with the Clark Foundation, citing among other things the history of successful collaboration with Clark both in the initial studies and the Morocco Pilot.

These interactions built understanding and trust, which are important building blocks for strategic alliances. Ongoing management of an effective alliance or collaborative venture requires a mindset and a set of attitudes that allows them to function in an environment characterized by risk, instability, and the unknown. Indeed, many collaborations evolve in rather unpredictable ways, depending to a great extent on trust and confidence (Das & Beng, 1998). Pfizer executive vice president for corporate affairs, Lou Clemente, observed, "We felt comfortable with Clark from the beginning. We didn't have to sell them on things that were important to us. They knew what we were about, what would be important to us. And I think we were sympathetic with what they wanted to achieve" (personal communication, December 15, 1999).

Austin's work on cross-sector collaboration supports the importance of an emotional connection. He has found that beyond traditional measures of effective leadership such as involvement, consensus building, and strategic implementation, these innovative partnerships are fueled by the emotional connection that key participants make not only with the social mission, but also with their counterparts in the partnering organization (Austin, 2000). Perhaps this personal connection is at the nexus of the confidence and trust that allows these collaborations to develop. Personal connections become invaluable in developing the necessary levels of trust to proceed as the alliance unfolds and matures. This is particularly important when operating in an uncertain environment without the clear benchmarks that are often used by corporate managers.

There was a range of personal connections that helped to facilitate and solidify the Clark-Pfizer relationship. For example, some of the researchers funded by Clark had worked previously with Pfizer's scientists, so the two organizations had a small historical base of cooperation. This scientific connection continued with the trials of Zithromax. At the corporate level, the positive relationship between Ms. Luff and Dr. Cook was facilitated by a personal connection that helped to initiate the relationship. Ms. Luff recounted:

> There were a couple of fortuitous things. I came to Pfizer from CARE and it was around that time Clark's Tropical Disease Research Program had hired someone who used to work for me at CARE. She informed her boss, Joe Cook, that I was at Pfizer, and so we had breakfast at the Harvard Club and that is how it all started. At the same time, internally, our marketing and clinical trials folks had been working with Joe and they came to us and said, "We've got a great opportunity here, but we do the commercial side of things and we need help figuring out how to launch an international humanitarian effort." (personal communication, November 8, 1999)

Both Dr. Cook and Ms. Luff were instrumental in building support for this collaboration within their respective organizations. Austin's research reveals that top leadership support for the business–non-profit collaborations studied was essential to their becoming strong alliances. Within Pfizer, Ms. Luff and the working group were able to present the program to senior management and to build a "business case." Ms. Luff stressed that they needed to demonstrate that it was a sound, workable program that would achieve results. The pilot program in Morocco provided an opportunity not only to learn about complexities of implementing this type of program, but also to build support within the company and strengthen the personal relationships between the two organizations.

Likewise, Dr. Cook was able to build support for this program within the Clark Foundation. The support of senior leadership at both the Clark Foundation and Pfizer for the trachoma program was clear and vital. As one Clark official put it, "If Mike Bailin [President of the Foundation] had not been convinced of this, it never would have happened" (personal communication,

September 1999). Indeed, Mr. Bailin worked with Dr. Cook to build support for this collaboration at the board level.

Achieving Strategic Congruency

In addition to making the connections, strong alliances require a congruency of mission and strategy. Both Clark and Pfizer had missions that were supportive of eradicating disease. Clark was dedicated to improving the lives of poor, disadvantaged, underserved communities, with one of its strategic program areas being tropical disease research. This program had a long history of funding scientific research on the epidemiology and treatment of tropical disease. It had also funded studies to analyze the issues surrounding drug availability. Pfizer's mission as a for-profit pharmaceutical company had both economic and social dimensions. As William Steere Jr., chairman of the board and chief executive officer, stated in Pfizer's 1998 annual report, the company was focused on "discovering, developing, and bringing to market innovative medicines to save, protect, and enhance the lives of humans and animals." Moreover, a Pfizer manager stated, "We want to make sure that we develop medicines that work, that actually help people. We also would like to be a very profitable company, so it's kind of a dual motivation. And I think increasingly society is not seeing anything wrong with that" (personal communication, November 8, 1999). However, while there was overlap in missions, the strategies of the two organizations were initially somewhat different. Clark's strategy involved funding research; Pfizer's involved developing and commercializing pharmaceuticals. Shifts in strategy on both sides were needed to create a strong convergence.

Clark's strategic shift and issues

The Clark Foundation, like other foundations, was concerned with finding new ways to increase its social impact and was reexamining its traditional approach. Its president, Michael Bailin, had come to the Clark Foundation in 1996 from an operating non-profit and, as such, had a perspective on the role of foundations that was somewhat different from Clark's previous leadership. In Clark's annual report, he outlined his view that foundations in general, and Clark in particular, had a unique opportunity to mobilize expertise and focus on building capacity in the field. He suggested "a more deliberative philanthropic investment needed to be made—of both dollars and ideas—in the organizational strengthening of our grantees and the strategic cohesiveness of the fields in which we work" (Bailin, 1998). He was advocating for a different approach to grantees:

Instead of simply developing our own strategy, say around system-wide reform, and funding organizations to assist us in implementing that strategy, we would think of ourselves as investors in good products, services and ideas. That is, investing in organizations that had developed their own strategies and were having a measurable impact on disadvantaged populations. We would then take a more entrepreneurial approach and provide funding to assist with the development of sustainable programs that would have a long-term impact. This also means that instead of a traditional grant application, we would be more interested in a business plan that focused on the grantee's plans for growth and self-sustainability with clear benchmarks for success. (personal communication, April 12, 2000)

Under Mr. Bailin's leadership, Clark was examining what this strategy shift meant to the organization in terms of its culture, staffing, and existing programs. As part of this transition the organization began to assess its existing programs in a more rigorous way. The trachoma program presented a unique opportunity to test this type of approach for several reasons. Mr. Bailin commented:

The Tropical Disease Program had the advantage of being a conceptually rigorous program, which was grounded in the scientific method and focused on outcomes. It had had a tremendous impact in the field of trachoma control, but there was still work to do in terms of applying this knowledge in ways that would have real impact on the people affected by the disease. Collaboration with Pfizer to build this organizational capacity was exactly the kind of strategic shift we wanted to make as a foundation. Although somewhat different in that it was a new organization, the ITI was a good opportunity for us. We hoped to learn from it and to see not only if it is successful in terms of its stated goals to eradicate trachoma, but also, just as importantly, whether this type of organization would be a model for us going forward. (personal communication, December 15, 1999)

In addition, by the mid- to late-1990s, Clark had reached a decision point with regard to its Tropical Disease Research Program and, more specifically, trachoma. Several researchers commented that Clark had had an enormous impact in trachoma, providing funding for over a decade that served to move the field forward. However, it needed to decide how, if at all, it should carry this program forward. Mr. Bailin explained:

We basically took the idea to our board. We explained that we had supported a lot of scientific research in trachoma and trachoma control and that this was an opportunity for us to focus on implementing the results. It also allowed us to remain involved, but at the board level. Instead of simply phasing out trachoma funding and leaving it to others to apply the research, which is what we typically did in the past, this gave us an opportunity to create some long-term sustainability for trachoma control programs. The board agreed with this. (personal communication, December 15, 1999)

This approach to trachoma and general strategy shift raised several issues for Clark.

- **Need to Partner.** Given both the complex nature of trachoma control and the legal constraints of foundations, Clark would need to partner with other organizations in order to build sustainable programs. It would need to rely on others to make operational the research that it had funded. This implies that Clark would need to be more cognizant of its partners' needs and work with them closely to ensure a coordinated approach. With this comes risk that the values and needs of a partnering organization, in this case Pfizer, might conflict with the needs of Clark.

- **Shift in Strategy Requires Different Organizational Capacity.** Shifting to an "investment" approach from its traditional funding approach requires different management and organizational resources, which Clark is still in the process of building. Like many strategic shifts, it also challenged the culture of the foundation.

Despite these challenges, Clark knew that collaboration with Pfizer presented a unique opportunity to understand some of the demands of its new strategy. More importantly, it was an opportunity to assist in implementing and applying the trachoma research it had funded and to have a real impact on the affected populations.

Pfizer's strategic shift and issues

Before partnering with Clark, Pfizer had been involved with philanthropic ventures, such as its "Sharing the Care" program in the United States, which makes available its advanced pharmaceuticals at no charge to the uninsured. But the donation of Zithromax focused on a single disease and involved developing countries, which presented a new and different type of undertaking. It created a distinct opportunity as well as significant challenges for Pfizer. The opportunity seemed clear. Pfizer possessed an antibiotic that had proved effective in controlling one of the world's leading causes of preventable blindness. Indeed, it was considered to be a significant improvement over the tetracycline treatment and was recommended by WHO as the antibiotic component of its SAFE strategy. However, it was also clear that there was no viable commercial market for this application, given the poor economic conditions of the countries affected by trachoma. Instead, if it wanted to see Zithromax used for the treatment of trachoma, Pfizer would need to find a way to provide the drug at no charge to those affected by this disease. In addition to the potential impact on the affected population, a move to donate the drug was an opportunity for Pfizer to demonstrate its commitment to improving the health of those in need. However, this proposition carried with it a number of risks.

In general, the pharmaceutical industry has a mixed history with regard to drug donation programs. Merck's donation of ivermectin, a drug for the treatment of river blindness, generally is viewed as having had a positive impact both inside and outside the company, which positively influenced Pfizer's deliberations. The ivermectin program was housed within an independent entity, the Task Force for Child Survival. Merck had committed to providing the drug for as long as it was needed (see chapters 2 and 5).

However, there have been problems with other donation efforts that raised concerns. For example, Eli Lily received criticism in the press for problems that occurred when it donated an antibiotic to assist in the treatment of wounded in the Rwandan civil war between the Hutus and Tutsis (Crooks, 1998). The company was accused of dumping expired drugs for the purpose of a tax write-off. And while the company contended that this was not true and that, in fact, the drugs expired due to logistical problems over which they had no control, the accusations did not help the company's public image. Glenna Crooks argues that this case is a leading example of what can go wrong with drug donation programs both in logistical and public relations terms (Crooks, 1998). Within this context, a decision to donate Zithromax for the treatment of trachoma raised a number of issues for Pfizer:

- **Logistical and Bureaucratic Issues.** In addition to legal and regulatory issues, Pfizer was also concerned that the existing infrastructure would not allow the drug to reach those in need. The experience of other programs had highlighted the complexity of this process. Indeed, any program would require coordination with the local ministries and support of each country's governments. Additionally, it was important that WHO support the use of Zithromax in the treatment of trachoma. The complexity of these issues necessitated a collaborative approach.

- **Leakage of Zithromax onto the Black Market.** Given the logistical issues, there was a risk that the donated drugs would make their way onto the black market and displace existing commercial sales (Pfizer, 1996). Zithromax was a valuable drug that could be used to treat a number of human conditions, including respiratory infections in both adults and children. One of Zithromax's advantages is that it is rapidly distributed from the blood serum into the tissues. This allows a shorter course of treatment compared to many other antibiotics. Importantly, migrating white blood cells absorb extra quantities of the drug, allowing it to be delivered to the site of the infection. Zithromax was also considered one of the most potent anti-chlamydia drugs known. By 1998, according to Pfizer's Annual Report, it was the most prescribed branded oral antibiotic in the United States and a leader in international markets, generating over $1 billion in revenue for the company.

- **Need for SAFE Strategy.** Research had shown that effective trachoma control included more than the antibiotic, such that simply providing the drug would only have a limited or temporary impact on the disease. In fact, prevalence after tetracycline ointment has usually risen to previous levels in about 12 months (Dawson, 1982; West, 1995). WHO's SAFE strategy recognized the range of components necessary for effective trachoma control. Thus, the long-term effectiveness of Zithromax in trachoma control depended upon the implementation of a broader program that encompassed all components of the SAFE strategy. Pfizer recognized and stressed that it was not considering a drug donation program, but a public health program based on the SAFE strategy.

- **Need for Collaboration with In-Country Organizations.** Pfizer and Clark had funded a report on the institutional dimensions of trachoma control to understand better what kind of organizational capacity was needed for an effective trachoma control program (Reich & Frost, 1998). Part of these findings pointed to the need to partner with a multitude of organizations including ministries of health and non-governmental organizations (NGOs) in the countries where the disease is endemic. While ultimately helpful, such partnering magnified the complexity of the undertaking.

- **Selection Process.** Another issue for Pfizer was ensuring that the decision to launch a program in a particular country was guided by objective criteria. These criteria would help to ensure that the decisions made were based on what was best for the development of the program. Pfizer and Clark provided funding for a study to develop country-selection criteria, which was completed in early 1998. These criteria included: political stability, government support and ministry level activities in trachoma control, strong partners on the ground, data on disease prevalence, and commitment to all components of the SAFE strategy.

  These criteria provided guidance for the expansion of the program, helped to protect the program from internal and external pressure, and provided support for the selection of certain countries over others. This was particularly important because Pfizer wanted a phased project that allowed it to learn from its experience. Thus, it did not want to launch programs in all 16 of the WHO priority countries in its initial phase. Instead, it wanted a staged implementation that allowed it to gain experience and better understand the complexity of trachoma control.

- **Damaging Public Relations Situations.** A problem with any of the above would open the company to criticism. Thus, Pfizer could begin the program as a philanthropic effort but, if it were to encounter implementation problems, it could be faced with a damaging public relations situation. Handling of this would require additional resources to manage and improve the situation. In addition, since Pfizer supported a phased project and not a program with an open-ended commitment, there was also a need to carefully manage expectations.

Creating Value

Strategic alliances seek to create value for each partner. Cross-sector alliances also create social value—value that could not be created by either of the partners independently. The greater the value and more balanced the mutual benefit, the stronger the alliance. Clark and Pfizer each brought unique assets to their relationship that were complementary and would help to manage many of the risks raised by the proposed trachoma control program. Clearly, each organization could independently add some level of value to the trachoma control efforts, but that value could be multiplied if they combined their complementary capabilities and entered into a more formal collaborative and strategic relationship.

Doz and Hamel argue that business alliances have at least three distinct purposes: co-optation, co-specialization, and learning and internalization (Doz & Hamel, 1998). The first of these, co-option, turns potential competitors into allies, effectively neutralizing potential rivals. Co-specialization results from combining previously separate resources, skills, and knowledge sources. When these resources are bundled together, they in fact become far more valuable than when they are kept separate. Bundling was clearly the opportunity facing Clark and Pfizer.

Pfizer brought the drug production and logistics capability and management skills, as well as financial and staff resources, and Clark brought financial resources, its network of relationships with in-country organizations, as well as its credibility with governments, WHO, non-governmental organizations, and the research community. Under the leadership of Dr. Cook, the Tropical Disease Research Program had developed relationships with the scientific community, ministries of health in some of endemic countries, and non-governmental organizations working in trachoma control, which would be instrumental to the program's success. Both organizations were using their core capabilities and combining them synergistically to create additional social value.

In addition to the social value, there were benefits to be gained by each partner. Pfizer could enhance its reputation with external stakeholders and create pride and motivation among its employees. Merck's ivermectin donation program had clearly demonstrated that sizable benefits in this regard could be gained. Moreover, in some but not all markets, it could create more awareness about the benefits of Zithromax in the treatment of other diseases. Clark could also realize benefits. Because of its strategy shift, Clark saw the partnership as an important learning laboratory. One Clark official stated, "We are very interested in the issue of the creation of a new intermediary institution, because it is a possible strategy of investment partnerships for some of our other programs" (personal communication, April 12, 2000).

Research by Austin, as well as Doz and Hamel, suggests that alliances may also be an avenue for learning and internalizing new skills that can in turn be leveraged into other activities at future points in time. If Pfizer learns to work effectively with a foundation and is able to manage an alliance and add value to the work it could accomplish alone, these skills are likely transferable and valuable to additional work with Clark, but also to other possible collaborations. In fact, cross-sector alliances are so complicated that the lessons learned in this arena might be enormously useful in intra-sector alliances. Likewise, the lessons for Clark would likely be applicable to other collaborations with both for-profit and non-profit organizations. Indeed, as it moves forward with its institution- and field-building strategy, how it manages its collaboration with Pfizer and its relationship with the ITI could offer important lessons for the management of similar relationships in other program areas.

Central to value creation is the ability to understand your partner. One Clark official observed that you cannot create value

> *unless from the very beginning you sincerely inquire into what the other partner needs. For instance, our communications office encouraged us to be receptive to what Pfizer was saying about its communication needs. I think some foundations might have shied away from some of their communications requirements and the negotiation over wording. If there is going to be some announcement, Pfizer wants to be absolutely clear about everything. And they were right about that. I think our foundation is learning about this. (personal communication, September 1999).*

Pfizer Senior Vice President Lou Clemente similarly observed, as noted earlier, "I think we were sympathetic with what they [Clark] wanted to achieve."

Strategic Integration: Launching the ITI

The experience with the Morocco Pilot had led to a decision within Pfizer to expand the program. However, it wanted to maintain its ability to manage the process and closely monitor the progress of the initiative. Of central importance to Pfizer was its ability to demonstrate an impact on trachoma and not simply donate product. Likewise, Clark saw expansion as an opportunity to institution-alize much of the research it had funded and to "finish the job." The key issue was creating a structure that allowed for appropriate control, program credibility, and multi-institutional collaboration in selected countries. That is, as the part-ners moved from the transactional stage into the integrative stage on the collab-oration continuum, they faced the decision as to how best fuse their resources to bring the trachoma control program to fruition.

The ITI was established with a $3.2 million grant from Clark, a $3.2 million grant from Pfizer, and a commitment by Pfizer to provide approximately $60 mil-lion worth of Zithromax. It was originally housed within Helen Keller International, a New York-based non-profit organization that had a long history of working internationally to prevent blindness, including work with the two organizations on the Morocco Pilot. The ITI sought to carry out its mission by supporting the implementation of the SAFE strategy and, as such, became a member of GET 2020.

The ITI attained independent status when it received its 501(c) 3 tax status in 1999. It is governed by a joint board of directors with equal representation from Pfizer and Clark. This joint ITI board represents a high degree of organizational integration at the governance level. In addition, the ITI consists of a small secretariat and the Trachoma Expert Committee (TEC), as well as a series of national and international implementing partners (see figures 3.1 and 3.2).

The ITI secretariat supports the TEC and the board of directors, as well as its partner organizations. It is led by its executive director, Dr. Cook (formerly head of Clark's Program in Tropical Disease Research). The secretariat coordinates technical assistance in program planning, monitoring and evaluating, and manages the application process for ITI support. In doing so, it works closely with country programs to assist them with the development of applications through workshops and other technical assistance. The secretariat also oversees external communications regarding ITI activities and makes recommendations to the TEC and the board of directors, including recommendations regarding funding country programs.

The TEC includes a range of experts including experts in trachoma as well as individuals with expertise in international philanthropic programs. Liaisons from Clark and Pfizer as well as from WHO also sit on the TEC, as do representatives from the non-governmental organizations. It meets at least twice a year to review country plans, monitor progress of trachoma control programs, and provide technical oversight of ITI-supported activities. The establishment of the TEC broadened the spectrum of stakeholders and expertise, thereby enhancing the credibility of the undertaking. Its membership is shown in figure 3.1. The ITI board generally accepts the technical recommendations made by the TEC. This, in effect, represents the integration of these technical experts into the governance decision-making process.

The ITI initially committed to working with partner organization in five priority countries that were selected prior to the launch of the ITI based on the criteria developed by researchers at the Harvard School of Public Health. These countries included Mali, Tanzania, Vietnam, Morocco, and Ghana. The ITI invited applications from governmental and non-governmental organizations to

Figure 3.1. International Trachoma Initiative*

BOARD OF DIRECTORS	TRACHOMA EXPERT COMMITTEE		ITI SECRETARIAT
C. Lou Clemente, Chairman Executive Vice President Corporate Affairs Pfizer Inc	Joseph A. Cook, MD, Chairman Executive Director of the ITI	Michael R. Reich, PhD Taro Takemi Professor of International Health Policy, and Chairman, Department of Population and International Health Harvard School of Public Health	Joseph A. Cook, MD Executive Director
H. Lawrence Clark, Secretary Trustee The Edna McConnell Clark Foundation	Chandler Dawson, MD (began 10/99) Director Emeritus, Francis I. Proctor Foundation for Research in Ophthalmology University of California, San Francisco, CA	Sheila K. West, PhD El-Maghraby Professor of Preventive Ophthalmology Dana Center for Preventive Ophthalmology The Johns Hopkins University School of Medicine	Jeffrey W. Mecaskey Program Director Jessica Rose Program Associate Jessica Calderon
Michael Bailin President and Trustee The Edna McConnell Clark Foundation	Donald A. Henderson, MD Director, Center for Civilian Biodefense Studies and Professor of Epidemiology The Johns Hopkins University School of Hygiene and Public Health	*NGO Representatives*	
Joseph Feczko, MD Senior Vice President, Medical and Regulatory Operations Pfizer Inc		Hannah Faal, MB, BS (ended 9/99) Sight Savers International Banjul, Gambia	
Edward C. Schmults Chairman, Board of Trustees The Edna McConnell Clark Foundation	Adetokunbo O. Lucas, MD, FRCP (retired) Professor of International Health, Harvard School of Public Health and former Director, UNDP/World Bank/WHO Special Program for Research & Training in Tropical Disease	Virginia Turner, DPH (began 10/99) Helen Keller International Arusha, Tanzania	
Mohand Sidi Said President Asia, Africa, Middle East Pfizer Inc		Volker Klaus, MD (designate) Christoffel Blindenmission Munich, Germany	
	David C. Mabey, BM, MRCP (term ended 9/99) Professor of Communicable Diseases London School of Hygiene ad Tropical Medicine	*Institutional Liaisons*	
		Bjorn Thylefors, MD World Health Organization Geneva, Switzerland	
	Nyi Nyi, PhD Director, Program Division (retired) UNICEF	H. Lawrence Clark The Edna McConnell Clark Foundation	
		Paula Luff Manager, Corporate Philanthropy Programs Pfizer Inc	

* Source: International Trachoma Initiative, 1999 Annual Report.

support trachoma control programs and stressed that the partners should "demonstrate the capacity to plan, manage, and evaluate trachoma control activities" (ITI, 1999). The ITI stated it would assist partner organizations with three types of support: technical assistance, donation of Zithromax, and targeted financial support.

Exhibit 3.2. Network of Partnerships (as of December 2000)

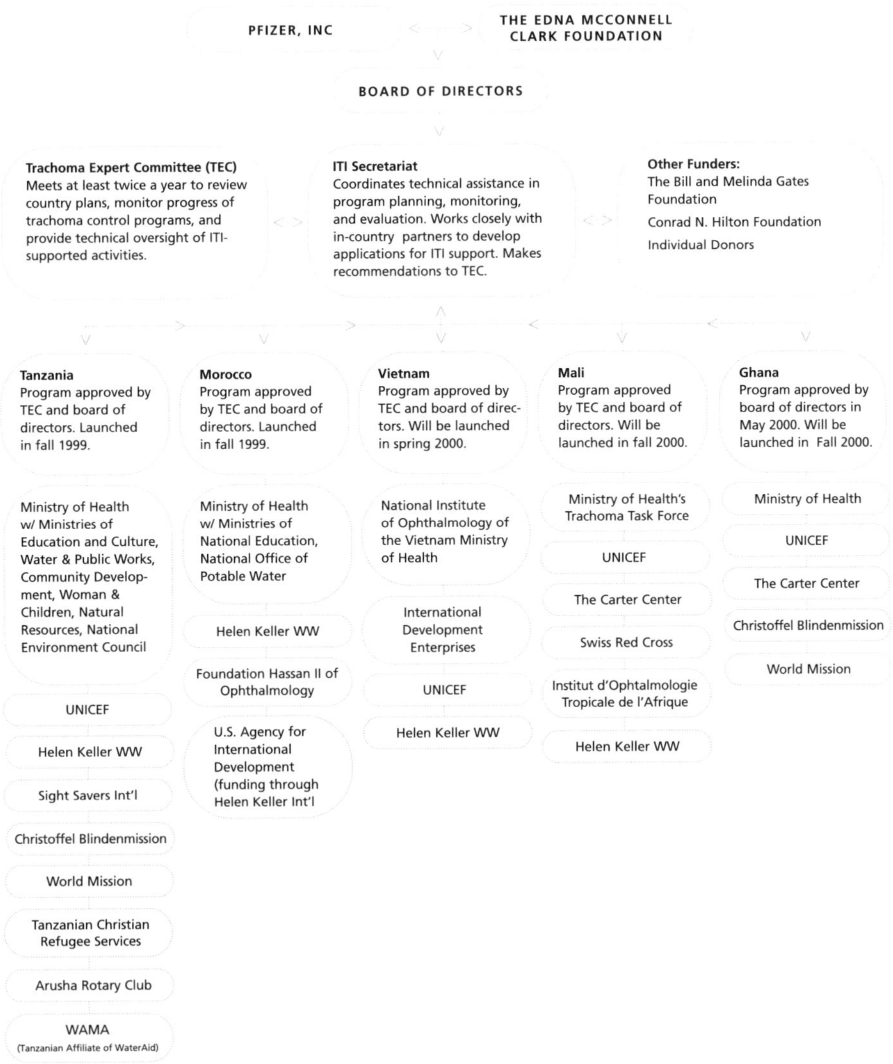

PFIZER, INC

THE EDNA MCCONNELL
CLARK FOUNDATION

BOARD OF DIRECTORS

Trachoma Expert Committee (TEC)
Meets at least twice a year to review country plans, monitor progress of trachoma control programs, and provide technical oversight of ITI-supported activities.

ITI Secretariat
Coordinates technical assistance in program planning, monitoring, and evaluation. Works closely with in-country partners to develop applications for ITI support. Makes recommendations to TEC.

Other Funders:
The Bill and Melinda Gates Foundation

Conrad N. Hilton Foundation

Individual Donors

Tanzania
Program approved by TEC and board of directors. Launched in fall 1999.

Morocco
Program approved by TEC and board of directors. Launched in fall 1999.

Vietnam
Program approved by TEC and board of directors. Will be launched in spring 2000.

Mali
Program approved by TEC and board of directors. Will be launched in fall 2000.

Ghana
Program approved by board of directors in May 2000. Will be launched in Fall 2000.

Ministry of Health w/ Ministries of Education and Culture, Water & Public Works, Community Development, Woman & Children, Natural Resources, National Environment Council

Ministry of Health w/ Ministries of National Education, National Office of Potable Water

National Institute of Ophtalmology of the Vietnam Ministry of Health

Ministry of Health's Trachoma Task Force

Ministry of Health

Helen Keller WW

International Development Enterprises

UNICEF

UNICEF

The Carter Center

The Carter Center

Foundation Hassan II of Ophthalmology

UNICEF

UNICEF

Swiss Red Cross

Christoffel Blindenmission

Helen Keller WW

U.S. Agency for International Development (funding through Helen Keller Int'l)

Helen Keller WW

Institut d'Ophtalmologie Tropicale de l'Afrique

World Mission

Sight Savers Int'l

Helen Keller WW

Christoffel Blindenmission

World Mission

Tanzanian Christian Refugee Services

Arusha Rotary Club

WAMA
(Tanzanian Affiliate of WaterAid)

The decision made by Pfizer and Clark regarding the ITI's structure and strategy, along with the two-year funding commitment, offered four advantages:

- **Joint Control.** This provided Pfizer with some protection from potential criticism as well as internal and external pressure, since it shared governance with Clark and the TEC, but gave day-to-day decision-making power to the secretariat. For Clark, it provided an equal voice that was important given Pfizer's size relative to Clark, which could distort the partnership.

- **Independence.** The structure allowed the collaboration to develop the management processes and culture that were appropriate for its strategy and working environment. It created some independence from the founding organizations, which would allow it to establish greater credibility. It also provided a path for the evolution into an organization that eventually could be governed and funded by other organizations in addition to just the two founders. This fit particularly well with Clark's desire to fund self-sustaining organizations.

  Many collaborations among companies have led to the formation of joint ventures designed to share known risks (Doz & Hamel, 1998). In this instance, it seemed as if the problems likely to occur were so predictable that the alliance needed to be set up as a separate business. This allowed the alliance managers to forge their own identity, an identity that is fundamentally different from that of either of the partner organizations. This guaranteed that the agenda did not become subsumed under the overall corporate or cross-sector agenda and will stay on center stage as it develops and matures.

- **Network Development.** For the trachoma initiative to be successful, a network of other international, governmental, and non-governmental organizations must be involved. This was demonstrated in the Morocco Pilot, which involved Helen Keller International and the Morocco Ministry of Health. Their involvement was cited as an important success factor in the pilot (Reich & Frost, 1998). Moreover, each country needed to establish a unique set of partnerships that were appropriate to its situation. For example, the Tanzanian effort requires partnership with eight partner organizations in addition to the Tanzania Ministry of Health. These organizations include: Helen Keller International, Sight Savers International, Christoffelblinden Mission, World Vision, Tanzanian Christian Refugee Services (now known as SEMA), the Arusha Rotary Club, and WAMA (the Tanzanian affiliate of WaterAid). The Morocco program involved the Ministry of Public Health, the Ministry of Basic Education, Helen Keller International, National Office of Potable Water, and Fondation Hassan II. See figure 3.2 for a list of the various partnerships at work. The ITI's strategy was designed to encourage these partnerships to develop with organizations and governments with in-country expertise and experience.

- **Integration of Lessons Learned.** The commitment of interventions in the five countries over an initial two-year period allowed the ITI and its partner organizations to manage some of the risks as well as expectations. It also provided a clear time frame for evaluation. Each of the partners understood that this was an evolutionary process that likely would require changes over time based on the lessons learned related to the partnership with in-country programs, as well as the relationships among Clark, Pfizer, and the ITI.

However, the structure and time frame also created a number of management and organizational challenges. Six are noted here:

- **Some Loss of Control by Founding Organizations.** This appeared to be a greater issue for Pfizer, which needed to ensure that Zithromax was used appropriately and its distribution was managed in a way that minimized the threat of leakage.

- **Need for Strong Leadership.** The ITI needed to develop its own credibility within the field. While the founding partners brought a history and credibility to the ITI, the ITI needed to establish its own credibility as an organization, which takes time and strong leadership. It also required that bridges and connections be built between the new organization and both of the partners—an ongoing management challenge. The downside of establishing a separate organization to achieve the goals of the alliance without such bridges is that the new organization will become insular, unable to draw on the skills of the existing partners or to provide new learning for the parent organizations. With the appropriate leadership, however, agendas should be reinforcing rather than competing. The separateness of the new entity should guarantee the necessary support to add value without the constant need to argue for additional financing in a resource-constrained environment

- **Additional Administrative Resources.** The establishment of a separate organization requires additional resources or overhead separate from the two founding organizations. Financial resources would need to be dedicated to staffing the ITI in addition to the in-country partner organizations.

- **Clear Communication and Reporting Mechanisms.** Research on other alliances points to the importance of communication between the partners as essential to preserving an effective relationship (Austin, 2000). This partnership evolved based on strong personal relationships and open communication. However, as the ITI matures it will be important to institutionalize these communications, so that they remain even if staff or leadership changes. This is particularly important as the needs of the two founding organizations and that of the ITI evolve.

- **Management of Other Stakeholder Relationships.** While ITI is governed and was initially funded by Pfizer and Clark, its success in achieving its ultimate goal is dependent upon relationships with other stakeholders. For example, WHO is an important stakeholder, as are the array of in-country organizations shown in figure 3.2 and any additional organizations that provide funding. The initial two-party alliance expands into cascading partnerships that form an implementation coalition. This increases the managerial and political complexity of the undertaking. One of the critical challenges will be to achieve a clear definition of institutional roles and responsibilities and create the coordinating mechanisms and incentives that ensure efficiency and accountability.
- **The Need to Demonstrate Short-Term Outcomes.** While the short timeframe provides focus, it also requires that the ITI demonstrate progress in a relatively short period of time.

Conclusion

It may be too soon to evaluate whether the ITI will attain its ultimate goal of improving the control of trachoma. However, early indications are quite positive. In December 2000, the ITI announced that the pilot projects in Morocco and Tanzania had cut the prevalence of trachoma by over 50 percent among two million people in just over one year. Based on the success in Morocco and Tanzania, the ITI was planning to expand its program to reach 30 million people at risk of trachoma-related blindness worldwide. Trachoma control programs were underway in Mali and Vietnam, and another was slated to begin in Ghana in early 2001. Moreover, the ITI had received an additional $6 million in funding over three years from the Clark Foundation, and from Pfizer 10 million doses of Zithromax for trachoma control and $6 million in funding over three years for operational expenses. In addition, the Bill and Melinda Gates Foundation committed to contribute $20 million over five years, and the United Kingdom's Department of International Development agreed to provide £1 million over the next year (ITI, 2000a).

At the time this chapter was written, the founding organizations and the leadership of the ITI were pleased with the progress so far. Ms. Luff commented that the ITI had done a "remarkable job," while Mr. Bailin was similarly enthusiastic about the accomplishments of the ITI. Dr. Cook in a press release commented on the ITI's work to date: "No other country or program has even attempted to deliver all four components of the SAFE strategy, appropriately balanced to a large population of people living in trachoma-endemic areas. The progress we have made exceeded our own expectations for our first year's operations" (ITI, 2000b).

However, the ITI and the founding organizations also recognized that they faced challenges in the future. By 1999, the ITI has already begun to think about additional sources of funding beyond those of the founding partners. It also had learned a great deal about the complexity of the relationships with its in-country partner organizations. For example, the ITI seeks to be a partner, but it is also a potential funder. This can create tension when working with in-country organizations, which understandingly may share different information with a funder than with a partner. In addition, as it considers expansion it would likely need to revisit the selection process for countries. In its initial phase, as a pilot, the founders had pre-selected the countries in which the ITI would work. However, as it expands, the ITI will have to determine a process that meets its needs as well as those of the founding organizations.

Pfizer and Clark will also need to manage their relationship with the ITI within the context of their own organizations. Pfizer will need to reevaluate the risks and benefits of the program within the context of the ITI's experience to date. While it is pleased with the progress so far, it still needs to closely monitor the use and distribution of Zithromax. Likewise, Clark will need to reevaluate its approach within the context of its evolving strategy and approach to its grantees. For example, as it more fully develops its approach to grant making, Clark will need to decide to what extent it will ask the ITI to meet the same criteria as other organizations, such as the development of a clear business plan that outlines it strategy for growth and benchmarks for success.

Clearly, the organizational model of the ITI offers some key lessons for foundations and organizations that are attempting to collaborate to solve politically charged and complex social problems.

From the standpoint of a for-profit entity, such as Pfizer, the model provides control while minimizing some of the risks by creating an independent organization that can establish credibility for a philanthropic program by protecting it from actual or perceived pressure from the for-profit organization. The model also allows the program to develop the operating mechanisms and expertise appropriate for the program, which might be somewhat different from those of the collaborating organizations. For foundations, this type of model can leverage expertise developed in program areas to build sustainable implementing institutions that can exist beyond the foundation's funding commitment.

That being said, if the ITI is going to be a sustainable social enterprise that makes a difference in eradicating trachoma, it must deal with considerable organizational complexity. This includes the management of the Clark-Pfizer relationship, which has moved to a highly integrative relationship of strategic importance to both organizations, involving high levels of engagement and managerial complexity. However, it also involves the establishment and maintenance of other alliances with organizations such as WHO, as well as the various nongovernmental and government organizations. This requires a complex structure that must exist in multiple countries and relies on symbolic as well as operational leaders. Moreover, it requires a commitment to a range of outcomes important to the various stakeholders.

Although the outcome of the ITI remains to be seen, the Pfizer-Clark collaboration provides a rich example of how the core capabilities of corporations and non-profit organizations can be powerfully combined to create mutually and socially beneficial undertakings. Cross-sector collaboration clearly holds significant potential for contributing to societal betterment.

References

Austin, J. E. (2000). *The collaboration challenge: How nonprofits and businesses succeed through strategic alliances*. San Francisco: Jossey-Bass.

Bailin, M. (1998). President's essay, 1998 Annual report. New York: Edna McConnell Clark Foundation.

Crooks, G. (1998). Drug donation: Protecting industry philanthropy. *Pharmaceutical Executive, 18*(8), 66–76.

Das T. K. & Teng, B.-S. (1998). Between trust and control: Developing confidence in partner cooperation in alliances. *The Academy of Management Review, 23*(3), 491–513.

Dawson, C. R., Daghfous, T., Hoshiwara, I., et al. (1982). Trachoma therapy with topical tetracycline and oral erythromycin: A comparative trial. *Bulletin of the World Health Organization, 60,* 347–355.

Doz, Y. L. & Hamel, G. (1998). *Alliance advantage: The art of creating value through partnering*. Boston: Harvard Business School Press, p.5.

Edna McConnell Clark Foundation (1988–1999). Annual reports. New York: Author.

GET 2020 (1997). Report of the first meeting of the WHO alliance for the global elimination of trachoma. Geneva: World Health Organization, p.3.

International Trachoma Initiative (1999). Program information, July 12 update. New York: Author.

International Trachoma Initiative (2000a). Press release, April 1. New York: Author.

International Trachoma Initiative (2000b). Press release, December 4. Geneva and New York: Author.

Pfizer Inc. (1996). Trachoma working group minutes, April.

Porter, M. & Kramer, M. R. (1999). Philanthropy's new agenda: Creating value. *Harvard Business Review, 77*(6), 121–131.

Reich, M. R., & Frost, L. (1998). *Institutional dimensions of trachoma control (Research report)*. Boston: Havard School of Public Health.

Thylefors, B., Negral, A. D., Pararajasegaram, R., & Dadzie, K. Y. (1995). Global data on blindness. *Bulletin of the World Health Organization, 73*, 115–121.

Social burden of blinding trachoma exceeds US $1 billion a year. (2000). *Trachoma Matters: A Newsletter of the International Trachoma Initiative, 2*(1).

West, S., Muñoz, B., Lynch, M., et al. (1995). Impact of face washing on trachoma in Kongwa, Tanzania. *Lancet, 345*, 155–158.

4

The Ethics of Public-Private Partnerships

Marc J. Roberts, A. G. Breitenstein, and Clement S. Roberts

MUCH WRITING ON PUBLIC-PRIVATE PARTNERSHIPS has assumed that such partnerships are a good thing. Success has been defined by whether the partnership flourishes, and authors advise managers on how to bring that about (Kanter, 1999; Smith, 1994; Birchard, 1999). This paper takes a different tack. We explore how participants in partnerships *should* behave from an ethical perspective. How can NGOs, CEOs, and WHO bureaucrats know whether they are doing the right thing in partnership undertakings? What obligations to engage in such ventures are incumbent upon those who manage the various companies and agencies that might become partners?

Our argument is quite general. We will, however, focus on international health, as this is both the context for much partnership activity and a potential example for other arenas of joint action. We begin by analyzing the current debate about corporate responsibility—which constitutes the general frame for corporate participation in partnership activities. Then we ask under what circumstances organizations and individuals have an obligation to try to create successful partnerships. Having argued that there are such obligations, we then go on to discuss what they might be.

We explore the question of corporate responsibility because that is where the most pointed ethical issues arise. Few would deny that the officers of not-for-profit organizations should not ruthlessly defend organizational interests at the expense of the social goals their organizations were created to pursue. We will, however, briefly treat the issues confronting non-corporate partners toward the end of the paper.

We hope that readers who disagree with our particular set of answers will at least accept the importance of our questions. Public-private partnerships raise important issues about national and international social policy and the appropriate role of the private sector. The Nike slogan "Just Do It!" is not a sufficient basis for thinking about these issues.

Not All Partnerships Are Desirable

This point may seem obvious, but it is widely ignored. Not all public-private partnerships are equally desirable. For example, a partnership between an advanced technology company and a grassroots organization, to help the latter acquire the former's products, might seem unambiguously good. But suppose that partnership is between an arms manufacturer and a street gang! Simply looking at whether the resulting partnership has succeeded in meeting the goals of the cooperating organizations is not sufficient basis for evaluating such an agreement.

The underlying point—that carrying out one's role in an organization does not insulate an individual from moral criticism—is broadly applicable. After all, the I-was-just-following-orders defense was rejected by the Nuremberg tribunal. We will argue that managers have an obligation not only to create partnerships, but also to use them to pursue particular ethical goals. Indeed, we believe the ethical appropriateness of a partnership's actions can only be evaluated in terms of such goals.

The particular ethical goal we advocate involves two elements. First, the ethical obligations of any particular corporation depend on its arena of economic activity. Automobile companies and drug companies are not the same. Second, the goal of providing minimum levels of opportunity to the poor of the world—especially in poor nations—should be a major priority. And health, as we will explain, is an important component of opportunity.

Can We Impose Obligations on Corporations?

What rights and responsibilities do corporations have? Our first argument is a negative one. Corporations do not have some fundamental or natural right to pursue profit and only profit. Hence, it is at least conceivable that they might have other obligations—like the ones to participate in certain kinds of partnerships which we are going to argue for shortly.

The conventional view of for-profit corporations is that they have all the rights of individuals, but none of the responsibilities (Moore, 1999, p. 329; see also Crossley, 1999). This perspective we call corporate libertarianism. It relies on a three-step analysis. The first claim is that the philosophical arguments that justify the existence of private property rights are correct. The second argument is that these rights are also possessed by corporations. The third argument is that no other obligations can be expected of, or imposed on, corporations.

As articulated by John Locke, the argument for private property rights is that individuals could legitimately appropriate unclaimed natural resources in pre-modern times (Locke, 1988). Such property was necessary for them to exercise their freedom and autonomy. With ample property to go around, such appropriation did not deprive anyone else of their livelihood. Locke then argued that *if* property had been transferred legitimately since then, the existing distribution of property in turn also would be acceptable.

The second step of the argument is the claim that individuals can transfer these rights as they wish—including giving them to corporations. As legal fictions, with the same rights as individuals, corporations can legitimately exercise these property rights (Iwai, 1999).

Now comes the critical third step. Since the directors and officers of a corporation are the agents of its shareholders, it is their obligation—and their *only* obligation—to act on shareholders' behalf. This means they must do everything they can to maximize shareholders' returns. Pursuing any other objective would constitute an illegitimate appropriation of shareholder property (Leung, 1997).

This view has a good deal of support in the law. Directors traditionally have been legally liable to suits from shareholders for decisions that did not meet the test of shareholder's interests (Orts, 1992, pp. 21–22). Interestingly, a few states have recently begun to modify that standard. So-called constituency or stakeholder statutes allow (but do not require) officers to consider interests of workers, customers, and suppliers in making decisions (Orts, 1992, p.16). Yet this new perspective is far from established compared to the traditional view.

For us, the effort to establish an unlimited right to pursue corporate profits based on individuals' natural right to property is fundamentally unpersuasive. How can the existing distribution of property—the product of generations of force, fraud, and the exercise of monopoly power—have any transcendent moral status?

In our view, the meaning and content of all property rights is not a matter of "natural law," but rather of legal convention (Moore, 1999, p. 333). Various legal and political processes have defined the particular bundle of rights attached to any piece of property. Regulations require property owners to control pollution, operate safe workplaces, refrain from discriminating, impose zoning limits on their construction activities, and so forth. This is especially evident in the case of intellectual property rights (such as patents and copyrights), which are the artificial creation of the legal system to begin with.

The same arguments apply even more strongly to the rights of corporations. Their internal governance, liability obligations, accounting requirements, etc., are all the product of legislative action and legal adjudication. As legal fictions, corporations are quintessentially legal artifacts. Not just individual corporations, but also their patterns of interaction in the marketplace are subject to social and legal processes. A market economy is a game played according to socially constructed rules. An enormous cultural and legal infrastructure defines the "teams," the "referees," and the "stadiums" (consider weights and measures, health codes, contracts law, banking and securities regulation, etc.). Moreover, the law itself is not enough. As Kenneth Arrow, the Nobel prize-winning economist has argued, if transactions are even to be possible, widespread voluntary adherence to an extensive set of specific norms and behaviors is required (Arrow, 1974).

So the question is not whether we can impose responsibilities and expectations on corporations. Because they are socially constructed entities, with socially constructed property rights, playing a socially constructed game, clearly we can. Instead, the question is, Is the existing set of formal contracts and informal rules the best we can construct to meet our objectives? That is an empirical question. Even FIFA, the governing body of world football (soccer) recently changed several rules (the offsides rule, and when goalkeepers could handle the ball) in order to improve the game. That doesn't mean the rules of football are now perfect. More tinkering may seem advisable in the future. Our claim is that some tinkering now—and perhaps in the future—with the norms of corporate governance could also produce some improvement in the game of world capitalism.

Evaluating the Arguments Against Corporate Responsibility

Should corporations be asked or expected to take actions that do not maximize shareholder value? (We are assuming that at least some partnerships will not maximize shareholder value—otherwise the whole question would be both easy and uninteresting!) The conventional argument against such calls for corporate responsibility is often not libertarian but utilitarian. It comes from the vision of general economic equilibrium in the presence of perfect competition. Given a large number of (empirically incorrect) assumptions, a perfectly competitive economy will be "efficient" in a certain narrow sense. It will produce a situation that economists call Pareto Optimal, where no one person could be made better off without someone else being made worse off. In the models used to derive this result, producers are presumed to maximize profit. Therefore, the argument goes, imposing social responsibility on corporations will lead them away from profit maximization and, hence, will diminish economic efficiency (Friedman, 1970).

The problem with this argument is that the real world is very far from being perfectly competitive. Well-established economic analysis reveals that once an economy is imperfect, we might be better off *not* trying to satisfy as many of the conditions of the pure case as possible. Instead, in a "second-best" world—which we surely inhabit—compensating imperfections might well produce the best available results (Lipsey and Lancaster, 1956). So the claim that responsibility will spoil perfection and necessarily make us worse off is not compelling. It all depends on the specifics of the situation.

Moreover, other things in life matter beside economic efficiency. The efficient outcome might be very unjust, and some efficiency loss might be acceptable to produce a more equal income distribution. To do this, corporations might have to act in ways other than maximizing profit. Again, such a possibility cannot be ruled out without further discussion.

The case for imposing additional obligations on corporations is reinforced by the realization that managers already use funds in ways that suit their—but not shareholders'—interests. Many corporations operate in markets that are imperfectly competitive. In such oligopolies, where there are only a few sellers, firms can make very substantial profits. Such potential profits are often appropriated by managers: to increase their own compensation, to pay for perquisites such as corporate airplanes, to indulge their desire for technological leadership, or simply to allow them to not work very hard (Simon, 1959). This is possible because the internal controls on managers, namely the ability of boards of directors to coerce them to maximize profits, is highly imperfect. Thus the discretionary use of corporate funds for objectives other than shareholder benefit already occurs on a substantial scale. Why not then subject it to some kind of social control or expectation?

While some defenders of corporate libertarianism criticize calls for social responsibility on the grounds that it would interfere with competition, others oppose such calls on the grounds that it would interfere with monopoly! They invoke the Austrian economist Joseph Schumpeter, who argued that by funding research and by providing the prize that motivated risk-taking, monopoly profits sustain technical progress (Schumpeter, 1947). Only large companies, he argued, were stable enough and protected enough from market forces to undertake long-term risky investments. This analysis has been used to oppose social responsibility on the grounds that such practices would diminish technical progress.

Even if Schumpeter's argument were empirically correct (which we doubt at least in part), it would not justify rejecting out of hand all proposals for changing corporate behavior. Surely it is possible to spend *too much* on new technology. The opportunity cost of what we give up elsewhere in the economy would, at some point, exceed the gains from more spending on research. Thus whether or not our proposals would produce more gain or cost, even if they did diminish technical progress, is an empirical question.

A final counterargument to new expectations is that society cannot renegotiate the social contract implicit in current corporate law without being unfair to those who made investments and commitments based on past rules. However, this too is an overly broad claim. Even under commercial contract law, there are situations in which contracts can be renegotiated—such as unanticipated circumstances or unconscionable outcomes. Courts have also declared contracts unenforceable on grounds of public policy—because, for example, they impair family relations or imply a promise to violate a fiduciary responsibility (Farnsworth, 1998). Following such logic, one might argue, for example, that the drug patent system was developed in a situation where the world HIV epidemic was unanticipated and that relying on that system will deprive tens of millions of people of treatment in a way that is unconscionable.

Clearly, new rules could raise fairness issues. But whether they do or not, in any specific case, needs to be looked at in detail. Moreover, there is at least some hypocrisy in making such a general claim, since industry often proposes changes in rules and regulations to benefit itself. And it seldom characterizes such modifications as unfairly violating society's expectations.

From the Organization to the Individual

Now we have to make the transition from organizations to individuals. The classic position on corporate managers is that they are mere employees whose responsibilities are exhaustively defined by their employment contract. This implies that individual managers should pursue corporate responsibility only to the extent that they are asked or told to do so by their superiors. In contrast, we want to claim that individual managers have a personal moral responsibility to behave in certain ways—even if pressured to do otherwise by the corporate hierarchy in which they operate (Moore, 1999).

One argument for conforming to corporate norms is rooted in the philosophical viewpoint called communitarianism. This doctrine sees individuals as embedded in communities, which give order and purpose to their lives. Communitarians believe it appropriate for communities to inculcate in their members the character and virtue that will allow the community to flourish (Roberts and Reich, 2002). If we analogize corporations to communities, it would follow that the duties of officers are whatever the corporation says they are. Some corporations might be altruistic—others rapacious. But just as, for at least some communitarians, there is no place to stand outside a community from which to judge it—on this theory, there would be no independent moral reference point for judging the behavior of members of a corporation.

We remain unpersuaded, however, either by this form of communitarian analysis or by its application to corporations. The undeniable sociological importance of communities in producing social values does not—it seems to us—oblige us to accept whatever social values any particular community happens to produce. The same can be said of corporations.

Instead, we would argue, the members of communities and corporations retain both responsibility for, and authority over, their actions. Individuals do acquire obligations by virtue of their membership in various groups. And such membership (whether by choice or historical accident) may be a self-defining, even self-transforming experience. But that membership does not allow one to escape from the web of moral discourse or moral responsibility. Particularly in the case of corporations, where managers can choose their "membership," they are responsible for their choices. This means that they should bring their moral sense, and that they do bring their potential culpability, into these relationships.

If individual corporate officers do retain their personal moral responsibilities, of what do these consist? We suggest that some of the aspects of professional responsibility—of the sort that society imposes on doctors, lawyers, or accountants—should be extended to corporate managers. Society relies on professional status as a mechanism of social control in certain typical situations that economists call agency relationships (Folland, Goodman & Stano, 1997). In these cases, certain experts—"agents"—have special knowledge and are delegated to make decisions on behalf of others (the "principals"). Because the principals lack knowledge, they are open to exploitation by the agents, especially when the agent's interests and the principal's interests do not coincide. The "professional" solution is to inculcate in the agents norms of conduct that limit their self-seeking. In return for such restraint, the organized members of the profession typically acquire certain forms of collective authority, including some capacity to regulate the training and behavior of the profession's members.

Agents' responsibilities may well extend to the institutional system within which they operate. Because society has limited capacity to monitor and discipline professional conduct, it needs to rely on professionals' internal norms to keep the system functioning smoothly. Thus, lawyers are "officers of the court" and have responsibilities to the court that can conflict with their responsibilities to their clients. CPAs, likewise, have responsibilities to users of their financial statements, apart from their obligations to the firm that hires them. So do engineers toward those who will live or work in buildings whose drawings they approve.

Today's managers do not have all the formal trappings of professionals. They do not have examination-based state licensing, a professional society that disciplines its members, or mandatory training in distinct institutions. However, we are moving closer to that model all the time. We propose a contribution to the code of ethics that the emerging managerial profession should and could adopt. Such a code could fill in the gaps left by the alphabet soup of regulatory agencies that currently constrain corporate managers. In areas of conduct filled with philosophical ambiguity and pragmatic difficulty, we believe that professional norms could be a more flexible mechanism for influencing behavior. The "invisible hand" of the market and the "visible foot" of state regulation may both produce less desirable results.

In overtly giving this task to managers, we are recognizing that managers confront conflicts between profit maximization and personal morality all the time. Telling people to obey the law does not contain enough content to guide many real choices. Motorists often feel it is acceptable to drive "just a little" above the speed limit—especially if "everyone is doing it." And managers can, and do, regularly make similar decisions. For example, just how strictly should they interpret ambiguous EPA or OSHA regulations? Just how aggressive a position should they take in interpreting some provision of the tax code? The reality of their discretion means that managers constantly balance various ethical norms against the pressure for profit. The question is just how far they should go in different situations.

What is Wrong in the World That We Should Try to Fix?

Since we take a "pragmatic" and "postmodern" view of the nature of ethics, we believe no knockdown argument can be made to compel all fair-minded readers to accept our particular values. Instead, since ethics are made, not found, moral philosophy has at least some of the features of an art or a craft. In judging alternative arguments, postmodernists believe it is necessary to use standards of ethical criticism that are internal to a particular tradition of discourse and for which no ultimate justification is available.

However, we are not paralyzed by this realization. Instead, we believe our task is to get on with the practical work of making the world a better place, as best we understand what that means. Yes, our definition of "better" is influenced by the particular cultural and historical matrix in which we are embedded. But it cannot be justified on *those* grounds exactly because it cannot be justified on *any* grounds. In arguing for a particular set of commitments, we are, as the contemporary philosophical pragmatist Richard Rorty points out, reduced to "poetry" and "prophesy" in an attempt to mobilize other peoples' sentiments in favor of our particular moral vision (Rorty, 1989).

The particular vision we advocate owes a great deal to the tradition of philosophical liberalism begun by Kant. The (modern) version of Kant's argument is that human beings are worthy of respect because they have the potential for rational action—for making plans and choices based on impartial norms as opposed to mere desire (Kant, 1998). The next step is to ask, What does respect for others require of us? One answer is simply to respect others' negative rights— to leave them free to do what they like. The alternative answer, which we find appealing, says individuals have positive as well as negative rights—rights to the resources and other preconditions that will allow them to make meaningful life choices. This implies not only a right to basic political liberties and a society where personal opportunity is not limited by law or prejudice, but also the income, education, and other resources to have real life chances and choices (Rawls, 1971).

Moreover, such reciprocal obligation—if it exists—would seem to extend across national boundaries. Philosophically (not to mention historically) such boundaries are highly arbitrary. If respect is due someone because of their humanity, then their citizenship is irrelevant. The recent development of international law with regards to human rights, war crimes, and labor standards suggests that we are at a moment in history when this principle is increasingly recognized.

Who in the world, then, really lacks the requisite basic opportunity that their humanity entitles them to? Our answer is the truly poor—especially the poor in poor nations. The poor in the rich industrial nations do not live in wonderful circumstances. But given the extensive public services typically available— health, education, housing, and income support—they are usually much better off than the poor in the developing world.

Moral Obligations in the Health Arena

Let us explore what this general claim would imply in the health arena, since so much of the interest in public-private partnerships has occurred in that context. The first issue is, What "health rights" do people have? While there is not general agreement on this point we are persuaded by Lauterbach's and Daniels' arguments for a right to a minimum quantity and quality of life (Daniels, 1985; Lauterbach, 1995). Arguing in slightly different ways, they both propose that the opportunity such a level of health provides is a necessary precondition if people are to develop and implement their life plans.

This analysis thus involves a focus on what might be called absolute—as opposed to relative—equality. The goal is not for everyone to have the same health care, or the same quality and quantity of life. The goal is to get everyone to a minimum level of health that allows for reasonable life choices. Thus, it is acceptable for the rich to have more care or better health than the poor, as long as the poor attain a certain minimum quality and quantity of life.

Admittedly, it is not easy to say exactly what that minimum level should be. But by any plausible standard, many of the world's poor do not reach that level (World Health Organization, 2000). Sophisticated health care is expensive. Poor people in poor countries cannot afford such services, either as private individuals or through public taxation. Financing is not the only problem, of course. Potentially available resources are often not mobilized due to a lack of political commitment. Furthermore, the available resources are often poorly managed and hence do not produce the health gains they could if the care system were better organized. But whatever the reasons, the question is, Who has what obligation to do something about all of these factors that limit the achievement of minimum health status among the world's poor?

Who Has What Responsibility?

The classic Kantian argument is that morality by definition must be universal and impersonal. This implies a particular answer to the question posed by the last heading. Everyone all over the world has responsibility for everyone else whose health falls below some—as yet undetermined—threshold.

To us such an argument is not persuasive in part because it fits so little with our sentiments. It is just not how most people view the world. Instead, most people feel a special obligation to those they know, or have harmed, or have benefited from. And employing the philosophical method of reflective criticism, we are led to conclude that the lack of correspondence between Kantian norms and normal human reactions may well reveal a lack in the former rather than the latter (Rawls, 1971, p.48).

As an alternative, the philosopher Thomas Pogge has argued that the obligation to correct inequalities is not, in fact, impersonal and universal (Pogge, 1998). Instead, it depends on exactly how we relate to, or are involved in the situation of a particular needy group. What is the relationship of the individuals concerned? Has one person caused another person's plight or profited from it? Does someone have particular power or competence to assist a certain group in need?

Pogge's suggestions resonate with the writings of the feminist philosophers who are part of the school of thinking called "ethics of care" (Baier, 1994). These writers argue that caring is not impartial, reciprocal, or universal—but instead reflects aid asymmetry and inequality of resources, power, and responsibility. It also involves particularity. We are not equally obligated to care for all. Thus these ideas have some of the same flavor as Pogge's.

We find this idea attractive on several grounds. Non-universal obligations are not as overwhelming and all-devouring as universal ones, and are thus more likely to be accepted. Modest human-scale redistributive maxims that help provoke real action have a lot to recommend them compared to Olympian councils of perfection whose intimidating severity leads them to be ignored. Making responsibility depend on capacity also has pragmatic advantages. We ask the most from those who can actually do the most. And using past benefit as a basis for obligation invokes feelings of guilt and responsibility—"sentiments," in Rorty's terms, that may have power to move us to action.

Taking this argument seriously implies that automobile companies do not have any special obligation to support the ballet, but that they do have a particular responsibility when it comes to reducing auto emissions, developing vehicle crash standards, and improving highway safety. They might well also have a special role in supporting the scientific study of the link between health and air pollution.

This same argument implies that the global pharmaceutical and medical device companies have a special responsibility to the sick poor—especially in poor countries. These companies have the competence, resources, and expertise to actually make a difference. In addition, many new compounds and treatment regimes have been tested in poor countries. Moreover, there are few segments of the economic world where the socially constructed nature of property rights is more evident than in pharmaceuticals. The foundation of the whole sector is the worldwide system of patent rights—each of which represents an "appropriation from nature" (to use Locke's vocabulary) that most assuredly diminishes the access of others to nature's bounty. Of course, the research-based companies risk their shareholders' capital to develop new compounds on the expectation that very high gains from a few very successful drugs will pay for all their unsuccessful efforts. And this deal, that both they and society have agreed to, has been advantageous to both sides. Still, given current profit levels and the socially sanctioned market imperfections that produce these, it is reasonable for society to ask for something more in return. And that something, we believe, should be voluntary efforts to ameliorate the health status of the world's poor, and thus help to provide them with a minimum level of human opportunity.

This case is strengthened by realizing that much of the industry's intellectual capital, in the form of modern molecular biology, and many of the critical individuals doing pharmaceutical research, have benefited greatly from government research and training funds. In a sense, these industries exist in part by privately appropriating some of the gains generated by public investments. This has been possible because the human and intellectual capital those investments have generated is not tightly fenced about with legal rules designed to prevent such appropriation. An obligation on the beneficiaries, of the sort we are proposing, would help the public retrieve some of those gains.

Why and How Partnerships

Suppose we accept, if only for the sake of argument, that there are the kinds of obligations we have suggested on both corporations and their officers (and we should note that, increasingly, companies accept that they have such obligations) (Birchard, 1999). Why should public-private partnerships play a significant role in carrying these out?

The basis of our position lies in the value of conceptual and intellectual diversity. Here is an example to help make that point. Many individuals who have gone through management training have encountered some form of the Desert Survival Exercise. In these exercises, individuals are asked to fill out questionnaires about how they would handle a particular desert survival situation.

Then they are put into groups of six to eight and asked to develop a consensus plan. Almost invariably, when the answers are compared with expert opinion, each group's performance exceeds the average of its constituent individuals.

The reason for this pattern lies in the way human beings think. At issue is the hold over us of what T. S. Kuhn, the historian of science, called "paradigms" (Kuhn, 1996), and the economist and psychologist Herbert Simon called "habits of mind" (Simon, 1966). The idea is that the mind creates models and theories of how the world works and about what is appropriate behavior. Moreover, these patterns of thought and action tend to persist once adopted. This is because the effort required to change our thought patterns is expensive in terms of mental time, energy, and analytical capacity. We hold on to our paradigms until events force us to change them. Indeed, the force of habit is so strong that even when we should change, we often refuse to do so. Such patterns make our thinking both rapid and limited—facile, yet trapped in well-worn grooves.

This reality helps explain why change and learning are so difficult—especially for experienced adults. It is also why multiple perspectives on a problem can be so helpful. A group whose members do not all think alike is less likely to fall into a rut or miss an obvious point. These advantages are likely to be especially large if the group includes individuals with quite different "habits of mind."

This is why we believe public-private partnerships are potentially so useful. Exactly because the participants come from varied organizational cultures and professional backgrounds, there is a great potential for creativity and mutual learning in such arrangements. An international drug company and an activist NGO might actually learn from each other—and both be transformed by their association. They might create something together that neither could have created separately. And if that something is a program or activity that serves the substantive moral goals we have sketched, then real good will have been accomplished.

In this context, it is interesting to refer to Allan Gibbard's work on encounters between members of different communities (Gibbard, 1990). Gibbard notes that such encounters might produce conflicts that are settled by force—by coercion or conversion. Or they might produce some form of live-and-let-live mutual toleration, which leaves both sides unscathed. A third possibility is that both sides enter into a serious conversation. In such an encounter, participants know that their views and values might be affected. They might learn or grow technically or ethically. In that sense, they cede authority over themselves to their future selves—to selves which, because they have been influenced by the intervening conversation, differ from their current selves in unpredictable ways.

That is exactly what can happen to organizations involved in any but the most superficial partnerships. Even as they pursue their own interests, they may come to redefine those interests. Even as they do deals, they may also create value by creating new possibilities.

This argument gets added force from both the need and the difficulty of improving the health status of the global poor. The health conditions of the world's poor differ enormously from those of the world's rich. Malaria, TB, schistosomiasis and dengue fever, and childhood diseases from upper respiratory infections to measles to diarrheal disease all result in enormous limits on human opportunity. And, unfortunately, tropical diseases rarely offer enough profit to induce much biomedical research. Drugs for such conditions are likely to not be very profitable because they occur primarily among the poor in poor countries. And the continued growth of HIV in these countries will only compound the problem. For those drugs that are developed, economic barriers are likely to make it increasingly difficult to get the fruits of the best science to those who would most benefit. This is an impending moral challenge to the world's economic and social order that is easy to foresee but not easy to deal with.

The strategy we are urging on corporations goes one step beyond the work by one of us over twenty years ago—about how electric utility companies responded to environmental regulation (Roberts & Blume, 1981). There, Roberts and Blume argued that companies that simply resisted all regulatory obligations often had a very difficult time, financially and legally. They also produced a fair amount of environmental harm in the process of forcing society to coerce them into reasonable behavior. In contrast, some companies were positively responsive. That is, they realized that criticisms of their behavior were often both legitimate and politically powerful. They decided to take some initiative—to propose solutions to environmental issues that responded to both their needs and to society's legitimate concerns. They thus gained both credibility and some control over the obligations they incurred. In the current context, public-private partnerships to improve access to drugs, devices, and healthcare services for poor people would constitute a similarly desirable positive response to a legitimate, and increasingly politically articulated, set of concerns. Moreover, we believe the companies involved need to take risks, incur costs, and go beyond that which is merely prudent. Partnerships simply as a self-interested strategy raise none of the moral issues we have been grappling with in this paper. Indeed one of the values of pursuing social goals through partnerships is that each participant can act as a check on the others. They can establish a dialogue in which the larger goal is kept in focus, and challenge each other's willingness to pay some real costs.

Another way to understand our suggestion is to invoke Robert Putnam's notion of "social capital" (Putnam, 2000). Putnam notes that some societies are better able to solve problems than others—in part because there is more trust and connection among their members. In a way, this argument echoes de Tocqueville's finding in his epic study *Democracy In America* (de Tocqueville, 2000). He attributed much of the effectiveness of American society to the vigor and successful action of non-government institutions that allowed communities to flexibly mobilize to deal with their problems.

We hope and believe that a growing network of public-private partnerships can serve these same goals. They can help build a new form of intersectoral and international social capital. They can create new problem-solving institutions through which different groups can come to know each other and work together. And these networks can function in a decentralized and flexible way outside the cumbersome legislative/regulatory framework of formal multilateral arrangements.

The Other Parties

If partnerships are good, doesn't that imply that all potential partners have obligations to participate, non-corporate as well as corporate? Yes. And doesn't that obligation require other organizations, and their managers, to take risks with their core missions and institutional interests in ways parallel to what we have asked of corporations? Yes. And doesn't that mean self-transformative learning might, and indeed should, occur on both sides of a partnership relationship? Yes, yet again.

The point is that NGOs or international agencies should not just look at partnerships from the self-righteous perspective of their own interests—anymore than for-profit corporations should. And the potential costs to these other players are also real. For example, the growth of private initiatives might loosen the control and diminish the role of bureaucrats at WHO or various UN agencies. But if the substantive moral agenda that we have identified is advanced, our claim is that they are obligated to support such efforts, despite potential personal and institutional costs. Similarly, hard-core, anti-capitalist humanitarians might fear the learning that such partnerships could bring about. For them, meeting with the representatives of global business is not risk free since they might acquire a corrupting understanding of business's legitimate needs and perspectives! Again that is a risk, we believe, purists on all sides need to take.

Final Points

We have argued that global health technology companies have special responsibilities for the health of the poorest citizens in poor nations. How far they can and should go will and should be a matter of social learning. Moreover, in the real world, the exact profit-maximizing strategy is seldom perfectly clear. Does whatever Timberland spends to help City Year, or Texaco spends to sponsor the Metropolitan Opera, pay off in profit terms more than all other possible uses of the same corporate resources (Austin, 1998)? No one can ever know. Given this ambiguity, the intuition, judgment, bias, ambitions, and moral vision of corporate managers all play a role in their strategy choices. To begin, we hope more companies will give "doing good" the benefit of the doubt in the same way they now do to other more conventional uses of corporate discretionary funds, like fancy offices and high levels of executive compensation. As morally accountable human beings, we believe there are ethical reasons for their officers to do as we recommend, as part of an emerging new definition of their professional responsibilities.

Rights without responsibilities are not a sound long-term basis for corporations to seek either social acceptance or social progress. However not every "good thing" is best approached through legislation or coercion. Internationally, the instrumentalities of government are relatively weak and cumbersome compared to the coordinated reach of a well-managed global corporation.

The voluntary efforts we recommend can lead to creativity and learning, both for the partners and for the larger international system. Hopefully, we will all develop a common understanding of what obligations are and are not reasonable and what risks are or are not defensible. We believe that both the need and the opportunity we have reviewed are large and important enough to demand/allow/require/legitimize the paradigm shift we have proposed.

We are not against property or profits. We do not want to end capitalism or abolish the patent system. But we do believe that the world would be a better place if the enormous gains those institutions have generated were used to a greater extent, and in a more purposive manner, for the important ethical goal of improving the health status of the global poor. We also believe that this could usefully be done in partnerships among those whose different perspectives can provide dialogue, self-correction, and creative self-discovery. And we believe such gains are available on all sides for those who respond to the challenge we have offered.

References

Arrow, K. A. (1974). *The limits of organization*. New York: Norton.

Austin, J. E. (1998). The collaboration challenge: Making the most of strategic alliances between nonprofits and corporations. *Social Enterprise Series No. 6*. (Working paper 99-063). Boston: Harvard Business School.

Baier, A. (1994). *Moral prejudices: Essays on ethics*. Cambridge: Harvard University Press.

Birchard, B. (1999). Doing well by doing good. *Harvard Management Update*, 4(12).

Crossley, D. (1999). Paternalism and corporate responsibility. *Journal of Business Ethics*, 21(4), 291–302.

Daniels, N. (1985). *Just health care*. New York: Cambridge University Press.

Farnsworth, E. A. (1998). *Farnsworth on contracts*. New York: Aspen Law & Business.

Friedman, M. (1970, September 13). The social responsibility of business is to increase its profits. *The New York Times Magazine*.

Folland, S., Goodman, A. C. & Stano, M. (1997). *The economics of health and health care* (2nd ed.). Saddle River, NJ: Prentice Hall.

Gibbard, A. (1990). *Wise choices, apt feeling: A theory of normative judgment*. Cambridge: Harvard University Press.

Iwai, K. (1999). Persons, things and corporations: The corporate personality controversy and comparative corporate governance. *American Journal of Comparative Law*, 47(4), 583.

Kant, I. (1998). *Critique of pure reason*. P. Guyer & A. Wood, (Eds. & Trans.). New York: Cambridge University Press.

Kanter, R. M. (1999). From spare change to real change: The social sector as beta site for business innovation. *Harvard Business Review*, 77(3), 122–133.

Kuhn, T. S. (1996). *Structure of scientific revolutions* (2nd ed.). Chicago: University of Chicago Press.

Lauterbach, K. (1995). Justice and the functions of health care [doctoral thesis]. Boston: Harvard School of Public Health.

Leung, W. S. W. (1997). The inadequacy of shareholder primacy: A proposed corporate regime that recognizes non-shareholder interests. *Columbia Journal of Law and Social Problems*, 30(4), 587–634.

Lipsey, R. G. & Lancaster, K. (1956). The general theory of second best. *Review of Economic Studies*, 24(1), 11–32.

Locke, J. (1988). *Two treatises of government*. P. Laslett, (Ed.). New York: Cambridge University Press.

Moore, G. (1999). Corporate moral agency: Review and implications. *Journal of Business Ethics*, 21(4), 329–343.

Orts, E. W. (1992, November). Beyond shareholders: Interpreting corporate constituency statutes. *George Washington Law Review*, 61(1), 14–135.

Pogge, T. (1998). *Rethinking redistribution obligation*. Unpublished working paper. New York: Columbia University Department of Philosophy.

Putnam, R. (2000). *Bowling alone: The collapse and revival of American community*. New York: Simon & Schuster.

Rawls, J. (1971). *A theory of justice*. Cambridge: Harvard University Press.

Roberts, M. J. & Reich, M. R. (2002). Ethical analysis in public health. *The Lancet*, (forthcoming).

Roberts, M. J. & Blume, J. S. (1981). *The choices of power: Utilities face the environmental challenge*. Cambridge: Harvard University Press.

Rorty, R. (1989). *Contingency, irony, and solidarity*. New York: Cambridge University Press.

Schumpeter, J. (1947). *Capitalism, socialism, and democracy* (3rd ed.). New York: Harper and Row.

Simon, H. A. (1959). Theories of decision making in economics and behavioral science. *American Economic Review*, 49(3), 253–283.

Smith, C. (1994). The new corporate philanthropy. *Harvard Business Review*, 72(3), 105–116.

de Tocqueville, A. (2000). *Democracy in America.* H. C. Mansfield, & D. Winthrop, (Eds. & Trans.). Chicago: University of Chicago Press.

World Health Organization. (2000). *World health report.* Geneva: Author.

5

A Partnership for Ivermectin:
Social Worlds and Boundary Objects

Laura Frost, Michael R. Reich, and Tomoko Fujisaki

THE DIRECT PARTICIPATION OF PRIVATE PHARMACEUTICAL COMPANIES in international public health disease control efforts has been a growing trend since the late 1980s. How do these private companies construct partnerships with health development organizations? When are these partnerships successful, and in what terms? This chapter examines these questions through the story of Merck & Co., Inc.'s donation of ivermectin for the treatment of onchocerciasis. It explores how two organizations, Merck and the Task Force for Child Survival and Development, with different organizational missions and productive pursuits were able to create common understandings and an effective partnership.

To explore the construction of partnerships, we use social worlds and boundary work theories. These theories guide our analysis of the contrasting missions, mandates and worldviews of organizations, and how "boundary objects" can bring together divergent organizations in cooperative pursuits. After presenting this approach, we analyze the divergent and intersecting worlds of the key participants that cooperated in the donation of ivermectin. We then examine the structure of the participants' relationships and the boundary objects that allowed diversity in organizational missions and activities, as well as cooperation in the donation of ivermectin. In the chapter's conclusion, we discuss whether this cooperative effort has been successful in terms of the partnership and in terms of the public health impact and the reduction of human suffering.

This study relies on information from published and unpublished documents, and key informant interviews carried out in 1996–97 with individuals involved in the conception, development, and implementation of the Mectizan Donation Program. We believe this analysis is timely because after more than a decade of Merck's experience with the Mectizan Donation Program, other pharmaceutical companies have begun to set up drug donation programs, often modeled on the this program. These other partnerships include Glaxo Wellcome (now Glaxo

SmithKline) and the Task Force for Child Survival and Development in the donation of Malarone for the treatment of malaria in drug-resistant endemic countries, SmithKline Beecham (now Glaxo SmithKline) and the World Health Organization in the donation of albendazole for the elimination of lymphatic filariasis, and Pfizer and the Edna McConnell Clark Foundation in the donation of Zithromax for the elimination of blinding trachoma (see chapter 3). This chapter examines the partnership of the Mectizan Donation Program and analyzes how the two different social worlds of a pharmaceutical company and a health development organization came together to donate ivermectin for the treatment of onchocerciasis.

The Problem of Onchocerciasis

Onchocerciasis is a chronic filarial disease associated with the parasitic worm *Onchocerca volvulus*. People are infected by the disease when they are bitten by infected female blackflies of the genus *Simulium*, which breed in fast-flowing rivers, leading to the other name for onchocerciasis: river blindness. When the blackfly bites, the larvae of *Onchocerca volvulus* move into the human host where they develop into adult worms. The adult female worm produces and discharges millions of microfilariae into the human host during its life of about 10 to 14 years. The microfilariae live for one to three years, during which time the clinical manifestations of the disease occur. Infected individuals may experience a number of symptoms: serious visual impairment, including blindness; rashes, lesions, intense itching and depigmentation of the skin; lymphadenitis; and general debilitation (Samba, 1994). The debilitation, disfigurement, and blindness caused by onchocerciasis can have serious psychological, social, and economic effects, including ostracism and low self-esteem (Ovuga et al., 1995), and decreased work productivity. In his study of Ghanaian coping strategies for onchocercal skin diseases, Awedoba (1999) found that the itching associated with onchocerciasis caused infected people to interrupt their work, caused skin laceration resulting in sores and "ugly" scratch marks, and kept people awake at night, leading to exhaustion and headaches. In her study of women in forest areas of Nigeria, Amazigo (1994) found that incessant itching brought on by onchocercal lesions affected the duration of breast-feeding among infected women.

Onchocerciasis is endemic in 35 countries, 28 of which are in Africa, plus Yemen and 6 countries in the Americas. In 1993, the WHO Expert Committee on Onchocerciasis Control estimated that about 17.7 million people were infected worldwide, of whom some 270 thousand were already blind, with another 500 thousand people severely visually disabled (WHO, 1995). The burden of onchocerciasis is particularly heavy in the hyper-endemic belt across sub-Saharan Africa. In these communities, high rates of visual disability caused by onchocerciasis—up to 40 percent of the population in some areas—often lead to declines in economic capacity and eventual abandonment of fertile agricultural lands.

Currently, the treatment of choice for onchocerciasis is one annual oral dose of 150 to 200 micrograms/kg of ivermectin (with tradename of Mectizan). The drug greatly reduces microfilarial loads—a single dose can reduce the level of skin microfilariae to near zero and, by virtue of its interference with embryogenesis, can delay build-up of microfilariae for a period of three months to two years. Another important aspect of ivermectin is that it is a very safe drug, as demonstrated by community trials from 1987 to 1989.[1] Among the millions of people who have been treated, only minor side effects have been reported, and these can be treated at the local level.

Ivermectin, however, does not completely eliminate the microfilariae because it only has limited effects on the adult worm, which recommences its reproduction several months after treatment with ivermectin.[2] Although ivermectin does not kill the adult worm, community studies have shown that the reduction of the microfilarial density in the skin can significantly reduce transmission by black fly vectors (Remme et al., 1989). These reductions are important, but studies have not gone on long enough to show complete interruption of transmission, after which time Mectizan treatment would be no longer needed. TDR and others continue efforts to discover a safe and effective macrofilaricide, to kill the adult worm in humans, which along with ivermectin could make eradication of onchocerciasis a feasible goal.

In the past, treatment of onchocerciasis included drugs such as diethylcarbamazine and Suramin, both of which have serious side effects that make them inappropriate for mass treatment. Other prior control strategies included the aerial application of insecticides to breeding sites of blackfly larvae in the rivers. Aerial spraying has been carried out for 15 years by the Onchocerciasis Control Program (OCP) in West Africa. When ivermectin became available for mass distribution in 1988, OCP quickly added this control strategy to its vector control activities. In those OCP areas where vector control is currently being carried out, ivermectin distribution programs are also being implemented to ensure the immediate prevention or alleviation of onchocercal manifestations in the eye.

Social Worlds and Boundary Objects

To assess how a for-profit pharmaceutical company and a non-profit health development organization maintained their separate missions and activities while at the same time cooperated on the donation of ivermectin, we draw from theoretical work developed in sociology on social worlds and boundary objects.

In her review of social worlds theory, Clarke (1990) identifies Shibutani (1955; 1962) as the theorist who initiated social worlds theory development. Shibutani focused on the idea of commitment as the basis of social action. In this approach, social worlds are groups with "shared commitments to the pursuit of a common task, who develop ideologies to define their work and who accumulate diverse resources needed to get the job done" (Gieryn, 1995, p. 412). In each social world, at least one primary activity is "strikingly evident" (Strauss, 1978, p. 122). Gerson (1983) points to three different kinds of social worlds: *production worlds* that seek to make something, *communal worlds* that pursue community and shared values, and *social movements* that focus on altering society beyond the boundaries of their world (see also Gieryn, 1995). Mixed worlds are possible, and people typically participate in several social worlds at the same time.

Gieryn points out three properties that are common to all social worlds: the potential for division and segmentation into sub-worlds; intersection with other social worlds; and legitimization through the definition and enforcement of standards and boundaries of a social world. Social worlds theory directs inquiry into how social worlds establish, maintain, or change boundaries between worlds, and how worlds gain legitimization.

The two organizations discussed in this chapter are representatives of two different production worlds. The stated mission of Merck, a leading research-driven pharmaceutical company, is "to provide society with superior products and services, innovations and solutions that improve the quality of life and satisfy customer needs, to provide employees with meaningful work and advancement opportunities and investors with a superior rate of return" (Merck, 1995). Merck is a part of a larger production world that focuses on producing and selling pharmaceutical products and on generating profits.

The Task Force for Child Survival and Development is a member of a different production world, one whose activities are focused on "producing" projects for the health development promotion of children and their families, mainly in poor countries. Established in 1984 with the WHO, the United Nations Children's Fund (UNICEF), the World Bank, the United Nations Development Program

(UNDP), and the Rockefeller Foundation as its sponsoring agencies, the Task Force for Child Survival and Development focused initially on global child immunization and vaccine research. In 1998, the Task Force became independent of its original sponsors, and its current mission is to promote "the health and development of children domestically and internationally by creating alliances, building consensus and leveraging scarce resources" (Task Force for Child Survival and Development, 1999). The Task Force can also be seen as a communal world that produces shared commitments to the improvement of health of children and their families worldwide.

How do diverse, bounded social worlds come together to do cooperative work? Social scientists have studied this question in various fields. For example, scientific work requires the involvement and cooperation of actors from diverse social worlds. Star and Griesemer (1989) argue that the central tension in science is that, on the one hand, scientific work is conducted by a diverse group of actors, including researchers from various disciplines, visionaries and functionaries, amateurs and professionals, all working individually. On the other hand, they argue, science requires cooperation to gather information, ensure reliability, and create common understandings. In analyzing the history of the Museum of Vertebrate Zoology in California, Star and Griesemer use the concept of "boundary objects" to explain how museum workers managed both diversity and cooperation. They define boundary objects as "objects which are both plastic enough to adapt to local needs and the constraints of the several parties employing them, yet robust enough to maintain a common identity across sites. . . . They have different meanings in different social worlds but their structure is common enough to more than one world to make them recognizable . . ." (p. 393). Gieryn adds, "boundary objects may be ideas, things, people, or processes; the requirement is that they be able to span boundaries separating social worlds, so that those on either side can 'get behind' the boundary object and work together toward some goal" (1995, p. 414–415).

In their analysis of the Museum of Vertebrate Zoology, Star and Griesemer found that the different worlds of sponsors, theorists, and amateurs shared the same goals of conserving and ordering the nature of California, although this goal had different meanings for the various actors. Boundary objects such as specimens, field notes, museums, and maps of particular territories spanned the various worlds to allow collaboration in the pursuit of shared goals. In addition, the state of California represented a boundary object. For the museum director,

California gave his research a delimited regional focus. From the perspective of the university administration, a regional focus supported its mandate to serve Californians. And for the amateur naturalists, research within the state boundaries supported their goals of preservation and conservation. Through their analysis of these boundary objects, Star and Griesemer found that decisions about how to bring together the different social worlds had material effects in shaping the character of the institution that was created and the content of its scientific claims.

The term *boundary objects* may suggest a lack of agency. For instance, it may suggest that such "objects" lack the power to act. However, boundary objects can be things, ideas, processes, and they can also be people. Boundary objects are locally specific and emerge through the processes of work when the work of multiple groups intersect (Fujimura, 1992). For example, the director of the Museum of Vertebrate Zoology did not create these boundary objects, but rather managed and reconstructed them as a way of coordinating the work of groups coming from different social worlds.

Boundary objects can also be important in managing the local uncertainties and risks associated with partnerships between organizations from different social worlds. Organizations that are forming partnerships for drug donation programs are faced with many uncertainties about the program, the product, and the partnership itself. For example, partners may be faced with institutional uncertainties: What will be the division of responsibilities between the partners? What are the interests of the partners? How will the divergent interests of the organizations be handled to avoid possible splits in the partnership? What obstacles will be encountered, and how will the partners overcome these obstacles? In addition, partners may have technical uncertainties: How can partners ensure that the drug reaches the people who need it most? Will the donation program actually reduce the burden of disease and human suffering? Political uncertainties also exist: How will countries or organizations be selected for participation in the program? Will the organizations' public images suffer or benefit from the program?

Managing these uncertainties is vital to the success of the partnership. Boundary objects, which may have different meanings to the partners but have a common identity across the social worlds, can be used to help manage uncertainties. Through an analysis of the partners involved in the donation of ivermectin, we will point to boundary objects that were crucial in creating a relationship of trust between partners and in providing legitimacy to a risky effort. An emphasis on diversity and cooperation between social worlds provides a useful conceptual lens to examine how Merck and the Task Force for Child Survival and Development cooperated.

The History of Merck's Donation of Ivermectin

Merck introduced ivermectin in 1981 as a veterinary product used for deworming both large and small animals. According to Merck's annual report of 1995, ivermectin became the world's largest selling animal health product after almost 15 years on the market (Merck, 1995). The report also states that the group of ivermectin-based parasiticide products was the fifth best-selling product group for Merck (including human drugs), with $740 million annual sales. In August 1997, Merck combined its animal health business (including its ivermectin-based animal health products) with the poultry genetics business of Rhône-Poulenc to form Merial Ltd., a new company. Merck, however, retains the rights to ivermectin, and the company's participation in the donation of ivermectin for the treatment of onchocerciasis has remained unchanged.

Ivermectin's role as a human drug began in April 1978 when Merck scientists, under the direction of Dr. William C. Campbell, observed that the drug was effective against microfilariae of *Onchocerca cervicalis* in horses. *O. cervicalis* in horses belongs to the same genus as *O. volvulus*, the cause of onchocerciasis in humans. Dr. Campbell was a member of the Filariasis Scientific Committee, established in 1977 by the UNDP/World Bank/WHO Special Program for Research and Training in Tropical Diseases (TDR). This committee was concerned that the high costs of screening facilities for drugs against tropical diseases were hampering the pharmaceutical industry's interest in tropical diseases (TDR, 1976). TDR therefore provided technical and financial support to academic and private research institutions to establish a biological screening system for macrofilaricides. In July 1978, Dr. Campbell sent ivermectin and the results of the horse trial to a TDR-supported tertiary screening facility using cattle in Australia. The results showed that ivermectin was "highly effective in preventing patent infections with both *O. gibsoni* and *O. gutturosa*," and thereby added evidence to the expectation that ivermectin would be effective against human onchocerciasis (TDR, 1983, p. 22).

On December 20, 1978, encouraged by these results, Dr. Campbell proposed to the Merck Sharp & Dohme Research Laboratories (MSDRL, now the Merck Research Laboratories) Research Management Council that "an avermectin could become the first means of preventing the blindness associated with onchocerciasis"[3] and that "discussions be held with representatives of WHO to determine the most appropriate approach to the problem" (Sturchio, 1992; J. Sturchio, personal communication, October 7, 1996). The senior management of MSDRL supported the lead taken by Dr. Campbell. In December 1978, Dr. Roy Vagelos, then president of MSDRL, approved research funding to investigate the potential use of ivermectin in humans. On January 16, 1980, Merck's senior management decided to proceed to clinical trials. This decision was a significant turning point in the history of ivermectin, shaping the course of events over the next eight years.

The first clinical trials of ivermectin began in 1981 in Senegal, with 32 infected but otherwise healthy subjects. The trials were independently organized and paid for by Merck (Aziz et al., 1982a). The study used placebos in a crossover design and began with a very low ivermectin dose of 5 micrograms per kilogram (µg/kg) for safety reasons. The study found that a single dose of ivermectin, as low as 30 or 50 µg/kg, substantially decreased the number of skin microfilariae. The effect was sustained in some patients for six months (Aziz et al., 1982b). No serious adverse reaction was observed. A second clinical trial was conducted in Paris with 20 West African immigrants (Coulard, 1983). This study confirmed the positive results of the trial in Senegal, showing that doses up to 100 µg/kg were well tolerated.

In 1982, Merck officials visited TDR and the Onchocerciasis Control Program (OCP) to present the results from the initial clinical trials. Although some observers were skeptical about the outcomes of the Senegal study (especially the apparent lack of severe reactions), which was conducted with lightly infected patients, both TDR and OCP became interested in the drug's potential.[4] In 1983 and 1984, trials were carried out as double-masked studies with both placebo and diethylcarbamazine controls. Following these trials, studies were carried out to compare ivermectin doses of 100, 150, and 200 µg/kg with placebo. These clinical trials of ivermectin were funded by Merck, TDR, and OCP. By 1986, the results of the clinical trials showed that ivermectin significantly decreased the number of skin microfilariae, the effect was sustained for at least six months, no serious adverse reaction was observed, and ivermectin was more effective than diethylcarbamazine in treating onchocerciasis.

Merck considered these trials sufficient to establish ivermectin's safety and efficacy, and submitted the registration of ivermectin for human onchocerciasis to French health authorities in 1987. TDR, however, argued that the data were not yet sufficient and that large-scale community-based trials were necessary to investigate adverse effects, ophthalmic pathology, effects on skin lesions, and effects on disease transmission in widely differing areas (WHO, 1987a). Eventually, funding for these community-based trials was made available by TDR and OCP, and studies began in 1987. The 13 studies conducted between 1987 and 1989 showed that ivermectin treatment was largely well accepted and could be administered in mass treatment campaigns with minimum medical supervision (De Sole et al., 1989; Pacque et al., 1989).

Merck and TDR's differing attitudes towards community-based trials reflect their contrasting views on the use of ivermectin and their different production and communal worlds. Merck viewed ivermectin as a therapeutic drug to be used for individual patient treatment, as with most of Merck's other products. TDR and OCP, on the other hand, saw ivermectin from a different worldview. For them, ivermectin was a public health drug that could potentially interrupt disease transmission and reduce disease prevalence in endemic communities. TDR and OCP regarded community-based trials under field conditions as a necessary step towards mass-treatment programs, beyond individual treatment in hospitals under professional supervision.

Pricing became the next stage in the drug's development. Merck had multiple objectives, according to one interview. First, the company hoped to make the drug available to the most people who needed it as possible because of its excellent efficacy and safety profile. Second, the company hoped to generate returns on its investment, although it was clear that the economic return of ivermectin as a human product would be limited. And third, the company wanted to protect its good public image by ensuring that ivermectin was handled responsibly (personal communication, September 10, 1996). Merck attempted to balance these three objectives as the development process moved ahead.

Merck faced four possible pricing options: 1) to sell the drug at some market price, as with other products; 2) to provide the drug at a discounted price for use in the public sector, with no charge to the patient and with financial compensation from third-party payers; 3) to donate the drug free of charge with no economic compensation; and 4) to abandon the plan for development altogether. In considering the first option, Merck used a benchmark price of US$3 per treatment in its registration materials submitted to the French authorities. The price level was calculated based on an economic analysis using available information about similar filarial drugs, advantages of ivermectin, production costs, and other factors (personal communication, September 9, 1996). In September 1987, just before the French approval was given, Merck representatives mentioned the idea of a discounted price of $1 per treatment in a meeting at WHO that included TDR and OCP representatives. WHO officials commented that $1 per treatment was not financially realistic in developing countries, and OCP officials told Merck that the total cost of the drug and distribution could not exceed $.50 (WHO, 1987b).[5]

Merck began to realize that selling ivermectin at any price would undermine its first objective to make the drug widely available to people who needed it. The second option of seeking a third-party payer then became viewed as a compromise that might accomplish the company's three objectives. The company approached U.S. government agencies and multilateral development organizations to purchase the drug from Merck and provide the drug free of charge to end users in endemic countries. At a meeting on February 2, 1986, Merck informed Dr. A. O. Lucas, then director of TDR, of its "high level decision to make special financial arrangements which would enable provision of the drug in endemic areas at a most favorable price" (Lucas, 1986).[6] Then, on June 20, 1986, Merck informed Dr. Lucas that it was making "appropriate arrangements, if necessary with other interested parties, to make needed quantities of the drug available to these [endemic countries'] governments and patients at no cost." The task of finding a third-party payer, however, turned out to be more difficult than Merck executives expected (WHO, 1987b; personal communication, August 19, 1996).[7]

The third option, donating ivermectin without any economic compensation, also appeared problematic for both Merck and WHO. Executives in other pharmaceutical companies reportedly pressed Merck not to make the donation out of concern that a donation of ivermectin would set a precedent that could reduce commercial incentives to invest in tropical disease drug development. Outside the pharmaceutical industry, concerns were raised that recipients of a free drug might doubt its quality and efficacy, and thereby damage its acceptability. And within WHO, some officials suggested that Merck be encouraged not to donate the drug (Tavis, 1996, p. 258).

The fourth option, terminating the development process, was also problematic for Merck. Once clinical trials showed its potential benefits to millions of people in preventing blindness, it was difficult for Merck to stop development for human use. Merck is proud of its corporate commitment to improved public health and would have found it ethically difficult to abandon ivermectin for human use. Such a decision could have produced serious damage to the company's public image and to internal morale, especially among scientists. After vigorous discussion and debate within the company, as well as with WHO, for more than three years, Merck made the final decision to donate ivermectin "for as long as it might be needed." Merck and WHO jointly announced the establishment of the Mectizan Donation Program in Washington and Paris on October 21, 1987.

There were three additional factors that helped Merck make the decision to donate the drug. First, Merck's business performance as a whole was very good at the time of the decision, and senior management felt that it could afford to donate the drug (personal communications, August 19 and September 10, 1996). Second, ivermectin was a huge success in the veterinary market, making it easier for internal advocates of donation to make their case inside the company. Lastly, ivermectin donations are tax deductible under the U.S. tax code for corporate donations. The total amount of tax deductions claimed by Merck to date is unknown, since this information is proprietary. One writer estimated "a $.57 production savings on each tablet due to the tax laws which allow an expense deduction against taxes of double the drug value plus an allowance of 75 percent for overhead" (Tavis, 1996, p. 258). These tax benefits associated with donating ivermectin would have also provided a supporting argument for donation proponents within Merck. Since 1988, the Mectizan Donation Program has enabled approximately 197.8 million treatments.

Structuring a Distribution Mechanism

After Merck decided to donate ivermectin, the company still needed to establish an effective distribution mechanism and to decide who should be in charge of that mechanism. Merck was concerned about two main issues related to distribution. First, it was concerned about adverse effects, particularly side effects that might be unreported because of the lack of an established monitoring system (as found in Merck's main markets). Serious side effects caused by ivermectin treatment in humans might even damage the drug's success in the veterinary market. Second, Merck was concerned about the possibility of the drug's diversion to a black market or to the animal drug market. In order to prevent such problems, Merck needed an effective distribution system and the ability to evaluate the distribution and control capabilities of interested parties, most of whom were presumed to be national governments. Such a system would need a capacity to monitor imple-mentation of the distribution and the use of ivermectin according to the agreed conditions. Merck also wanted to avoid involvement in publicly expressing its judgment about an individual government's capability to participate in the program.

Merck initially turned to WHO to design and implement the ivermectin dis-tribution system. The letter of agreement signed by TDR and Merck on July 10, 1985, contains the first public record of Merck's desire for WHO, with national health authorities, to establish appropriate programs for the efficient distribution of the drug (R. D. Fluss, personal communication, May 17, 1985).[8] Merck repeat-edly urged WHO to take active leadership in building a distribution mechanism for the drug but did not receive a clear response (WHO, 1987b).[9]

Documents suggest that this was due to the fact that WHO was contemplat-ing the pros and cons of various options for WHO's involvement in distribution. WHO had two concerns: its legal status as a multilateral organization, which would not allow its association with a committee jointly run by a private firm; and the degree of control that WHO could exert over the process in various options.[10] At one end of the spectrum of options, WHO could merely remain as an advisor to a committee established by Merck and to individual countries that wished to receive the drug. This form of participation would not have any con-flict with provisions of the WHO Constitution, but WHO's control over deci-sions would be limited. At the other end of the spectrum, WHO could establish a group of experts who would assess the capacity of governments that requested ivermectin to implement an onchocerciasis treatment program using ivermectin. This option also would not involve any conflict with the WHO Constitution, but it would allow WHO to exert a high degree of control over decisions. However, WHO hesitated to choose this option, because a negative assessment could deprive some countries of access to ivermectin.

On September 22, 1987, just before the announcement of the registration approval, WHO sent Merck its proposal on the ivermectin distribution mecha-nism: to create an informal mechanism of tripartite consultation among WHO, Merck, and the individual requesting country, instead of setting up a formal com-mittee (W. Furth, personal communication, September 22, 1987).[11] WHO saw this approach as more effective in guiding the requesting countries to fulfill the necessary requirements to distribute and use ivermectin properly. But this format did not accommodate Merck's desire for some organizational distance from the decision process. Five days later, on September 27, 1987, Merck informed WHO of its intention to establish an independent expert committee to review and approve drug requests (J. T. Jackson, personal communication, September 27, 1987).[12] Merck decided to house this expert committee within the Task Force for Child Survival and Development, a non-profit, Atlanta-based non-governmental organization. In short, Merck discovered that it needed a partnership with a non-governmental organization to create an acceptable distribution mechanism for its donation of ivermectin.

The Mectizan Expert Committee and its Secretariat make up the program that has become known as the Mectizan Donation Program. The Mectizan Donation Program donates ivermectin to community-directed programs that treat large populations in endemic areas. The donation of ivermectin involves five major players: the Mectizan Expert Committee and its Secretariat, Merck Corporate Contributions, Merck's Export Department in Riom, France, and the government and non-governmental organizations' treatment programs in endemic countries. Applicants to the Mectizan Donation Program send their completed application forms to the program's office at the Task Force for Child Survival and Development in Atlanta, Georgia. Once the Mectizan Expert Committee's Secretariat determines that an application is complete, the application is sent to the Mectizan Expert Committee for consideration. If the application is approved, it returns to the Secretariat, which notifies Merck Corporate Contributions of the approval. Merck Corporate Contributions contacts the company's Riom Export Department in France to begin the process of shipping the tablets to the recipient government or non-governmental organization in the endemic country. Merck Corporate Contributions tracks the product until the recipient certifies that the product has been received.

The decision about the distribution mechanism for ivermectin reflects the different social worlds of Merck and WHO and their inability to create a formal partnership. During the clinical trials of ivermectin, as pointed out, Merck was primarily interested in developing a drug to be used for individual patient treatment for therapeutic purposes. This is the for-profit pharmaceutical company's standard interest in all of its normal products. When Merck discovered that the company was not going to be able to sell the drug, they realized that they would have to rethink their purpose in making the drug available. On the other hand, OCP and TDR/WHO saw the drug as a tool for interrupting disease transmission and contributing to the reduction of disease prevalence on a large scale. Their interests reflect a social world that seeks to produce health development in poor countries and consists of shared commitments to the improvement of global health.

Both Merck and WHO were concerned about giving negative assessments of governments' capacities to implement ivermectin treatment programs, but for different reasons. As a private company, Merck sought to be perceived as independent of the decisions about donation. Giving negative assessments to particular countries could damage the company's public image and harm its ability to sell pharmaceutical products for profit in those and possibly other countries. For WHO, a negative assessment could deprive some countries of access to ivermectin and would conflict with the goals of WHO's social world. The WHO Constitution specifies that the objective of the World Health Organization is the attainment by *all peoples* of the highest possible level of health (WHO, 1946). Furthermore, the constitution specifies that a function of the agency is to assist governments, upon request, in strengthening health services.

WHO was also concerned about its legal ability to create a formal partnership with a private company. The WHO Constitution states that the organization may make "suitable arrangements for consultation and co-operation with non-governmental international organizations" (WHO, 1946). But the agency's ability to create partnerships with industry is not specified.

Ultimately, Merck decided to locate the program at the Task Force for Child Survival and Development—suggesting that the company had already begun to look beyond the WHO for an alternative distribution mechanism. In sum, Merck and WHO were unable to find acceptable boundary objects that could span their divergent social worlds, and therefore could not construct an effective partnership.

Boundary Objects for a Partnership

By contrast, Merck and the Task Force for Child Survival were able to construct an effective partnership through their use of three boundary objects: 1) the drug, ivermectin; 2) Dr. William Foege, the Executive Director of both the Task Force for Child Survival and Development and the Carter Center; and 3) the Mectizan Expert Committee. Although these three objects had different meanings for Merck and the Task Force, the objects were plastic enough to allow the creation of a common identity. The two organizations used the boundary objects to construct bridges across their two social worlds, helping them to achieve agreement on shared goals and to create a relationship of trust. These boundary objects also help explain how the partnership could gain the support of WHO, governments, and non-governmental organizations to fulfill its shared goal of donating ivermectin for the control of onchocerciasis.

Ivermectin

When Merck made the decision to donate ivermectin, it also made the decision that it did not have the in-house expertise to design and implement a distribution system for the drug. At that time it turned to other participants—first the WHO, and then the Task Force for Child Survival and Development—to provide the needed expertise. In order to connect the different worlds of a pharmaceutical company and a non-profit organization, Merck needed to connect its goal of donating ivermectin with the mission of the Task Force.

Ivermectin was at the center of the donation program, but the drug had a different meaning for the partners. For Merck, ivermectin was the reason for the donation program. The company did not start by seeking a product for a donation program, but arrived at its idea of donating ivermectin after discovering that the drug was effective against human onchocerciasis. The company did not arrive at this decision to donate the drug in a linear way, but did so after years of searching for third-party payers and debating alternative strategies within the firm.

Ivermectin had a different meaning for the Task Force for Child Survival and Development. The promotion of the health of children and their families internationally is central to the mission of the organization. While the Task Force did bring expertise in international public health and health development, the organization did not have previous experience working with a pharmaceutical company for the donation of drugs internationally. Ivermectin donation supported the mandate of the Task Force and became a way to further the organization's activities in new directions. Despite the different meanings that ivermectin had for the two organizations, Merck and the Task Force were united in their goal to donate ivermectin through the donation program. Therefore, ivermectin acted as an important boundary object in that it was plastic enough to allow the drug to have different meanings to the social worlds but robust enough to have a common identity for the two partners.

Dr. William Foege

At the time Merck was considering whether and how to donate ivermectin, Dr. William Foege had just left his position as the director of the federal Centers for

Disease Control and Prevention (CDC) to become executive director of the Carter Center. Because he also was executive director of the Task Force for Child Survival and Development, one of the conditions of his new job was that the Task Force be housed in the Carter Center.[13]

Dr. Foege had a deep commitment to disease control programs, given his previous involvement in directing the CDC smallpox control program as part of the global elimination effort in the 1970s. Merck's decision to house the Mectizan Donation Program in the Task Force for Child Survival and Development depended on the involvement of Dr. Foege, and his expertise, credibility, and visibility. From the beginning of the program, Dr. Foege acted as a boundary object between Merck and the Task Force for Child Survival and Development, particularly in his appointment as chair of the Mectizan Expert Committee, which he has held since the beginning of the donation program. He provided a personal connection between the two organizations and the basis for creating a relationship of trust.

Dr. Foege's involvement has had different but overlapping meanings for the two organizations. For the Task Force for Child Survival and Development, Dr. Foege's directing and chairing roles in the Carter Center, the Task Force, and the Mectizan Expert Committee have provided continuity among the various involved organizations but also have led to a certain amount of identity confusion between the Carter Center and the Task Force. For Merck, on the other hand, Dr. Foege's involvement brought visibility and credibility to its donation effort because of his legitimacy and stature in the international health community. From Merck's perspective, the legitimacy he offered the donation effort has been crucial both internally and externally. Social worlds theory argues that a fundamental characteristic of social worlds is the partners' need to create legitimacy for their actions and interests (Strauss, 1982; Clarke, 1990; Gieryn, 1995). By asking Dr. Foege to participate in the donation effort, Merck sought legitimization for the intersection of the two production/communal worlds in a cooperative pursuit.

Mectizan Expert Committee

The Mectizan Expert Committee represents an important boundary object for the cooperative pursuit of the partnership. It is composed of seven independent experts in the fields of public health and parasitic diseases. Three liaison, non-voting members representing WHO, the Centers for Disease Control, and Merck also participate in the Mectizan Expert Committee. The Mectizan Expert Committee meets twice a year at a place and time agreed to by the members.

According to its charter, the main goal of the Mectizan Expert Committee is to "facilitate the earliest and widest possible application of Mectizan in public health programs consistent with good medical practice and the approved prescribing information in all areas where onchocerciasis is endemic" (Mectizan Donation Program, 1987). The Mectizan Expert Committee has four main functions. The first is to develop guidelines and standards for community-directed treatment programs, including a lengthy application form. The second function is to review applications and, when necessary, to work with applicants to bring their proposals into compliance (Mectizan Donation Program, 1987). Third, the Mectizan Expert Committee advises and assists applicants in the implementation of treatment programs. Its fourth function is to monitor the progress of programs.

The Mectizan Expert Committee sits at the intersection between Merck and the Task Force for Child Survival and Development, and the two organizations have different responsibilities toward the committee. The Task Force has administrative responsibility for the Mectizan Expert Committee. The staff persons with these administrative responsibilities make up the Mectizan Expert Committee Secretariat. Merck's responsibility for the committee is to pay for all committee expenses and honoraria. Both partners maintain that the Mectizan Expert Committee is independent from Merck.

Two different kinds of boundary work occur around the Mectizan Expert Committee.[14] On the one hand, the Mectizan Expert Committee is a boundary object in that it *sustains* a boundary between Merck, a private company that wishes to remain independent from the donation process, and international public health experts who are viewed as qualified to make judgments about governmental and non-governmental participation in the donation program. On the other hand, the Mectizan Expert Committee *spans* the boundaries between the separate social worlds of a pharmaceutical company, international public health experts, health and development organizations, and governments in endemic countries. It does this by creating an organizational locus that brings these diverse actors together in the functions of applying for ivermectin, reviewing applications for ivermectin, and shipping ivermectin to endemic countries.

A Successful Cooperative Pursuit

In evaluating the success of the partnership, we first consider the *outputs* of the partners' ivermectin donation program. In examining outputs, we look at the physical resources that the program makes available, such as the ivermectin treatments, as well as other quantifiable processes associated with the donation program, such as the applications for ivermectin. We then look at *outcomes* of the ivermectin donation program. We define outcomes as the end results, such as changes in health status, that are triggered by outputs. Because "success" is contingent on the perspective being employed, these measures of success will be considered from the perspectives of the partners in the ivermectin donation program, disease sufferers, and the global onchocerciasis control effort.

The number of applications and tablets approved since the establishment of the Mectizan Donation Program points to the impressive outputs of the partnership's cooperative effort. Since 1988, 105 applications have been received and approved for initial community-directed mass treatment programs. In addition, 306 applications for the continuation of these programs have been received and approved. Through these programs, a total of 195 million treatments have been approved for the community-directed mass treatment programs between 1988 and 2000 (see also table 2.3).[15] The Mectizan Donation Program estimates that 25 million people have received at least one dose of the drug and many of these people are receiving annual doses. Community-directed mass treatment programs for onchocerciasis are extensive, existing in 32 of 35 endemic countries (the exceptions are Mozambique, Burundi, and Angola). In 25 of the 35 endemic countries, community-directed mass treatment programs have been continually ongoing for nine or more years.

There are also other outputs associated with the Mectizan Donation Program. From the perspective of global onchocerciasis control efforts, one indicator of success has been the growing level of support and participation from the international community for onchocerciasis control. In November 1990, the health ministers of six central African countries (Cameroon, Central African Republic, Chad, Congo, Equatorial Guinea, and Gabon) passed a resolution for the acceleration of onchocerciasis treatment programs. The following year, in September 1991, the Pan American Health Organization and WHO approved a resolution to eliminate onchocerciasis as a public health problem in the Americas by 2002, through a program known as the Onchocerciasis Elimination Program in the Americas (OEPA). And in 1994, the World Bank approved funding for the

African Program for Onchocerciasis Control (APOC), a program that was launched in December 1995 to expand onchocerciasis control activities to the 16 onchocerciasis-endemic countries in Africa not covered by the Onchocerciasis Control Program (OCP) in West Africa. APOC's goal is to eliminate onchocerciasis as a disease of public health and socio-economic importance in the non-OCP countries in Africa—where more than 85 percent of people (about 15 million) who are currently affected by the disease live—by establishing sustainable community-based ivermectin treatment programs over a period of 12 years (African Program for Onchocerciasis Control, 1996).

Outcome indicators for the Mectizan Donation Program are related to the program's health impacts. Measures of health impact include whether the program has reduced the disease burden of onchocerciasis, whether treatment has interrupted disease transmission, whether the clinical manifestations of the disease (such as blindness, itching, and general debilitation) have been prevented, and whether human suffering associated with these clinical manifestations has been reduced.

Research on the disease burden of onchocerciasis has demonstrated that annual treatment with ivermectin has reduced the prevalence and incidence of infection. A study by Taylor et al. (1990) in Liberia showed that community-based distribution of ivermectin over a three-year period had a measurable impact on incidence of infection. Only individuals older than 12 years were treated with the drug, and incidence was assessed in children aged less than 12 years. The research found that overall incidence of infection in children aged 5–12 years fell from 14.9 percent in 1988 to 9.7 percent in 1989 and after adjusting for age, the overall incidence of infection in children aged 7–12 years fell from 16.4 percent in 1988 to 9.1 percent in 1989. Prevalence of infection in 5 year olds decreased from 23.7 percent in 1987 to 19 percent in 1989. Later studies assessing the medium- to long-term impact of ivermectin on transmission also found a decrease in incidence and prevalence of infection following community-based treatment with the drug (see, for example, Boussinesq et al., 1997).

The impact of treatment on disease transmission is less clear-cut. In a review of the entomological and epidemiological evidence, Boatin et al. (1998) report that several studies have shown considerable reduction in transmission after treatment with the drug. This assessment of the entomological evidence demonstrates that mass treatment with the drug significantly reduces the numbers of infective blackflies and the transmission of O. *volvulus*. However, similar doses of ivermectin yield considerable variability in the reduction of transmission in different studies, ranging between 65 to 97 percent. Boatin et al. attribute this variability to differences in the competence of blackflies as vectors, differences in treatment coverage, and different levels of endemnicity before treatment. The limited ability to interrupt disease transmission fully is also due to the fact that ivermectin does not kill the adult worm, which can live up to 15 years in the human host, although repeated treatment seems to reduce the worm's fecundity and lower its production of microfilariae. It is believed that long-term treatment with ivermectin (for example, for 15 years, to allow the adult worms to die) will completely interrupt disease transmission, but this has not yet been demonstrated. In addition, Boatin et al. point out that unless coverage of ivermectin treatment can be expanded, transmission of O. *volvulus* will continue. The Mectizan Donation Program thus confronts the two challenges of expanding treatment coverage while continuing annual treatments for many years, in the hope of interrupting disease transmission.

The clinical manifestations associated with onchocerciasis include blindness, itching, and general debilitation. The Mectizan Donation Program does not have statistics showing numbers of blindness cases or itching prevented through their donation activities. However, the Onchocerciasis Control Program (OCP) in West Africa, which uses the primary strategy of vector control but combines this strategy with large-scale ivermectin distribution, has calculated numbers of blindness cases prevented through their activities. According to Kate (1998), the OCP has achieved the following successes, since the beginning of its activities in 1974, in the 11 West African OCP countries: "about 30 million people are no longer at risk of infection and therefore of blindness; up to 1.5 million people originally infected have been relieved of infection; up to 200,000 people have been prevented from going blind; and 25 million hectares of land have been freed for cultivation and resettlement." The OCP also estimates that the combined vector control and ivermectin distribution strategies have an effect that would only be obtained after several years of larviciding when carried out alone. Because the OCP began carrying out vector control activities well before the Mectizan Donation Program started donating ivermectin, and because the West African OCP countries represent only a portion of countries that have received the donated ivermectin, these OCP figures do not accurately reflect the donation program's full impact on onchocerciasis.

In contrast to the OCP, the African Program for Onchocerciasis Control (APOC) focuses its onchocerciasis control activities only on large-scale ivermectin distribution. Furthermore, APOC was established after the Mectizan Donation Program started donating ivermectin. APOC activities, therefore, are a better indicator of the Mectizan Donation Program's impact on onchocerciasis. But the onchocerciasis control activities of the APOC have only recently begun. Benton (1998) predicts that if APOC activities reach the bulk of the target population by 2002, then the cases of blindness prevented will be 434,527 in the 12-year project horizon of 1996–2009.

The partnership to donate ivermectin has also affected the public images of the partners (although this consequence does not represent an outcome as we have defined the term above). For the Task Force, creating the partnership with Merck helped enhance its image within the international public health development community. The Task Force's expanding role in pharmaceutical donation programs, as evidenced through its involvement in Glaxo Wellcome's Malarone donation program, suggests that the partnership has been successful from this perspective. Similarly, Merck's pride in the program is represented by the sculpture that stands in its corporate headquarters of a child leading a blind man. The same sculpture is on display at the World Bank, a major player and donor in the APOC program, at the Carter Center, a non-profit organization involved in ivermectin distribution, and in front of the World Health Organization's headquarters in Geneva, Switzerland. The public image of the Mectizan story is one of success, and a number of other pharmaceutical companies have initiated donation programs for international disease control efforts modeled on the Mectizan Donation Program. Comparative research is necessary to assess the experiences of these new partnerships modeled on the Mectizan Donation Program, and to evaluate the intended and unintended consequences of these cooperative efforts on health development activities, both globally and nationally.

A final question is whether the Merck-Task Force effort has been successful as a partnership. In simple terms, the partnership is a success because the partners together are achieving a cooperative goal that each partner could not accomplish alone. In addition, the partnership has persisted for more than a decade, suggesting that the partners view the experience as worthy of a long-term commitment. It also suggests that the partners have been able to overcome the institutional, technical, and political uncertainties that they have encountered over the past decade. We argue that the persistence and adaptability of the partnership is explained in part by the existence and maintenance of the three key boundary objects.

Conclusion

This analysis has broader implications for pharmaceutical companies and non-profit health development organizations that seek to form partnerships in cooperative disease control efforts. The social worlds framework used in this chapter emphasizes that drug donation programs involve partners with sharply different missions and work activities. These different social worlds do not easily come together in cooperative pursuits. The critical question is how to maintain heterogeneity, which is crucial to the divergent activities required in getting the work done, while creating common understandings, which is necessary for effectively working together.

In the case of the Merck-Task Force partnership, the boundary objects have three important properties. One property is that the boundary objects are plastic enough to be meaningful to different social worlds yet robust enough to maintain a common identity across the social worlds. However, by the very nature of their plasticity, these boundary objects may require ongoing reconstruction as they continue to span divergent worlds. A second property of these boundary objects is that they provide legitimacy to the new social world created by the partnership. This legitimacy is not only important for the partnership within the international public health development community, but it is also critical for creating a relationship of trust between the partners. A final property identified in the case of the Merck-Task Force partnership is that boundary objects provide a distance for the partners from the risky effort. For example, Merck vested the independent experts in the Mectizan Expert Committee with the responsibility for assessing governmental and non-governmental capabilities to distribute the drug. This gave Merck the distance it perceived was necessary from decisions about the beneficiaries of the donation program.

These properties of plasticity, legitimacy, and distance explain part of the success of the partnership between Merck and the Task Force. In addition, for the partnership to work effectively, the two organizations needed to come to agreement on shared goals and to establish a relationship of trust. The success of the partnership also relied on having adequate resources to carry out its work. Merck has provided these resources to the Mectizan Donation Program since the program's inception. Comparative research on other partnerships is needed to help us understand how organizations rooted in divergent social worlds can construct effective partnerships and how these partnerships can contribute to reducing global disease burden and human suffering.

Acknowledgments

We would like to thank the Edna McConnell Clark Foundation for providing funding for this research. We would also like to thank Brenda Colatrella at Merck & Co., Inc., various officials at WHO and TDR in Geneva, and Stefanie Meredith, Mary Alleman, and others at the Mectizan Donation Program for providing information for this study and reading various versions of this manuscript.

Notes

1. The safety of ivermectin treatment has been questioned in cases with heavy co-infection with *Loa loa*. Beginning in 1990, reports of adverse central nervous system (CNS) events in cases with heavy co-infection with *Loa loa* were reported in an area of Cameroon. Investigations into this problem found that "severe CNS complications following treatment with ivermectin in patients with loiasis and onchocerciasis are extremely rare and the most important factor is very high levels of Loa microfilaraemia." Furthermore, these investigations stated that "more important . . . was the evidence that any patient experiencing a severe CNS event will recover without sequelae if proper medical support therapy is given immediately" (Mectizan Donation Program, 1997). Currently, researchers are identifying areas at risk, studying whether the level of endemicity of loiasis can be rapidly assessed, and developing a method for identifying those individuals who are hypermicrofilaraemic for Loa loa using blood samples but not a microscope (Boussinesq et al., 1998).

2. Research suggests that the microfilarial loads in each individual are successively less after each treatment than they were following preceding treatments. See Plaisier et al., 1995, and Alley et al., 1994.

3. Ivermectin is derived from the *avermectin* class of compounds, a class of highly active broad-spectrum antiparasitic agents.

4. Skepticism about the apparent lack of side-effects of ivermectin was expressed strongly by Rougemont (1982), formerly with the OCP, who wrote that the conclusions of Aziz et al. (1982a) were "over optimistic." See also the response by Aziz et al. (1982b).

5. Minutes of a joint meeting between representatives of WHO and Merck Sharp and Dohme (MSD) in Geneva, September 14, 1987 (TDR file, WHO/Geneva).

6. Travel Report Summary by Dr. A.O. Lucas, March 5, 1986 (TDR file, WHO/Geneva).

7. Minutes of a joint meeting between representatives of WHO and Merck Sharp and Dohme (MSD) in Geneva, September 14, 1987 (TDR file, WHO/Geneva). Also interview 9 with Merck official (August 19, 1996).

8. This letter from Merck includes a signature for agreement by Dr. A. O. Lucas of TDR, dated July 10, 1985.

9. For example, a letter from Mr. R. Vagelos, CEO/Merck, to Dr. H. Mahler, director-general of WHO, dated September 26, 1986; and "Agreed Subsequent Steps" at the Merck/WHO meeting on January 21–22, 1987.

10. WHO internal document (sometime after October 1986–precise date unknown, TDR file, WHO/Geneva).

11. Mr. W. Furth, Assistant Director-General of WHO, wrote to Mr. J. Lyons, executive vice president of Merck, on September 22, 1987.

12. Telegram from Mr. J. T. Jackson, senior vice president for human health marketing of Merck, to Mr. W. Furth, Assistant Director-General of WHO, on September 22, 1987.

13. Although still in Atlanta, the Task Force for Child Survival is no longer housed in the Carter Center. It has always been a non-profit organization separate from the Carter Center, with its own staff, budget, and programs.

14. In his analysis of Star and Griesemer's research, Gieryn calls this kind of boundary work "double-edged" (Gieryn, 1995).

15. Between 1988 and 2000, a further 2.8 million treatments have been enabled through the Merck's Humanitarian Program, bringing the total treatments enabled in this time period to 197.8 million treatments. The Humanitarian Program is managed by Merck and makes ivermectin available to individual practitioners for treatment of patients who do not have access to community-directed mass treatment programs.

References

African Program for Onchocerciasis Control (1996). *Programme document: African Programme for Onchocerciasis Control.* Joint Action Forum, Second Session, Cotonou.

Alley, E. S., Plaisier, A. P., Boatin, B. A., Dadzie, K. Y., Remme, J., Zerbo, G., & Samba, E. M. (1994). The impact of five years of annual ivermectin treatment on skin microfilarial loads in the onchocerciasis focus of Asubende, Ghana. *Transactions of the Royal Society of Tropical Medicine and Hygiene,* 88(5), 581–584.

Amazigo, U. O. (1994). Detrimental effects of onchocerciasis on marriage age and breast-feeding. *Tropical and Geographical Medicine,* 46, 5, 322–325.

Awedoba, A. K. (1999). Help-seeking behavior and coping with onchocercal skin disease in endemic communities of southwestern Ghana. Research Paper. Boston: Takemi Program in International Health, Harvard School of Public Health.

Aziz, M. A., Diallo, S., Diop, I. M., Lariviere, M., & Porta, M. (1982a). Efficacy and tolerance of ivermectin in human onchocerciasis. *The Lancet, 2*(8291), 171–173.

Aziz M. A., Diallo, S., Lariviere, M., Diop, I. M., Porta, M., & Gaxotte, P. (1982b). Ivermectin in onchocerciasis. Letter. *The Lancet, 2*(8313), 1456–1457.

Benton, B. (1998). Economic impact of onchocerciasis control through the African Programme for Onchocerciasis Control: An overview. *Annals of Tropical Medicine and Parasitology, 92*, supplement 1, S33–39.

Boatin, B. A., Hougard, J-M., Alley, E. S., Akpoboua, L. K. B., Yaméogo, L., Dembélé, N. Sékétéli, A., & Dadzie, K. Y. (1998). The impact of Mectizan on the transmission of onchocerciasis. *Annals of Tropical Medicine and Parasitology, 92*, supplement 1, S47–60.

Boussinesq, M., Prod'hon, J., & Chippaux, J. P. (1997). Onchocerca volvulus: Striking decrease in transmission in the Vina valley (Cameroon) after eight annual large-scale ivermectin treatments. *Transactions of the Royal Society of Tropical Medicine and Hygiene, 91*, 1, 82–86.

Boussinesq, M., & Gardon, J. (1998). Challenges for the future: Loiasis. *Annals of Tropical Medicine and Parasitology, 92*, supplement 1, S147–151.

Clarke, A. (1990). A social worlds research adventure: The case of reproductive science. In T. Gieryn & S. Cozzens (Eds.), *Theories of science in society* (pp. 15–42). Bloomington: Indiana University Press.

Coulard, J. P., Lariviere M., Gerevais, M. C., Gaxotte, P., Aziz, A., Deloul A. M., & Cenac J. (1983). Traitement de l'onchocercose humaine par l'ivermectine. *Bulletin de la Société Pathologie Exotique, 76*, 681–688.

De Sole, G., Remme, J., Awadzi, K., Accorsi, S., Alley, E. S., Ba, O., Dadzie, K. Y., Giese, J., Karam, M., Keita, F. M. (1989). Adverse reactions after large-scale treatment of onchocerciasis with ivermectin: Combined result from eight community trials. *Bulletin of the World Health Organization, 67*(6), 707–719.

Fujimura, J. (1992). Crafting science: Standardized packages, boundary objects, and "translation." In A. Pickering (Ed.) *Science as practice and culture* (pp. 168–211). Chicago: University of Chicago Press.

Gerson, E. M. (1983). Scientific work and social worlds. *Knowledge, 4*, 357–377.

Gieryn, T. F. (1995). Boundaries of science. In S. Jasanoff, G. E. Markle, J. C. Petersen, and T. Pinch (Eds.) *Handbook of science and technology studies* (pp. 393–443). London: Sage Publications.

Kale, O. O. (1998). Onchocerciasis: The burden of disease. *Annals of Tropical Medicine and Parasitology, 92,* supplement 1, S101–115.

Lucas, A. O. (1986). Travel report summary. Geneva: TDR file, WHO.

Mectizan Donation Program (1987). *Mectizan donation program charter.* Atlanta: Author.

Merck & Co., Inc. (1995). *1995 annual report.* Whitehouse Station, NJ: Author.

Merck Sharp & Dohme (1991). *Mectizan: Hope for patients suffering from onchocerciasis, a vision of tomorrow.* Whitehouse Station, NJ: Author.

Ovuga, E. B., Ogwal-Okeny, J. W., & Okello, D. O. (1995). Social anthropological aspects of onchocercal skin disease in Nebbi District, Uganda. *East African Medical Journal, 72*(10), 649–653.

Pacque, M. C., Dukuly, Z., Greene, B. M., Munoz, B., Keyvan-Larijani, E., Williams, P. N., & Taylor, H. R. (1989). Community-based treatment of onchocerciasis with ivermectin: Acceptability and early adverse reactions. *Bulletin of the World Health Organization, 67*(6), 721–730.

Plaisier, A. P., Alley, E. S., Boatin, B. A., Van Oortmarssen, G. J., Remme, H., De Vlas, S. J., Bonneux, L., & Habbema, J. D. (1995). Irreversible effects of ivermectin on adult parasites in onchocerciasis patients in the Onchocerciasis Control Programme in West Africa. *Journal of Infectious Disease, 172*(1), 204–210.

Remme, J., Baker, R. H. A., De Sole, G., Dadzie, K. Y., Adams, M. A., Alley, E. S., Avissey, H. S. K., & Walsh, J. F. (1989). A community trial of ivermectin in the onchocerciasis focus of Asubende, Ghana. I. Effect on the microfilarial reservoir and the transmission of *Onchocerca volvulus. Tropical Medicine and Parasitology 40,* 367–374.

Rougemont, A. (1982). Ivermectin for onchocerciasis. Letter. *The Lancet, 2*(8308), 1158.

Samba, E. M. (1994). *The onchocerciasis Control Programme in West Africa: An example of effective public health management.* Geneva: World Health Organization.

Shibutani, T. (1962). Reference groups and social control. In A. Rose (Ed.) *Human behavior and social processes: An interactionist approach* (pp. 129–147). London: Routledge.

Shibutani, T. (1955). Reference groups as perspectives. *American Journal of Sociology*, 60, 562–569.

Star, S. L., & Griesemer, J. R. (1989). Institutional ecology, "translations" and boundary objects: Amateurs and professionals in Berkeley's Museum of Vertebrate Zoology, 1907–39. *Social Studies of Science*, 19, 387–420.

Strauss, A. L. (1978). A social worlds perspective. *Studies in Symbolic Interaction*, 1, 119–128.

Strauss, A. L. (1982). Social worlds and legitimation processes. *Studies in Symbolic Interaction*, 4, 171–190.

Sturchio, J. (1992). *The decision to donate Mectizan: Historical background.* Unpublished manuscript, distributed by Merck.

Task Force for Child Survival and Development (1999). *About the Task Force for Child Survival and Development. www.taskforce.org.*

Tavis, L. (1996). *Power and responsibility: Multinational managers and developing country concerns.* Notre Dame: University of Notre Dame Press.

Taylor, H. R., Pacque, M., Munoz, B., Greene, B. M. (1990). Impact of mass treatment of onchocerciasis with ivermectin on the transmission of infection. *Science, 250* (4977), 116–118.

UNDP/World Bank/WHO Special Program for Research and Training in Tropical Diseases (1976). *Participation of the Pharmaceutical Sector.* TDR/WP/76.30, Geneva: TDR.

UNDP/World Bank/WHO Special Program for Research and Training in Tropical Diseases (1983). *Report of the scientific working group on filariasis for 1980–83.* Geneva: TDR.

World Health Organization (1946). *Constitution of the World Health Organization.* New York: United Nations.

World Health Organization (1987a). Minutes of the meeting with TDR, OCP and USAID on June 26, 1987. Geneva: TDR file, WHO.

World Health Organization (1987b). Minutes of a joint meeting between representatives of WHO and Merck Sharp and Dohme (MSD), September 14. Geneva: TDR file, WHO.

World Health Organization Expert Committee on Onchocerciasis Control (1995). *Onchocerciasis and its control.* Geneva: Author.

6

The Last Years of the CVI and the Birth of the GAVI

William Muraskin

THE CHILDREN'S VACCINE INITIATIVE (CVI) WAS CREATED IN 1990 with the goal of saving the lives of tens of millions of poor children in the Third World through the development of new and improved vaccines. The CVI was designed to bring together all the major participants in the international health community—scientists, national and international health bureaucrats, foreign aid donors, and private and public sector vaccine manufacturers.[1]

The core of the CVI was made up of the five founding organizations—UNICEF, the World Health Organization (WHO), the United Nations Development Program (UNDP), the World Bank, and the Rockefeller Foundation—which constituted its standing committee. The rest of the vaccine community made up the consultative group (CG), which met once a year, and a smaller management advisory committee (MAC), which represented the CG and met twice a year.

If the CVI were to succeed in helping the international health system produce and deliver new vaccines for the children of the Third World, it was vital that it help facilitate better and more extensive communication and cooperation between the public and private sectors. This was crucial because the two sectors focused on different, though ultimately interdependent, areas of vaccine creation. The public sector did basic research, helped with large-scale clinical trials, and delivered vaccine to the poor in Third World countries. Some of its breakthrough scientific research was quite high profile and well publicized. The private sector did something called vaccine product development. This long, laborious, unglamorous, and unheralded type of work involves creating high quality batches of a candidate vaccine for testing, carrying out clinical trials to demonstrate safety and efficacy, finding appropriate doses, meeting complex licensing requirements, solving the problems of scale-up to high volume manufacturing, and arranging for packaging, shipping, and marketing. What goes into product development is relatively unknown outside industrial circles.

The existing vaccine system was badly fractured and disarticulated: the lines of communication between the public and private spheres, other than among scientists, were often weak or nonexistent. Basic researchers, product developers, and vaccine deliverers often worked in ignorance of the interests or needs of the other groups in the continuum. As far as the generation of vaccines for the industrial world, where normal market mechanisms (i.e., profit seeking) functioned adequately, the process operated relatively effectively, despite the system's basic disorganization. For the production of new and improved vaccines for the Third World, where the prospects of profit appeared dim to nonexistent, it did not work and could not work unless the relations between the two sectors improved radically.

Bringing members of the public and private sectors together constituted a daunting challenge for the Children's Vaccine Initiative. There existed a great gulf of distrust, often bordering on outright contempt, between people in the two sectors. A significant part of their estrangement was ideological. Most of those attracted into national and international public health saw their work as partaking of a calling to benefit mankind. Especially in the area of vaccines, with their ability to prevent suffering from deadly infectious diseases, the work was seen as quintessentially humanitarian in nature. The idea that the profit motive should play a key role in determining which life-saving vaccines were produced was seen as fundamentally immoral; vaccines should be a public service, even a public right, not something bought and sold.

For those in the private sector, the situation was seen totally differently. The search for profit was the engine of innovation. It made new life-saving products possible and spurred creative individuals to do their best. Since it enabled the private sector to be both efficient and productive in the health field, it saved lives. The public sector, on the other hand, was seen as bureaucratic, inefficient, and wasteful of limited resources. It was inherently incapable of generating constant innovation, but by its heavy-handed interventions was able to stifle efficient enterprise through excessive taxation, complex regulation, price and profit control, or unfair subsidized competition.

This ideological divide was compounded on the public sector's side by a profound lack of understanding of what the private sector actually contributed to vaccine creation. For most people in public health, the job of vaccine generation was accomplished primarily by basic scientists working in government-funded laboratories. It was they who discovered what would work and what would not. It was in their laboratories that breakthrough ideas were made real, taken to the point of "proof of principle," and then turned into proto-vaccines. What the private sector did was "simply" take those researcher-created proto-vaccines, mass produce them, and make excessive profits. When it came to R&D, the public sector understood and valued the research component highly, but saw the development component as more an add-on than anything else.

The private sector thoroughly disagreed. While they appreciated the research done in government and university laboratories, they believed that until that work was put through the long and arduous process of development, it was worthless. Most of the basic research, given the limited amount of capital available for development, would of necessity remain little more than laboratory curiosities. The gap between proof-of-principle or proto-vaccines and real vaccines that could actually be utilized by a population was enormous. The real work of vaccine creation was done by the unheralded vaccine developers in industry, not basic researchers in public-sector laboratories.

One of the most important and lasting achievements of the CVI during its later years was its role in legitimizing the presence of the private sector at public-sector vaccine gatherings. It helped make clear to everyone that inviting companies should not be seen as a gimmick or done just for show, but because moving the immunization agenda required it. The CVI laid the foundation for accepting the private sector not simply as an invited guest, but as an active, and ultimately equal, partner with the public sector.

The Early Years of the CVI: High Hopes, Complex Realities

Since the leaders of the Children's Vaccine Initiative saw bridging the gulf between the public and private sectors as so vital, it was not surprising that the original leader-designate of the CVI was someone whose experience made him knowledgeable about the importance of intersector cooperation, and who actually knew the fundamental role played by vaccine developers in industry. That leader was General (Dr.) Philip Russell, newly retired commanding general of the Army Medical Research Command. The Army, because its troops often fought in the tropics, was concerned that vaccines be available to protect its personnel even though normal market forces would not produce such vaccines. As a result, the Army financed basic research for a variety of vaccines, and then went to the private sector to contract for the creation of the needed products. Unlike most scientists in the public sector, General Russell had focused on the "end-to-end mission"—the whole vaccine continuum from basic research, through product development, to actual delivery of vaccine into the arms of service personnel. Russell knew that his scientific colleagues in the international health community didn't have an accurate understanding of what the private sector actually did, and that he and the CVI would have to educate them to the importance and legitimacy of stronger public-private relations. Otherwise, the CVI could not succeed.

The CVI tries to bridge the gap

One of the most important means to close the gap between the two sectors was to bring the private sector into social and personal contact with the public sector by including representatives of industry in meetings of the international health community. It was important that when vital vaccine issues were discussed in public-sector gatherings that organizers and participants alike think inclusively and invite industry. That was a radical departure from the way things were customarily done.

Even before the CVI took shape as an organized structure—the building of which Russell took the lead—the process of bringing the private sector into dialogue with the public sector had already begun. The Institute of Medicine organized a series of meetings to deal with the question of the new Children's Vaccine Initiative and invited the heads of a number of pharmaceutical companies. For the first time, public scientists and policy makers heard from company heads: what industry wanted, what it rejected, where it would gladly cooperate, and where it would "never" collaborate. While much that was said was unpalatable, a real dialogue had begun. The CVI proceeded to build upon that initial interaction by making sure that industry was invited to the CVI's consultative group meetings, where the entire vaccine community (now defined as including both the public and private sectors) could come together and talk. The CVI also set up a series of task forces to work on specific problems, and one of the key task forces involved public-private cooperation. In addition, a number of product development groups for specific new and improved vaccines were established, with the goal of ultimately interfacing.

The creation of a social space where private entrepreneurs and civil servants could come into contact on a regular basis was quite important because it allowed actual interaction with the possibility of generating practical collaborative activities. But, no less important, it was part of a CVI educational process in which the public sector learned that no meeting was complete without industry being present, and industry recognizing the public sector as a willing, able, and reliable partner for future cooperative ventures.

It was originally assumed that the task force on relations with development collaborators would be of key importance for the success of the CVI. Here the two groups could interface and the necessary cooperation on vaccines be hammered out. In order to give industry a sense of ownership, the chairmanship of the task force was given to Richard Arnold, vice president of the leading pharmaceutical trade association, the International Federation of Pharmaceutical Manufacturers Associations (IFPMA). The second ranking position in the task force, that of secretary, was given to one of the CVI's leading proponents of private-public cooperation, Dr. Richard Mahoney.

Unfortunately, the task force was stillborn. The chairman, instead of seeing the group as an ongoing pillar of the new organization, felt that the task force should meet infrequently, do little, and rapidly disband. He appeared to feel that his responsibility was primarily to limit the exposure of the trade association— and himself—to risk. He certainly did not see himself or the IFPMA as trailblazers looking for new ways to connect the public-private sectors. As an official in a loose, industrywide association lacking a broad mandate to act for the private sector, some circumspection on his part was quite understandable, though in this case, rather excessive. At the least it demonstrated the inherent weakness of assigning a key leadership role to an individual on the basis of title rather than personal commitment. Apparently, the CVI assumed that the dedication of the secretary of the task force would mold, educate, and ignite the enthusiasm of the titular chairman, but it was not to be. Fortunately, while the task force figured prominently in the CVI's organizational chart, in reality it was of limited significance. Increased public-private interaction flourished in many other areas of the CVI structure, and the task force could and did wither away without disrupting the increased contact.

In fact, as we see later, an unintended consequence of Arnold's abortive involvement with the CVI ultimately proved extremely positive for the future of public-private relations. Arnold was very uncomfortable with his role as representative of industry to the CVI and decided to ease the pressure on himself by revitalizing the IFPMA's biologicals committee and reorienting it to deal primarily with vaccine problems. Jacques-Francois Martin, one-time CEO of Pasteur-Merieux, Chiron, and Biocene, became the chairman of the biologicals committee. Martin proved to be little less than a visionary, with a deep commitment to the moral urgency of saving children's lives. He became the key force on industry's side working to create a full-fledged partnership between the private and public sectors.[2]

The CVI's original mandate was very broad and in keeping with General Russell's vision that the "end-to-end mission" could justify focusing on any problem in the vaccine creation continuum from "bench to bush." In fact, however, the initial enthusiasm for the CVI, which sparked its creation and came predominantly from the scientific community, was the lure of innovative work in the technical nature of the vaccines and their method of delivery. The official goal of the CVI was the development of a "magic bullet" vaccine (e.g., multi-antigen, administered near birth, preferably orally, utilizing novel delivery systems such as time release, and requiring only one administration).

The product development groups—which dealt with improved versions of measles, polio, and tetanus toxoid vaccines—and the CVI's aggressive championship of using the DPT (diphtheria, pertussis, tetanus) vaccine as the platform upon which other, newer vaccines should be added, all required that the CVI deal with the private sector in an intimate way. Of special importance was the question of how to deal with intellectual property rights that increasingly controlled the vaccine landscape. However, it was in this area that the CVI possessed a major structural flaw that severely limited its ability to engage the private sector successfully.

The difficulty's source

The problem hearkens back to the origins of the CVI. The initiative was partially motivated by the widespread feeling in the vaccine community that the World Health Organization, which held the United Nations' mandate to protect humanity's physical well-being, was unable or unwilling to carry out its role effectively. The WHO was supposed to be helping to lead and unify the vaccine development community—plugging its gaps, bringing groups together, spearheading technological innovation, and helping bring those scientific discussions to fruition by facilitating agreements with the private sector. The CVI, to a large extent, was filling a vacuum left by WHO's failure to aggressively carry this mission out.

One of WHO's major weaknesses as far as the CVI was concerned was its difficulty in dealing with private industry when profit and royalties were involved. The World Health Organization was concerned that, in dealing with the private sector, it should not be accused of favoring one company over another, and that it avoid both the appearance of being motivated by financial gain—which would hurt its prestige and reputation—and the actuality of its agents being corrupted by the lure of personal profit. This organizational anxiety was strongly reflected in its legal staff, which operated at the interface between the institution and the private sector. As a result, WHO had great difficulty in working constructively with industry to commercialize therapeutic products, especially where profits could accrue to the public sector.

The CVI saw itself as being able to innovate new arrangements with the private sector that would encourage private-public cooperation where WHO would not. The CVI's flexibility and aggressiveness would be its hallmark where WHO was hamstrung by legal and bureaucratic concerns. Unfortunately, the CVI, as a consortium with limited resources and personnel, was dependent upon its core membership for a variety of vital functions. One of the services that WHO provided for the CVI was use of its legal staff. Thus, for example, when questions of intellectual property rights came up, the CVI and private enterprise talked innovatively and flexibly about them. But the matter would ultimately be referred to the legal advisors of the very group whose failure to successfully deal with such issues provoked the CVI's creation in the first place. Such a situation guaranteed frustration, both on the part of the private sector and those in the CVI dedicated to pioneering a rapprochement with industry.

The most glaring example of the CVI's severely limited ability to independently encourage public-private cooperation occurred around what appeared to be the its greatest triumph: the decision of industry to help the public sector develop a product that it had expressly declared it would never work on—a more heat-stable polio vaccine. Industry had explicitly declared its opposition to such a venture because the existing polio vaccine worked very well in the developed world and presented problems only in places that by definition could not pay for an improved vaccine. Pharmaceutical companies, they said, were not in the charity business but owed a fiduciary obligation to their stockholders to make profits. That obligation still left a lot of room for private-public cooperation, but not when it involved such fruitless projects. Top business leaders had made this clear as early as the Institute of Medicine meetings on the new CVI.

Despite this line-in-the-sand position, industry in fact did decide to help the CVI develop such an unprofitable vaccine. When it was discovered that deuterium oxide ("heavy water") might be able to stabilize the polio vaccine and make it more heat resistant, Jacques-Francois Martin championed industry cooperation on the grounds that a major humanitarian goal could be achieved, children's lives could be saved, and the cost would be minimal—even though no short-term financial profit would accrue. In addition to the invaluable lives saved, a firm foundation for public-private cooperation would be laid which could in the future produce both profit for industry and a benefit for mankind. "Doing well by doing good" was a form of honorable business.

For Martin, industrial cooperation on a heat-resistant polio vaccine showed that industry was a responsible and reliable partner in an idealistic cause. In turn, the public sector could demonstrate that it was a dependable collaborator by buying large quantities of the vaccine that it had commissioned. The latter was particularly important because of the widespread belief within industry that the public sector was a fickle and unreliable partner in joint ventures because it too often unpredictably shifted its position, depending upon the latest political pressures. Thus, for Martin and the CVI, the polio vaccine was a good test of the new spirit of cooperation that both sides now hoped to nurture.

Unfortunately, internal divisions within the CVI now manifested themselves in the most damaging way possible. While the quest for a heat-resistant polio vaccine was a major official goal of the CVI, there were many within the public sector who never supported it. The leaders of the Expanded Program on Immunization (EPI) of WHO-UNICEF felt that polio eradication could be achieved without an improved vaccine and that the enterprise was a waste of time and effort. The fact that the new stabilizing agent was deuterium oxide, "heavy water," could play into the hands of anti-vaccination groups throughout the Third World, who would falsely claim that the vaccine was radioactive and panic people.

Given these attitudes and fears, the stage was set for a crisis when it became clear that polio eradication was moving forward at an unexpectedly rapid rate due to the adoption of National Immunization Days, in which countries inoculated whole cohorts of children on specific days rather than piecemeal during the year. The mass immunizations made the problem of temperature sensitivity far less of a problem than did the traditional method. In addition, a new form of packaging with internal temperature monitors that would allow vaccinators to know specifically which vials of vaccine were good and which ones were spoiled would soon be available, making the problem of heat stabilization much less important.

At a meeting in Washington, D.C., representatives of WHO, UNICEF, the U.S. Centers for Disease Control, and other groups agreed that a more heat-resistant polio vaccine was simply not needed, and if developed should not be purchased because it was not needed, it would be more expensive, it might not be available until after eradication, and its controversial new component would lead to bad publicity that might endanger the whole anti-polio campaign. This decision was reached without any consultation with industry, the CVI, or any of the major proponents of an improved vaccine.

One could not have planned an action that embodied industry's worst fears of the public sector if one had tried. Industry started out with the widespread belief that the public sector was unreliable and fickle as a partner, that they would commission a product or a project and, for purely internal reasons, would back out after industry had spent time and money on it. Private sector leaders had made clear that under "no conditions" would they get involved in a heat-resistant polio vaccine since it held no prospect of profit for them. But despite that pledge, they had cooperated anyway. And now, without consultation, in what was perceived as a high-handed unilateral decision, the public sector had backed out. Where a major bridge connecting industry to the public sector had been constructed, now only a bombed-out ruin existed.

The polio project had promised to be the greatest achievement of the CVI, but turned out to be the last gasp of its original leadership, who saw vaccine product development as the paramount goal for the CVI. That leadership, especially Dr. Scott Halstead of the Rockefeller Foundation and Frank Hartvelt of the United Nations Development Program, had controlled the CVI through the power concentrated in the small standing committee. However, long-term discontent by members of the consultative group—which represented the entire vaccine community—and management advisory committee—that represented its more active members—led to a "donors' revolt" that shifted power away from the standing committee to a larger and (theoretically) more representative group, the meeting of interested parties (MIP). Unfortunately, the members of this group had little interest or commitment to vaccine product development and placed its concerns elsewhere.[3] Simultaneously, and somewhat coincidentally, the original leaders retired or shifted to different posts, which removed them from any connection to the CVI. Most important of all, the CVI, which had fought for years to maintain its relative independence from the World Health Organization, was de facto absorbed into WHO after it was decided that the executive director of WHO's newly reorganized Global Program on Vaccines (GPV) would also head the CVI.

The CVI is successful in unexpected ways

As a result of all these changes, the first and most dramatic phase of the CVI ended. The efforts of the CVI to directly impact vaccine product development ended in failure, as did its attempts to do large-scale fundraising for its activities and remain an independent entity. Nevertheless, the first phase of the CVI was far from a total failure. In fact, it was amazingly successful, but in areas far removed from the vaccine product development that had inspired its original founders. It was in the less glamorous area of vaccine procurement that the CVI's greatest success in laying the foundations for public-private cooperation actually occurred.

The original CVI mandate covered all aspects of the vaccine continuum, and for some of the partners, UNICEF especially, dealing with problems of vaccine supply and quality were of particular concern. One of the CVI's most significant contributions to solving vaccine problems was its ability to create a space outside the agency bureaucracies where creative people could work freely across organizational lines. This was especially important for people within WHO, where the rigidity of the rules and structure of the agency made innovative and speedy work hard to accomplish. The CVI, with its task forces, created a place where activities could be carried out that WHO's "organizational chart" made no provision for.

Two exceptional people—Peter Evans and Amie Batson—both working with the EPI in WHO's Geneva headquarters, found themselves desperately in need of the flexibility that only the CVI could provide. They had created in their spare time a graphic representation—using population size and gross national product as the two axes—to reveal the extent to which the countries of the world could meet their individual vaccine needs by foreign purchase or local vaccine production. This grid demonstrated that the world could be divided into a series of groupings vis-à-vis their vaccine needs: those that were rich and populous, therefore capable of producing their own vaccines; those that were rich and sparsely inhabited, which meant they could afford to buy vaccines from others; those that were poor but so populous that they could create a vast internal market for locally produced vaccines; and those that were poor and sparsely inhabited, thus lacking the ability to buy or produce vaccines for themselves. The exciting thing about the grid was that it could be easily turned into a practical guide for the international donor community.

According to Evans, the grid provided "a framework for working out for a given country whether aid money is really needed to support its vaccine supply and, if so, whether the support should go more to [local] production or [foreign] procurement, so that the country will need less and less aid as it becomes more and more vaccine-independent."[4] The payoff from the grid was almost instantaneous once people became aware of it through the mechanism of the CVI's task force on situation analysis. The grid strikingly revealed that some rich countries had been receiving free vaccines while some countries too small and poor to justify the investment were attempting to produce their own vaccines.[5] Within a very short period of time USAID and UNICEF used the grid to map out such anomalies with the hope of coordinating the activities of current and future donors.[6]

Batson and Evans also played a pivotal role in UNICEF's decision to obtain an outside study of the international vaccine industry by Mercer Management Consultants. The study "concluded that, as the world's largest purchaser of vaccines, UNICEF has sufficient leverage to influence the price and availability of new vaccines through its global procurement strategies." Based on the Mercer study's findings (and heavily influenced by both the Batson-Evans Grid, and the work of the task force on situation analysis) UNICEF announced a fundamental change in policy. It would no longer purchase vaccines and distribute them to all the countries of the Third World that asked, but would systematically differentiate and target assistance to only the neediest countries. In addition, the plan was to "move UNICEF from merely supporting immunization to assisting governments to take complete responsibility for their vaccine supply and immunization programs."[7]

In order to achieve that goal, UNICEF took the Batson-Evans Grid (which looked at GNP/capita, total population size, and total GNP) and overlaid it with a series of four bands that divided the world into groupings from the poorest to the richest nations.[8] Band A countries needed outside support because without it they could not maintain their existing vaccine programs—let alone add new vaccines. Band B countries were capable of significantly moving toward supporting their own vaccine programs—though they would need outside help at first. All of the Band B nations had the resources to finance at least 80 percent of their current EPI vaccine supply within four years. Band C nations were seen as capable of achieving vaccine self-sufficiency by local production or foreign procurement; however, they might need help in setting up national vaccine quality control systems and making local production stronger. Band D countries could achieve immediate vaccine independence, though they might require a one-time external investment in their vaccine supply systems.

The effects of this change in strategy were manifold, but for our purposes the effect on the private sector is the most striking. As far as industry was concerned, what Amie Batson, Peter Evans, and their closest colleague, Julie Milstien, had helped achieve was to radically change the way the public sector saw its role—a change that made its viewpoint much more compatible with that of the private sector. Industry leaders felt that these public servants truly understood what the private sector needed.

The fundamental importance of the foundation laid by these individuals is made exceptionally clear by Dr. Thomas Vernon, executive director of medical, scientific, and public health affairs at Merck's vaccine division. According to him, the basis of increased cooperation between the public and private sector that occurred in the last years of the CVI (1994 to 1999) was the result of UNICEF's commissioning of the Mercer study, which showed that children could not benefit from new and improved vaccines if price alone were considered. The creation and use of the Batson-Evans Grid was also a major event for industry because it carried a message that the public's responsibility lay where the market failed, but "where it doesn't fail that is private territory. I think that was a message not previously heard or expressed from the public sector," said Vernon.[9] According to him, the fact that public-sector people like Batson, Evans, and Milstien were willing to say out loud that UNICEF's policy of lumping together countries that were fully capable of buying vaccines at market prices with countries drowning in poverty was a counterproductive policy for everyone, meant that real negotiation and cooperation between the sectors was possible. Many in industry believed a strong argument could be made for helping countries so poor that market mechanisms could not function, but vehemently protested against public-sector policies that undercut the natural development of private markets where they could flourish.

Reinforcing what the private sector considered a pro-industry message, the CVI and its task forces also championed the idea that vaccines are the most economical means of preventing disease, and the world has undervalued them by assuming that, unlike curative medicine, vaccines must be dirt cheap to be worth purchasing. The old vaccines (e.g., measles, polio, DPT) were indeed inexpensive, but the new ones (e.g., hepatitis B, Hib) would of necessity be more costly, and yet they would still be the cheapest and most effective form of medical intervention. Industry strongly believed this, and now the public sector was starting to take a similar view.

This change in perspective and policy pioneered by the CVI's task forces created a foundation for public-private cooperation that was firm enough that even the heat-stable polio vaccine fiasco could not significantly undermine it. Thus, when the CVI as an independent entity under the control of the standing committee was transformed into a weaker entity subordinated to the World Health Organization, it nevertheless maintained and even strengthened its attractiveness to industry as an indispensable place for the incubation of better public-private relations.

An Older and Smaller CVI Finds Its Niche by Championing Vaccine Introduction

The "transformed" CVI was officially headed by Dr. J. W. Lee, who served as its executive director, though his main role was as head of the World Health Organization's Global Program for Vaccines and Immunization (GPV). With Lee's loyalties and interests focused primarily on the WHO program, and the CVI's old protector, the standing committee, effectively submerged into an often indifferent meeting of interested parties, the CVI was left orphaned. What saved it from simply withering away or becoming a Potemkin village for WHO's fundraising efforts, was that Lee turned over practical control of the CVI to Dr. Roy Widdus, a committed advocate for the initiative.

The most daunting task for Widdus as de facto head of the severely reduced CVI was to find a justification for its continued existence. At the fifth meeting of the CVI consultative group in Sao Paulo, Brazil, in 1995—billed as a "birthday party" for the CVI—the minutes report that "Dr. Widdus took a moment to answer the often asked question, 'What is the CVI?' "[10] For some people the question was meant literally. An African representative said that "people in the WHO regional office and in the UNDP field office in Africa did not know about the CVI."[11] The fact that Lee and others spoke at the general sessions of the Sao Paulo meeting almost exclusively about the accomplishments of WHO's Global Program on Vaccines certainly did not help matters. While developing country representatives were unsure what the CVI was, many of the European donors (including members of the CVI's "controlling" body, the meeting of interested parties) were unsure why there was any need for the CVI now that WHO had reformed its vaccine activities and created the Global Program on Vaccines.[12] As late as the sixth consultative group meeting in Dakar in late 1996, a sympathetic observer from USAID could still say that he came away from the meeting not knowing exactly what the CVI did or how it differed from WHO-GPV.[13]

The problem for Widdus was that the original focus of the CVI was on vaccine product development, with the CVI playing an active and catalytic role through its product development groups. That effort had failed, and its champions were no longer active in the organization. In fact, (European) bilateral donor hostility to what they perceived as an overly "technological fix" state of mind dominating the CVI was one of the reasons the meeting of interested parties forced the standing committee out of power. The original leadership also had been proponents of the end-to-end mission concept and had seen the whole vaccine continuum as the CVI's responsibility. For a downsized CVI to survive, Widdus would have to find a different and narrower focus for the CVI's activities, even though he would continue to keep the ideal alive.[14]

The introduction of new vaccines

Certain new areas for the CVI to concentrate on looked very promising to Widdus. One of the most important was the problem of introducing new vaccines such as hepatitis B into developing countries. While the old leadership had seen its task as helping to actively create new vaccines, the fact was that existing ones were not being adequately utilized. While for five years the bottleneck in the system had appeared to be vaccine development, it was increasingly clear to many that the true bottleneck was vaccine introduction.[15] While fostering vaccine introduction had always fit into the CVI's mandate, it had actually not received much attention by the leadership.

Many groups in the vaccine community were increasingly disturbed by this lack of attention to vaccine usage, and this created a potential constituency and niche for the CVI. Dr. Gustav Nossal, chairman of the prestigious Scientific Advisory Group of Experts (SAGE) of WHO, had mentioned the issue in his summary and closing remarks at the Sao Paulo CVI meeting.[16] Its importance was vigorous discussed at the SAGE meeting in 1997,[17] and Nossal's view represented that of many in the public sector, in both the developing and developed world.[18]

Of special importance, industry saw successful introduction of existing vaccines as an absolutely fundamental issue. The public sector's claim that industry and the free market had failed the Third World because they did not produce vaccines for diseases that primarily effected the poorest countries (e.g., malaria, tuberculosis, schistosomiasis), would not be convincing to the private sector as long as Yellow Fever vaccine (selling for pennies) and hepatitis B vaccine (purchasable for quarters) were not being utilized in countries desperately needing them.[19] As far as industry was concerned constructive talk about cooperation on future "orphan" vaccines would have to wait on a solution to the vaccine introduction problem. Business looked very favorably upon any help that the CVI could give to solve the problem, and the CVI under Widdus was very happy to oblige.

A focus on vaccine introduction was not only a good place to win support, but it was a good activity to differentiate the CVI from the GPV, and especially its Expanded Program on Immunization (EPI). The EPI, which had created the system for universal immunization of the children of the Third World, had long been fixated on the problems of maintaining and increasing coverage of the original six vaccines (i.e., DPT, measles, polio, BCG). It was also deeply concerned about the aging of the vaccine delivery infrastructure, especially the "cold chain." It had little enthusiasm or interest in the introduction of new vaccines such as hepatitis B and Hib, which were seen as additional burdens on an already ailing system. Thus, the EPI had left the field wide open for the CVI.

However, for the CVI to highlight its achievements in this area was exceptionally difficult and fraught with danger because CVI activism on the issue would of necessity be seen as an implicit rebuke of the GVP-EPI's relative inactivity. To make matters worse, Lee, the formal leader of the CVI, was also executive director of the GVP. For Lee to emphasize CVI success was tantamount to criticizing his own leadership of the larger and better funded WHO program. The conflict of interest built into Lee's position continually placed the CVI in an impossible situation: to act was dangerous and threatening to WHO, but not to act left the CVI appearing a superfluous and redundant appendage of GPV. Even more aggravating to the CVI staff, on various occasions when a CVI activity proved unexpectedly successful, credit for its work was claimed by WHO-GPV, and the CVI's role correspondingly downplayed or ignored.

The key document in reorienting the immunization community in the new direction was "What Actions Will Accelerate the Introduction of New

Vaccines?"[20] prepared for the Scientific Advisory Group of Experts by Roy Widdus and the CVI secretariat.[21] The SAGE was the main advisor to the Global Program on Vaccines, as well as the Children's Vaccine Initiative, and the most prestigious scientific body advising on vaccine policy in the world. Its advice and criticism was of paramount importance for the international vaccine community. For example, when the Bill and Melinda Gates Children's Vaccine Program (CVP) came into existence and established a presence on the internet, it highlighted the report on its website. According to Scott Wittet, director of communications for the program, the whole purpose of the CVP could be summarized as an attempt to "simply implement the SAGE report"—which in reality was the Children's Vaccine Initiative's policy report on the introduction of new vaccines.[22]

The general analysis of the problem and the kinds of activities recommended to rectify it which the report suggested were in total harmony with the private sector's assessment of the situation. The report maintained that the under-utilization of hepatitis B, Hib, yellow fever and rubella vaccines had to be corrected, "even though they would fit easily within current NIP (National Immunization Program) efforts." The report recommended studying how decisions were made about introducing new vaccines, identifying what delayed the process, and creating a conceptual framework to "help in developing a general understanding of the dynamics of the process."[23]

A number of studies were undertaken to create this more systematic approach, most being carried out by the CVI itself. They included CVI staff surveying Third World countries that adopted the Hib vaccine relatively soon after licensure; assessing the significance of the association between adoption of hepatitis B vaccine and factors such as per capita GNP; studying magnitude of disease burden and vaccine program effectiveness in order to ascertain the "best predictor of adoption"; and constructing a model that used these markers plus others (e.g., private sector use, neighboring country utilization, year of adoption, and price) to specifically discover the "factors most predictive of the time of adoption for HB and Hib vaccines."[24]

Of special importance for industry, the prototype the CVI was building was a comprehensive model that would "help avoid an undue emphasis on single facets . . . such as vaccine price," in favor of seeing vaccine adoption as a multifaceted process that included the whole range of influences determining how decision makers perceived the situation. While perception was influenced by the existence of studies of disease burden, vaccine safety, logistical feasibility, and financial resources—all of which needed to be supplied to policy makers—ultimately it was not purely a rational, scientifically informed accounting process. The CVI people found that any accurate model would have to take perception seriously as a factor "in and of itself"—even if it were too often based on inaccurate or unscientific information.[25] As a result, they found that the answer to the issue of vaccine affordability "lies in changing the perception of the value of vaccination, i.e. making governments and donors more willing to invest in health through vaccination"—a position resolutely supported by industry.[26]

The report went on to recommend that the public sector help Third World governments to better understand the value of vaccines by

> communicating the economic benefits of investment in vaccination, not just to NIP [National Immunization Program] mangers, but to ministries of finance, and others concerned with providing resources to vaccination programs, including donors, and lending agencies, who can view investment in health interventions from a broader societal and development perspective.[27]

No one in the private sector could have put it better. This vision of the problem was identical to the one that Batson, Evans, and Milstien of the CVI's task force on situation analysis had been championing for years, and which had laid the original foundations for a lasting private sector interest in the Children's Vaccine Initiative.

In many ways the CVI report for the 1998 SAGE meeting was an embodiment of the agreements reached between the private sector and the public sector the year before at a historic conference at Bellagio, Italy, hosted by the Children's Vaccine Initiative and the Rockefeller Foundation. The conference was on the global supply of new vaccines. Dr. Alan Shaw, chair of the biologicals committee of the International Federation of Pharmaceutical Manufacturers Associations (IFPMA), later stated that at that meeting industry had "gone from being a passive partner in [the] CVI to becoming an active participant," which he considered a major watershed in public-private relations.[28] The meeting had been called to find common ground between the two sectors to make new vaccines available to the Third World. The participants had agreed to adopt key positions favored by industry as a basis for cooperation. These included

- Full implementation of the CVI task force on situation analysis–inspired UNICEF-WHO strategy for targeting supply and assistance for new vaccines to only those countries in greatest need

- Tiering prices for new vaccines offered by manufacturers, with broad communication by the public sector to achieve governmental and popular acceptance of this strategy
- Protection of, and respect for, intellectual property
- Earlier forecasts of demand for new vaccines, based on epidemiological criteria
- Advocacy to raise awareness of the high value of a vaccines[29]

All of these items were of crucial importance to industry.

Some might see the willingness of the public sector to support these positions as little more than a capitulation to private power, but such an assessment misses the key aspects of the situation. Tiered pricing for new vaccines (as opposed to old vaccines like polio, measles, and DPT, whose development costs had long since been paid off) was a requirement industry needed help in "selling" to national governments. It was simultaneously, and more importantly, a major concession by industry to those championing public-private cooperation. For example, according to Jacques-Francois Martin, when Richard Arnold of the IFPMA first looked at the concept of tiered pricing for new products in 1994 he disapproved of it, and felt that industry would simply reject it. Industry would not agree to sell new vaccines at discount prices until they matured— many years down the line. In fact, the American pharmaceutical companies were so uncomfortable with the concept—having been burnt by negative publicity during congressional hearings in the 1980s—that when the IFPMA started discussing the issue in 1994 the Americans "often left the room" rather than be involved. According to Martin, since Europeans were more liberal on this issue than Americans, and the American companies didn't sell to the Third World public sector anyway, "it allowed the Europeans more flexibility."[30] But, he emphasized, "We have to have political support to keep prices higher in the developed world" in order to recoup costs and make a reasonable level of profit "or no one will invest in vaccines." This is hard for both intermediary countries (i.e., developing countries above the level of the "truly poor") and the rich developed world to accept without political will.[31] Martin and others in the private sector "wanted the CVI to be the body to create the political will."[32]

In addition to the creation of political will, all of the goals agreed to by the participants at Bellagio needed someone to help coordinate, build consensus, and foster mutual respect between the partners. The entity most likely to play that role was the CVI. In addition, industry believed that it would be primarily through a renewed CVI that the private sector could achieve the status of full partner with the public sector.[33]

Widdus understands industry

Widdus believed that the solid support of industry for the CVI was founded on the realization that people closest to the CVI understood industry's position in a way that was unique in the public sector.

> *I think the private sector trusts me as an individual and [realizes] I wish to include them and understand them. I think only Amie [Batson] and Peter Evans and I in the public sector have fully realized what drives industry and what terms they need to collaborate. . . . The Mercer studies say volume of vaccine production is the key to low prices for the poor. To get the volume, the intermediate countries must get the vaccines fast [since] only they can make the [sales] volume big enough to lower the price [for the poor]* [34]

He described the rest of the vaccine community as still naïve, despite all that they have learned about industry's needs. For most of the vaccine community, getting vaccines to the poorest countries is "the" overriding goal, and as a result, the issue of the intermediate countries, while not ignored, is seen as far less important. This perspective misses the fact that the solution to one problem depends on the prior solution of the other. According to Widdus, the big problem is, therefore, how to accelerate introduction of new vaccines in those places like Brazil, Mexico, etc., that can pay middling prices—*before* you introduce them into the poorest countries. That, said Widdus, is "the *big picture*" constituting the need for a comprehensive strategy.[35] Such a strategy would insure maximum private-sector support, proving practical, while a purely poorest-countries-first approach would not.[36]

Hib vaccine

The CVI not only innovated in creating a general model for vaccine introduction, it also actively championed a specific new and under-utilized vaccine—the Haemophilus influenzae type b (Hib) vaccine. Since action to widen the market for Hib was especially important to industry, it was very reasonable for the CVI to act as "point man" on the issue.

The Hib vaccine is a remarkably effective product that had almost eradicated infantile meningitis in the industrial world. More importantly, it held out the promise of preventing a large proportion of infantile pneumonia deaths in the developing world, thus saving the lives of literally hundreds of thousands of young children. Unfortunately, outside of Latin America, it simply wasn't being used in the Third World. Part of the problem was that most decision makers—both in the political and health areas—didn't think that Hib was a significant problem in their countries. In order to change that perception, detailed studies of its epidemiology, disease burden, and cost-benefit were urgently needed. The EPI was leery of getting involved with Hib vaccine since it was seen as still another threat to its already overburdened system. Thus, the CVI was able to take a leading role in promoting the use of the life saving vaccine, differentiate itself from WHO-GPV, justify its continued organizational existence, and help create closer public-private relations, all at the same time. In addition, since carrying out the needed studies would require the cooperation of a number of different international groups, the CVI could demonstrate anew its indispensability as a coordinating mechanism.[37]

As part of its effort to accelerate the introduction of Hib into the Third World, the CVI arranged with the CDC to have Dr. Jay Wenger move to Geneva to work on the vaccine. His position, while technically a joint one with the CVI and EPI, was in fact primarily with the CVI. While Widdus and many outside observers were quite critical of the EPI's slowness regarding introduction of Hib vaccine, Wenger was more charitable in his assessment of the EPI's situation:

> There were researchers working on Hib here at WHO—[e.g., evaluating the utility of Hib], but an implementation program through EPI wasn't there. [However,] it was the same pattern at the CDC: first a research group does the vaccine, then as the vaccine is licensed and promoted, then someone would take on introduction. There is natural evolution in these organizations. So it was not surprising or unnatural that EPI didn't have a person [dealing with Hib] yet. Ideally, you want to anticipate new vaccines—we want in the future to look at issues of implementation earlier. They [WHO, EPI] admit that they were late with HB and Hib. . . . I think that EPI would have gotten to it after a while.[38]

Wenger's generous evaluation may indeed be accurate, but the whole problem of vaccine introduction revolves around the question of timing, and many strongly felt that "after a while" would be much too long a time in the lives of Third World children. In addition, many observers believed that as long as WHO was organized along disease specific lines, with people focused exclusively on their "own" disease, no serious attention could be paid to Hib unless there was a designated advocate for it. Even when Wenger became Hib's champion in Geneva, there were many who wanted Hib, as the new vaccine on the block, placed at the bottom of the EPI's list of priorities. The odds were already heavily stacked against Hib introduction given the vaccine's high price and the lack of resources for it and knowledge about it, without the additional burdens of bureaucratic inertia, and competitive go-to-the-end-of-the-line-ism.

Clearly, the EPI did not like being pushed faster than it wanted to go, nor did it like being made to appear slow and inept. The long-standing tensions between EPI and CVI made Wenger's job extra difficult since he was the classic man-in-the-middle; it was hard for EPI to hear his message as long as he was so closely associated with the CVI. WHO's disposition toward new vaccines would later change for the better as a result of its radical reorganization under Director-General Gro Brundtland's administration. Wenger described the change of attitude that went along with the restructuring: "We are building a much more substantial program for introduction and assistance for introduction of new vaccines. . . . Many of the CVI agendas are now part of the work plan of the vaccine program—a substantial part."[39] These ideas are now incorporated within EPI rather than emanating from an outside competitor, so they aren't weighed down with the politics and bad feelings resulting from bureaucratic clashes.[40]

In acting as the champion of Hib vaccine introduction, the CVI held meetings each year to bring key officials and experts together to look at the problems that introduction would involve. According to Wenger, the meetings would look at efficacy, supply and quality, finance, and technical issues such as disease burden. The outcome was a work plan. "Different groups did parts. You could see progress and identify new issues as they came up. This is the key tool for getting different partners to work in a similar direction," he said. The CVI was also in a good position to further this process because it had specified funds from USAID to distribute to its partners in a manner that would further the CVI's Hib agenda.[41]

In the period before the Brundtland reorganization of WHO, Widdus, while pleased with the progress of the Hib project, was concerned about the long-term future for the activity. In his view the ideal role for the CVI was to take the initiative in areas that the partners were neglecting. Once the groundwork had been laid, the task could be handed off to the appropriate agency. In the case of Hib vaccine, Wenger should be moved totally into the EPI as things progressed. However, with EPI unenthusiastic and lacking a structure that concentrated on vaccine introduction, Widdus was afraid that Wenger would be isolated and his work marginalized and ignored. The desirable movement from CVI to partner agency didn't look feasible under such conditions—a situation Widdus was uncomfortable with, but felt he had no choice about.[42] Unfortunately, this prolonged Wenger's awkward status and continued to exacerbate the problem. There was no satisfactory solution until the reorganization of WHO radically changed things.

Industry Is Inspired by the Vision of a Revitalized Vaccine Alliance

In everything having to do with vaccine introduction, we see the concern of the CVI leadership with building bridges between industry and the public sector. This is not accidental, since making the private sector comfortable as a full part-ner with the public sector was, along with new vaccine introduction, the place where Widdus saw the CVI as uniquely capable of making its mark and justify-ing its continued existence. As early as 1995, his efforts to win over industry leaders had already started to bear fruit. At the Sao Paulo CVI meeting, Thomas Vernon of Merck talked of industry's expectations, disappointments, and hopes for the future. According to the meeting's official report, "Dr. Vernon's hopeful-ness stems from the repeated references in CVI materials to the importance of the private sector and the acknowledgment that industry has a great deal to offer . . . something clearly stated in a recent letter written by Dr. Roy Widdus to industry leaders. The ability of the private sector to work successfully with the public sector, however, was handicapped "largely due to ideological differences . . . and the continued misunderstanding that industry, driven by the profit motive, cannot at the same time utilize its resources for a positive societal bene-fit." But Vernon remained optimistic about the future because of Widdus's dedi-cation to including industry in the planning and ongoing work of CVI, and acknowledged Widdus's efforts to reach out to industry leaders and to ask their views on how the CVI secretariat might facilitate industry's participation in CVI objectives. If such a partnership can be achieved, "the potential for private-sec-tor contribution to the work of CVI is tremendous."[43]

For industry, having a sympathetic and determined ally occupying a pivotal role in the CVI was a major asset, and Widdus was that ally. This was especially important because many industry leaders had strongly negative feelings toward WHO. According to Harvey Bale Jr., director-general of the International

Federation of Pharmaceutical Manufacturers Associations, industry had doubts about WHO because of the organization's history of handling AIDS and other issues. Complaining about WHO's baronies and lack of leadership, he said, "Business companies are result oriented. There hasn't been a performance standard at WHO. They say the right things but nothing happens."[44] Nevertheless, there was an unresolved problem with the CVI from industry's perspective. Despite the yeoman service expended by Widdus, his staff, and supporters such as Batson, Milstien, and Evans, the CVI's extreme financial and political weakness severely compromised its usefulness. Widdus had kept the idea of the "grand global alliance" alive, but was fundamentally unable to expand and carry it out. Widdus was not even the official head of the CVI—Lee of WHO occupied that position. Thus, the CVI was not an independent force capable of making the private sector a full and active partner, since it was primarily a satellite of the World Health Organization, which still took a hands-off position vis-à-vis business. As Widdus starkly put it:

> The CVI secretariat is most closely affiliated in perception and reality with WHO. This is due primarily to . . . [its] location . . . within the WHO head-quarters [since the appointment of a joint head for CVI and WHO-GPV in 1994]. . . . This structure has permitted the WHO to provide direction to the . . . CVI secretariat . . . disproportionate to other cosponsors and collaborators. . . .The operation of the CVI within the legal framework of the WHO's constitution requires conformance to that of other WHO programs and has led to the exclusion of industry membership on the CVI decision-making bodies . . . . and contributed to the perception of the CVI as having "puppet-status" in relationship to WHO.[45]

The best way to understand the complex attitude of the private sector toward the Children's Vaccine Initiative is to understand how Jacques-Francois Martin saw the CVI and what he tried to do about it, because it was his view that came to be accepted by industry at large.

Martin had originally hoped that Lee as joint head of GVP-CVI would bring the two groups together and end competition and conflict between WHO and the CVI. In Martin's opinion, Lee was a good leader for the first two years, though he—and the organization in general—lacked vision. The result was that enthusiasm disappeared and CVI sponsors were not on board any more.[46] What Martin felt was needed was a "new" CVI which, by concentrating only on the poorest children, would made sure that they had the same fast access to the new vaccines as the children of the rich nations.

Of special importance in crystallizing Martin's thinking was his experience at the 1997 CVI-Rockefeller meeting at Bellagio discussed earlier. We saw that industry had very positive things to say about the meeting. But the private sector's full response was not so simple. What Martin and his colleagues saw in Bellagio was a unique opportunity to move forward based upon a set of agreed upon principles. The existing CVI helped point the way to the promised land, but it was clearly incapable in its present, weakened form to lead the way there. The industry participants at Bellagio talked freely among themselves about the "insufficiency of the CVI to do the job" but carefully kept that view out of public discussion. The last thing they wanted was to seem critical of Widdus and his team. They were not the reason the CVI was weak; they were the victims of that weakness.[47] What Martin felt was needed was "a new global organization with a *real* identity, strong leadership, efficient management, adequate financing, and a good business plan."[48]

The vital moment for Martin at Bellagio was during a dinner with Dr. Seth Berkley, acting director of the health division of the Rockefeller Foundation, and Phil Russell, one of the original architects of the CVI, when a revolutionary idea was presented. While the idea was too extreme for Martin to fully accept, it nevertheless set things in motion. Berkley suggested to Martin that the way to get out of the difficulties of a weak and crippled CVI was for industry to take over the organization.

> I did think something had to be done but the political aspects were important and we had to be prudent. If the CVI was seen as an arm of industry it would be dead. I told him, if you mean we [IFPMA] take real control, I disagree. . . . [Since] I was seen as the industry person who was really loyal to the poor children of the world . . . people thought I could play [such] a role in the new organization. . . . I said no. We need to find something different.[49]

Martin and Walter Vandersmissen, director for governmental affairs, SmithKline Beecham Biologicals, brought back to the IFPMA's biologicals committee their views of what had transpired at Bellagio. The committee was told that the Rockefeller Foundation, World Bank, and UNICEF were not happy with the current functioning of the CVI. Many participants wanted the CVI restructured and thought the IFPMA should take the leadership role in the new structure. Berkley had met with various vaccine manufacturers to talk about a stronger industry representation in CVI. He emphasized his belief that the R&D pipeline for diseases specific to the Third World, which lacked commercial markets, had to be dealt with better. He also requested that a CEO-level meeting be convened by the end of 1997 for a "celebration" of industry's commitment to the CVI. Martin told of Berkley's preliminary discussions with the CEOs of the major vaccine companies to find out if they were willing to make a greater commitment to the CVI if the public sector (e.g., the World Bank, UNICEF) were willing to increase their financial support for the initiative. The biologicals committee's response was to agree that a restructuring of the CVI was desirable and perhaps a CEO meeting should be arranged along with it. However, industry management of the CVI would be undesirable since it would look like the CVI was just a promotional scheme for business.

Martin, who was very friendly with Widdus, kept him informed of everything that was going on, and believed that Widdus "shared our views generally speaking."[50] As a result of Bellagio and the discussions at the biologicals committee, it was decided that Martin should write a paper that put forward the options for the future.

Martin's paper was called "Immunization Strategies: A Vision by Industry" and was presented in late 1997 to the IFPMA biologicals committee, where it was adopted. The paper reviewed the recent history of the global vaccine alliance from the private sector's perspective. First came the praise: the superb work done by Batson, Evans, and Milstien to increase understanding of the economics and technical basis of vaccine development and production. Martin then listed the negative aspects of the recent past. They included: lack of commitment by many of the sponsors of the CVI, many of whom had not even bothered to attend the June 1997 SAGE meeting; many CVI sponsors carrying on activities at cross purposes to the CVI's global strategy; the growth of donor fatigue; the "perceived lack of institutional leadership of WHO as the main sponsor of CVI," and the fact that "CVI's secretariat is facing difficulties in securing the necessary financing of its activities, including its [vital] advocacy work."[51]

According to Martin, there was a solution at hand because the "international community now has in [its] hands all necessary tools to bring about a new initiative." That initiative would have:

- Vision—i.e., that the poorest have the same access to protection that the richest have
- A clear target—insofar as all the poorest children would receive 'free of charge' access to HBV, Hib, pneumococcus and rotavirus vaccines
- A global organization with identity—including not only the current sponsors of the CVI but others willing to participate
- A strong leadership
- An efficient management—where industry would be willing to provide its expertise
- Adequate financial resources

The commitment of large economic resources by the World Bank or the European Union was mandatory if industry was to support the new initiative given the "necessary investment in terms of industrial capacity and the very low (if any) return on that investment that is envisaged." Martin's paper ended with the call for a business plan for a new initiative made up of a small working group, with industry included. The ultimate rallying cry of the new initiative would be the "five million young lives" that could be saved at the cost of only one billion dollars a year. Martin closed with a statement that he deeply believed in: "It is our personal responsibility to make it happen. We are all liable to the children."[52]

After the biologicals committee endorsed the Martin paper it discussed what industry should do to promote it, and how industry could use its management capabilities to help make it happen. Should they go to the five CVI founding sponsors (i.e., UNICEF, Rockefeller, United Nations Development Program, WHO, and the World Bank) and share it with them? Would they support it? WHO was not happy with the plan since Lee, executive director of both WHO-GPV and CVI, initially saw it as the private sector personally attacking him. But by the time of the CVI consultative group meeting in Dakar, Senegal, in late 1997, Lee had come around to the position that the CVI structure and location could be rethought—something he had never said before. Martin had shown the paper to key people at the Rockefeller Foundation and they had warmly praised it, though nothing concrete came from the discussions. A friend at UNICEF discouraged Martin from raising the issue there—despite Martin's growing concern over rumors that UNICEF was dropping vaccination to a lower rung on its agenda.[53] Despite many attempts, UNDP couldn't seem to even set up a meeting with him. As one knowledgeable observer put it, "Vaccination was not [even] on the radar screen at the big [UN] agencies."

Martin goes to the World Bank

At that point, Martin went to the World Bank to speak to Dr. Richard Feachem. Feachem, ex-dean of the London School of Hygiene and Tropical Medicine, was the director of health, nutrition, and population at the Bank. Coincidentally, at the very time Martin met with Feachem, Feachem was himself in the process of thinking through the whole question of the Bank's role in vaccination. He reached the conclusion that "childhood immunization was not in good shape, and the Bank was under-shooting considerably what its contribution could be."[54] Martin spoke to Feachem at length about the private sector's understanding of what was wrong with immunization and what required fixing. While Feachem met with many people over time to discuss the problem, he described the discussions with Martin as particularly important in the evolution of his own thinking.[55] From his talks with Martin (and Gus Nossal, chairman of the SAGE), Feachem concluded that the chief problem with immunization revolved around three problems: the EPI was declining, existing new vaccines were not being introduced, and there was insufficient investment in R&D for additional vaccines for Third World diseases.

One of those other meetings was especially important for the future because of what did not happen. Berkley met with Feachem and told him that with all the changes in leadership in the UN (e.g., at UNICEF and WHO) now was the time for the Bank and the Rockefeller to stage "a coup." If industry could be convinced to put up 49 to 51 percent of the money that the CVI needed to become independent, and the Gates Foundation put up the rest, it could be done. If this were done, according to Berkley, this outside body could bring in industry, which WHO can't legally do, do advocacy, build a truly international alliance and let WHO do the technical stuff it does best. Feachem rejected this suggestion, by simply saying he was "too busy" to get involved in such an undertaking. Berkley considered this an unfortunate "missed opportunity."[56] As we will soon see, many observers, both friends and foes, would attribute to Feachem's actions the exact motivation that Feachem cast aside when it was suggested to him.

When Martin met with Feachem he was told that Feachem had already been in communication with James Wolfensohn, president of the Bank, and a conference restricted to top international health leaders would be called to look at the problem of what should be done.[57] That meeting occurred in Washington, D.C., in March 1998. At the meeting a dialogue was structured around Feachem's three themes:

- New vaccines: Why are they not being introduced into the poorest countries?
- The Expanded Program for Immunization: Why are national programs stagnating and, in some cases, declining?
- Research and Development: How can we increase the inadequate level of R&D investment in vaccines of low market value?[58]

The participants accepted Feachem's propositions and agreed that

> *the development and introduction of new vaccines must be supported by the key agencies and by active public-private alliances . . . [and a] mechanism which can facilitate the interaction and contributions of all of the key partners is needed. . . . A mechanism which involves all the partners but which can work outside the system, identifying the inevitable gaps and problems and stretching thinking.*[59]

The high profile, by-invitation-only conference would ultimately raise hopes throughout the international vaccine community that the global alliance would be reignited and strengthened, the public-private sector relationship put on a new footing, and the financial underpinnings of immunization revolutionized.

Momentous Gathering Tries to Reorganize the Playing Field

The World Bank meeting turned out to be a major point in the history of the Children's Vaccine Initiative, but not in the way people expected. First, the community at large—including industry and supporters of the CVI—misunderstood the exact nature of the World Bank's intentions. It was widely assumed that the very act of the Bank calling such a high level meeting (which included the heads of UNICEF, WHO, the World Bank, and the CEOs of Pasteur-Merieux-Connaught, Merck, Chiron, Wyeth-Lederle, and SmithKline, plus the director-general of the International Federation of Pharmaceutical Manufacturers Associations) which raised the issue of "Vaccine Development and Delivery: Leadership for the 21st Century" meant that the Bank had finally decided to truly commit its resources to immunization as an economic development tool. It was widely believed that the Bank intended to put "billions" of dollars (ten billion was a popular figure) of its own money into a fund for vaccines for the Third World, and directly underwrite a revitalized and reformed CVI or CVI-type entity.

It was assumed by many observers that the Bank was making a bid for leadership in the vaccine area because the World Health Organization had continued to fail in that role, and the CVI as it was currently situated within WHO was unable to carry out its functions adequately. The fact that the Bank had very good relations with industry, and understood business needs and requirements in a way that no other United Nations agency did, made the possibility of a true partnership between the public and private sectors seem achievable in a way it had never been before. The fact that both WHO and UNICEF had new leadership—Dr. Gro Brundtland actually attended the Bank meeting as director-general designate, not having been officially installed yet—all pointed to a new and commanding role for the World Bank vis-à-vis the other UN agencies.

The truth was far more complex and less sanguine. The Bank did not have billions of dollars of its "own" money to put into a fund or with which to directly finance a revitalized CVI. The Bank was in the business of lending money to countries, and was bound by banking rules and practices that had little in common with the "Daddy-Warbucks" institution that most people imaged the Bank to be. The Bank wanted to bring its lending resources to immunization by encouraging countries (including the ministries of finance) to think of vaccines as a form of capital investment, but that was quite different from "giving" vast sums of money away.[60]

The Bank had neither the desire nor ability to take leadership in health or immunization away from the World Health Organization, since it lacked the expertise and technical know-how that were required for such an undertaking. Pushing WHO to act was not the same as trying to usurp its role.

The political situation within the Bank also radically differed from outsiders' perceptions. To some extent the conference was an attempt by Feachem to raise the level of awareness in the Bank of the importance and usefulness of immunization. Most officials of the Bank were not used to thinking of vaccines as a tool of economic development, and the Bank's in-country task managers—who dealt directly with Third World governments—did not normally raise the issue of immunization or encourage its inclusion in loan applications. Thus, the high-profile meeting was at least partly an exercise in self-education for the Bank, designed to highlight immunization's importance and the strength of President Wolfensohn's concern with it. In other words, the Bank's commitment to immunization and a revitalized global alliance was as much a work-in-progress as an extant reality.

This was especially true because of the extreme decentralization of power within the Bank structure—a decentralization that far surpassed that of WHO and UNICEF. Outsiders might talk about "the" Bank position, but that was more a figure of speech than an actuality. The Bank was divided into a variety of divisions,

the leaders of which had the power to make policies for their areas, and when policies involved more than one section, leaders had to be convinced to cooperate. As
one Bank official put it, "If we in our particular vice-presidency [i.e., division]
agree, then that is the Bank position. We are not highly centralized." The impli-
cation of this situation was quite far reaching. If the Bank were faced with determined opposition to its ideas or activities on immunization from WHO, it would
compromise rather than fight. There was no way that the Bank would ignore or
push aside WHO, and in any showdown the World Health Organization would
have the last word. The basic limitations of the Bank's sponsorship of change were
not widely understood.

Feachem's view

In the period before the Washington meeting, Feachem's views about immunization had been slowly maturing. We have already seen that Martin was a major
influence, as was Nossal, the head of the SAGE. Feachem became convinced by
his discussions with them that things were getting worse and the Bank was doing
very little about it. Feachem came to agree with Nossal and Martin that the Bank
could do more.[61] He believed the situation in immunization presented an excellent opportunity to actualize a model for how the Bank should deal with the area
of health in general that he strongly supported.

The controlling concept was greater Bank activity, but in a way that stayed
focused and avoided over-extension. This was especially important since the Bank
lacked any technical expertise in health and immunization, and had only a tiny
staff to deal with those problems. The Bank could use its "comparative advantage"
(i.e., financial muscle) only in close collaboration with other partners—especially
the World Health Organization. Thus, the Bank could use its resources to lend in
the area of vaccines, but since it lacked the ability to determine which vaccines
were important, WHO would have to take the lead in determining priorities.

Increasingly Feachem's analysis of the problem of vaccines for the Third
World came to emphasize the extreme complexity of the task at hand, the limited knowledge, staff, and resources available to all of the major players, and the
resulting dependence of each agency on all the others. This perspective was
shared by his chief colleague, Amie Batson, and later by Feachem's replacement
at the Bank, Chris Lovelace.

This position was a significant departure from the view held by the original
creators of the Children's Vaccine Initiative in 1990. At that time most of the

founders of the CVI felt that it would have been unnecessary to create the organization "if only WHO did its job." The World Health Organization should have been the leader, planner, implementer, and coordinator of the entire immunization effort—with everyone else giving support where and when it was asked for. WHO's insufficiencies forced the CVI to be formed. The long Nakajima regime at WHO (1988–1998) did nothing to undermine the judgment that WHO was falling short of its obligations, and something else had to fill the gap.

However, the Feachem-Batson-Lovelace reassessment was that things had matured to the point that no single organization—no matter how well managed and run—could do it all. The World Health Organization's weakness under Director-General Hiroshi Nakajima was hopefully correctable with the right leadership, but the vaccine job had grown so complex that only a highly committed partnership of international organizations, each with its own specific strengths, could successfully tackle it.

As a result, the Washington meeting that Feachem and the Bank called together in March 1998 was not aimed at explicitly or implicitly criticizing the World Health Organization; if anything, it contained a fair amount of Bank self-criticism for its failings in the vaccine area. Unfortunately, the situation appeared quite differently to outsiders. The reason for the general misperception is easy to understand. For many in the international vaccine community, the World Health Organization was still seen as the key problem, and despite the election of a new leadership team, many people despaired of any real change occurring within the entrenched WHO bureaucratic subculture. They still believed that WHO should be doing what needed to be done, but had given up on expecting anything to happen. Many had long hoped that the World Bank would take over the leading role in immunization, thereby marginalizing WHO, and they interpreted the Bank meeting in a way consistent with that hope. As a result, many of the Bank's "supporters" misunderstood what was going on.

The World Health Organization read the Bank's intentions in a very similar way, but with the opposite slant: as a threat. To many WHO careerists, it looked like a traditional United Nations turf fight, with the Bank trying to grab power during the confusion created by the change of administration at WHO. That this view was not simply paranoid thinking is obvious from what we know about what other people outside the Bank hoped and believed was happening, and what Berkley had in fact explicitly suggested to both Feachem and Martin. Thus, regardless of what Feachem, Batson, Lovelace, and the Bank actually intended, almost everyone else in the international vaccine community perceived them engaged in a power and turf fight.

If many in the World Health Organization had a general knee-jerk reaction to the Bank holding a meeting on immunization, Lee, the head of both the WHO's Global Program for Vaccines and Immunization and the Children's Vaccine Initiative, had a very specific reason to recoil from it. The original title of the meeting asked why immunization "failed." Lee saw this as a direct attack on himself and his leadership of GPV and CVI. And if the implicit criticisms were not stinging enough, the new director-general-designate, Gro Brundtland, the person who would determine his fate in WHO, would be attending the Bank's meeting.

When Feachem and Batson tried to defuse the situation by changing the title of the conference, they chose the name "New Leadership for the Twenty-First Century," which accomplished nothing, since it still seemed to imply that Lee and WHO had failed in their leadership duties and needed to be replaced. This unfortunate tempest over titles did nothing to undermine the assumption that the Bank was engaged in a bid for more influence at WHO's expense.

In addition, Feachem's assessment that the EPI had stagnated and lacked aggressive leadership not only stung Lee, but could not help but cast aspersions on the leadership of Dr. Bjorn Melgaard, the EPI chief, as well. So with all the best will in the world, the Feachem group had gotten off to a bad start in creating bridges to WHO.

The new view at WHO
Director-General Gro Brundtland and most of her top advisors were not WHO careerists.[62] They didn't move up in the organization after years of surviving within the agency as did Nakajima and his closest confidants. Thus, one would expect that they would not see the situation in the same way as long-term WHO officials. To some extent this was true. According to Jonas Store, one of her top advisors, Brundtland objected to colleagues in WHO that blamed the World Bank for showing interest in immunization. "Brundtland said you can't talk like that—you can't say stay out of our area because it is our mandate. If the World Bank gives more money for vaccines that is *good*."[63]

However, fights over power, influence, and turf were not something alien to the politically suave administration coming into WHO, and being concerned about such fundamental issues did not require them to be immersed in the WHO bureaucratic subculture. According to Store, the World Health Assembly elected new leadership to effect change, including innovation and partnering with the private sector. The new leadership saw their election as requiring them to revolutionize the agency, and part of that was to take back control over areas that had been relinquished under the previous regime:

> *But while we appreciate new players and new dynamism, we wanted to send a clear message: Don't count on WHO in this partnership as you did a year ago. This is a new WHO. The Initiative was based on the assumption that WHO was losing its leadership. Now that is going to change. We can now lead, but in cooperation with our partners. She [Brundtland] felt immunization was the place WHO should exercise leadership. . . .* We saw in Washington that WHO had been gradually sidelined in the area of vaccines in the 1990s.[64] *(emphasis added)*

There was nothing unreasonable or objectionable about a new leadership's confident determination to take charge, nor their fear that to do less would be an abdication of responsibility. Nevertheless, such an attitude lent itself to a turf-protection state of mind that could easily parallel and be influenced by the traditional WHO bureaucratic mentality. It is true that the new leadership kept emphasizing its desire for partnership and made explicit references to its recognition that other agencies had strength where WHO did not. Nevertheless, that was more than counter-balanced by the explicit concern that WHO exert leadership in relationship to its partners. For outsiders, the difference between WHO exercising leadership and the traditional "we can do it all" mentality was often obscure. The new WHO seemed very much like the old WHO—and outsiders (and perhaps some insiders as well) easily lost sight of the change in attitude toward the alliance that Store felt was basic to the new administration.

If the Brundtland administration, by the very fact of its election, had good reason to be concerned about reestablishing WHO's prerogatives, that tendency could not help but be exaggerated by what it heard from long-time WHO officials. While Store and Brundtland might have tried to combat what they saw as excessive territorialism at WHO, they nevertheless had to rely on the bureaucracy for background information, advice, information, and guidance in key areas as they acclimated themselves. There was no way they could totally insulate themselves from the bureaucracy's views of the World Bank and, even more importantly, of the Children's Vaccine Initiative, which was destined to become the focus of concern in the year following the Washington meeting.

Feachem and the CVI

Oddly enough, the Children's Vaccine Initiative, which became strongly identified with the World Bank's immunization initiative, was of little or no interest to Richard Feachem himself. As he put it:

> I had no feeling about the CVI before the March meeting! It was never a matter of interest for me, nor a matter of motivation for me. Jacques Martin didn't influence me on the CVI, rather he and Gus [Nossal] influenced me on the appropriateness of Bank involvement and the lack of Bank contribution [to immunization].[65]

As a result, the CVI was not a focus of discussion at the Washington meeting. As far as Feachem could see, the problems of the Expanded Program on Immunization (EPI), which were of fundamental significance, had nothing to do with the existence or nonexistence of the Children's Vaccine Initiative. And when the CVI did become the focus of discussion in the months after the Washington meeting, Feachem said, "I never found interesting the pros and cons of the CVI."[66]

What Feachem was concerned about, and what would ultimately be a major point of interagency contention and conflict, was his growing belief that a new hub of focus for the collaboration was necessary in order to challenge partners and to hold them accountable for their commitments—a view very much like that of Martin, except less concerned about using the Children's Vaccine Initiative as that vehicle.

Regardless of the storms that might occur in the future, the immediate results of the Washington meeting looked very good to everyone. Feachem sent out a letter summarizing the areas that the conference participants had felt were vital: "increased private-public cooperation; higher levels of sustainable financing for vaccines; enhanced recognition of the importance of vaccines and increased advocacy for them; and production of more accurate market data to help industry plan ahead." They also agreed that a way to foster a sense of ownership by all parties in the alliance was needed, but while "the Children's Vaccine Initiative was cited as a good model . . . [it was] in need of greater independence and flexibility to foster a sense of ownership by all the partners." The CVI would be a good starting point to look at possible mechanisms for a reinvigorated alliance. What was needed was "a mechanism which involves . . . all the partners but which can work outside the system, identifying the inevitable gaps and problems and stretching thinking beyond today's immediate concerns."[67]

A Working Group Is Created, But Carrying Out
Its Task Is Harder Than Anticipated

The major outcome of the meeting was the creation of a working group made up of representatives of UNICEF, WHO, the World Bank, the Rockefeller Foundation, and industry "to work with all of the participants in the meeting and other partners in immunization to further elaborate the key issues which have been raised and to develop proposals on ways to move forward."[68] The working group was supposed to hold meetings with key members of the immunization community—from bilateral donors to Third World countries[69]—and "listen, analyze, synthesize, and present the ideas of key partners about the priority areas of work in the vaccine development and delivery continuum and the mechanisms which would optimize both the efficiency of a multipartner, coordinated effort and broad participation and ownership."[70] One of the group's chief questions was "the advantages and disadvantages of a mechanism like the CVI or some modification of it."[71] The results of the working group findings were supposed to be presented at a second high level meeting within approximately six months.

This all sounded very good on paper, but the situation was far more complicated. The working group was slow to get off the ground and there were fundamental problems that had to be addressed before the process could move forward. According to Tim Evans of the Rockefeller Foundation, they found the plan lacking in detail and doubted that, given the limited human and financial resources, the group could produce results.[72] Evans spoke to Feachem and said the Foundation wanted to be part of the working group, and suggested that since a person with technical expertise in the area of vaccines was totally missing from the working group, that Myron [Mike] Levine, a noted academic and researcher, would be a valuable addition.[73] After Levine joined the working group, Rockefeller became more active in overseeing the process.

Evans noticed that the mobilization of the working group was very slow, and when he ultimately met with Suomi Sakai of UNICEF in September (fully six months after the Washington meeting), he found it still lacked any resources despite its "gigantic agenda."[74] Notwithstanding the lack of progress of the working group, there was mounting pressure to convene the large follow-up meeting that had been agreed upon at the Washington conference. No one wanted to lose the momentum or risk the diminution of industry's interest in the project. However, as the fall of 1998 progressed, both Evans and Levine increasingly felt that an early meeting would be a great mistake because not enough background work had been done to go to the heads of the UN agencies. "There was not enough on the table being put forward, [not enough] substance for the organizations to respond to," said Levine. He expressed concern that the working group was doing nothing but "renaming the CVI."[75]

The situation was made worse by the fact that so many of the UN agencies were in flux. Feachem, who initiated the whole process, had announced he would soon be leaving his position at the World Bank. As a result, according to Evans, Feachem "wasn't giving his oversight and input into this [project]."[76] At the same time, the World Health Organization was being radically reformed by its new leadership, but "vaccines were nowhere to be seen on its agenda."[77] Rather, the big projects were "Roll Back Malaria" and an anti-tobacco initiative. The situation at UNICEF vis-à-vis vaccines was even worse. According to Evans, vaccines had been off of UNICEF's agenda for a long time. Senior Health Advisor Suomi Sakai was seeing budget cutbacks for vaccine projects, while her new boss, David Alnwick, knew very little about vaccines.[78] Of the major players, only industry, led by Martin, was strongly focused on vaccines and the issue at hand—and that was because he "was instigating this process to some extent" and had been urging it for months before the Washington meeting.[79]

Evans met with Batson, who was leading the hardworking but overwhelmed working group. She was despondent that they would ever get it right and felt that it was better to have an early meeting in December while enthusiasm was still high, rather than delay it on the chance that the working group would get something better together, risking industry disillusionment.[80]

When Evans was in Geneva in October 1998, he met with Jonas Store of WHO. Store asked what was going on and Evans told him that he did not see "anything on the table substantially different than what we have now," a position Store agreed with. Later, Evans met with David De Ferranti at the World Bank. De Ferranti, Feachem's superior at the Bank, had assumed responsibility for overseeing the Bank's role in the working group after Feachem's departure.[81] He, like Evans, "felt this was a seriously undeveloped . . . concept [with] no sufficient substance for a new entity."[82]

As a result of these concerns, a high level meeting was held in early January 1999 at the World Bank in Washington, D.C., with Feachem, members of the working group, and their immediate superiors (i.e., De Ferranti and Chris Lovelace for the World Bank, Evans for Rockefeller, David Alnwick for UNICEF, Mike Scholtz for WHO and Harvey Bale for the International

Federation of Pharmaceutical Manufacturers Associations [IFPMA]) in attendance.[83] At that gathering it was agreed to postpone the follow-up meeting to the Washington conference. Instead, the group decided to meet at UNICEF in late January or early February, when hopefully the working group would be able to submit a plan that would justify the long-wished-for follow-up to the Washington conference. That large meeting would hopefully be in March 1999, at the Rockefeller Foundation's center in Bellagio, Italy.

The determination to put off the major meeting was coupled with the decision to downgrade it by not inviting the heads of the UN agencies. This position caused significant dissension. According to Tim Evans—reflecting the view of the World Bank, WHO, and UNICEF—it was necessary that it be a working meeting which would need "to have people who could talk substantially about the issue, not just signers of a grand declaration."[84] The agency heads would not be required until the actual launch of the new entity was possible. Thus, excluding the UN agency leaders from Bellagio was primarily based upon the "immaturity of the process." However, Levine, Feachem, Martin and Bale expressed great disappointment with the decision and emphasized that industry in general would be quite displeased with it.[85] This disagreement was significant because it represented the growing uneasiness on the part of industry with how slowly the process was moving forward. However, it is important to note that the decision to downgrade the Bellagio meeting was not the result of any disagreement between the UN agencies themselves—as most outsiders later believed—but rather the consequence of their unified position.

At the next meeting of the group at UNICEF, the participants decided that they could go forward with planning the Bellagio meeting, and they charged the working group to create an agenda for it.

Expectations are dashed

As the Bellagio meeting approached, the expectation on the part of industry and most participants was that a major change was about to be occur, and that a new era in public-private relationship was about to begin under the auspices of a reformed and strengthened CVI. Not only would industry be an equal partner for the first time, but many expected that the new CVI (or CVI-like entity) would be headed, at least temporarily, by Martin.

What was not clearly understood by those with such high expectations was that a "near" consensus that included the key players but excluded the World

Health Organization was not going to produce the desired results. If the leadership of WHO decided that a reinvigorated and independent CVI was not to its liking, was not needed, or was a threat, and was willing to dig in its heels and to fight against it, there was no one—certainly not the World Bank—who would stand up to it for long. And that is exactly what happened. WHO said it would not accept an independent CVI with a substantial secretariat that could hold the partners accountable. WHO said it was willing, even eager, for a renewed global alliance, but it wanted the partners to do the work of coordination themselves; the failures of WHO which had led to the creation of the CVI in 1990 was a thing of the past; the new administration under Dr. Brundtland would make sure that WHO carried out its mandates; indeed, with a reinvigorated and proactive WHO even the existing CVI was superfluous, and there certainly was no need for a new, enlarged organization. As a result, WHO shockingly announced that the CVI would be dismantled and terminated by the end of the year.[86]

Most participants at Bellagio, and especially industry representatives, were stunned. They were appalled not simply by the outcome, but the way the outcome was reached. The basic decision about the CVI was not determined in open debate during the Bellagio conference, but in a small, closed, pre-conference dinner the night before the meeting's formal opening. In turn, that dinner was shaped by a series of phone calls previously made by Brundtland to Wolfensohn of the Bank and Carol Bellamy of UNICEF. Brundtland made it clear that WHO didn't want a new uncontrolled independent bureaucracy whose actions might rebound negatively to WHO, and she expected UNICEF and the World Bank would feel the same. Regardless of what the members of the working group and their immediate superiors might have believed, they did not "represent the major players" until the top leadership gave their stamp of approval. Brundtland believed that Wolfensohn "did not know" what his subordinates were doing, and by directly reaching out to him she could remedy the situation. Wolfensohn said nothing to contradict her perception.[87]

The immediate result of the Bellagio meeting was apparently disastrous. Industry was outraged and alienated, supporters of the CVI (especially in America) were appalled and offended, and the working group was shaken and demoralized. While there was an attempt to salvage the meeting, and put the best possible face on it by Gus Nossal, head of the SAGE, and Barry Bloom, dean of the Harvard School of Public Health, the fact was that the CVI was now the walking dead, and no specific replacement for it had been agreed upon. Instead of the global alliance being revitalized, it appeared to have collapsed. There were many who felt that the atmosphere was so charged with animosity and recrimination that there was a danger that it could never be repaired.

Of all the groups distressed by the turn of events at Bellagio, industry was probably the most upset. In an unprecedented gesture, a joint letter of protest was sent by the CEOs of the four largest vaccine companies—SmithKline, Pasteur-Merieux, Merck, and Wyeth Vaccines—to WHO, UNICEF, and the World Bank. A number of drafts of the letter were written—the original ones quite strong and angry—but the one actually sent was fairly mild.[88] Yet the very fact that a letter was sent, and signed by all four CEOs, spoke louder than anything specifically written on the page. According to Bale, at least part of industry's concern was the desire to be "free of political controls [and] the letters to WHO reflected this fear of WHO control."[89] There was a feeling that the agency "wanted to do it alone" and leave the rest of the partners out.[90] The CEO letter specifically said:

> After Bellagio we are seriously concerned that the challenges raised last March [at the World Bank meeting] remain unanswered. We write now with the hope of restoring the sense of urgency to this process. . . . The outcome [of Bellagio] was disappointing—with little agreement on action steps, financing options, or the revitalized mission of the proposed coalition . . . the discussion did little to advance that vision from an operational viewpoint. It is our strong hope that we will not come to remember this meeting . . . as a missed opportunity.[91]

That letter was soon followed by a considerably stronger protest by the CEO of Chiron.[92] After the letters, many people went to WHO in person to protest the situation. While WHO expected some reaction from industry, the intensity of the reaction caught them by surprise.[93] The outrage from other partners in the public sector was also quite intense.

An attempt to repair the damage

In the months following Bellagio there was a determined effort to undo the damage to the alliance that occurred. The working group, despite the recent repudiation of its yearlong labor, was charged with helping create a mechanism for revitalizing the alliance. Logically, if things had remained the way they were, this second effort would have failed. However, with the matter of the CVI behind it, there appeared to exist a major change in attitude on the part of all participants. A true spirit of cooperation appeared for the first time between agencies that had shown very little of it in the past. Many observers felt that the realization by the community of how close they had come to the abyss—the total unraveling of the global alliance—had awakened everyone to the need to overcome rivalries and work together—or, failing that, to hang separately.[94]

The Bill and Melinda Gates Foundation's Children's Vaccine Program, a newcomer on the scene, offered money to help lubricate the places where scarce resources exacerbated interagency friction. It willingly took on the role of godfather to what became the new alliance, the Global Alliance on Vaccines and Immunization (GAVI), and became an active part of it.

GAVI had many of the attributes that proponents of a revitalized CVI had wanted. It had the active and enthusiastic buy-in of the major agencies, the presence on the board of directors of the heads of those agencies, and it provided a seat on the board for industry. While WHO had originally wanted no secretariat separate from the agencies, it had compromised and a small secretariat was created under the leadership of Tore Godal, the widely respected ex-chief of TDR (the UNDP/World Bank/WHO Special Program for Research and Training in Tropical Diseases). In addition, the working group became a major component of the new alliance. The good relationships existing among the members helped strengthen the sense of interagency cooperation, and also took over some of the burden the small secretariat normally would have had to deal with.

As a result, there was increasing hope that the death of the CVI was leading not to the end of the global alliance but to its true fruition. Even among critics of Bellagio, there was growing optimism and enthusiasm. Whether it is justified, only time will tell. What is clear is that industry for the first time occupies a place of equality in the alliance with the UN agencies. It not only sits on the board of directors, but also has a representative on the working group. Many of its partners in the working group, such as Batson, continue to be committed to building public-private bridges and educating the larger community of the necessity of understanding and adjusting to the economic realities of the vaccine system.

Conclusions: What Have We Learned?

Was the CVI's relationship with the private sector a success or failure? And what lessons if any can be learned from that experience?

In some respects the Children's Vaccine Initiative's interaction with industry was strikingly successful, in other respects a discouraging failure. The failed aspects came directly out of the founding structure of the CVI. The initiative represented the public sector, but the public sector was badly divided in its goals, attitudes, and interests. The original CVI was run by a standing committee of five founders: UNICEF, WHO, Rockefeller, United Nations Development Program, and the World Bank. Those agencies did not coexist in harmony. WHO felt the CVI was forced upon it by outsiders against its will. The other agencies were united, but only in their opposition to WHO. Among themselves they had different goals and purposes for the CVI and pulled in different directions. Outside the standing committee was the management advisory group, which included the most important bilateral donors. Many of them disliked the standing committee and strongly opposed the vaccine-development emphasis that the CVI pursued in its early years. They saw it as a "technological fix" that avoided the hard questions of socioeconomic conditions in the developing world. It was very hard for industry to work with a group that had such divided attitudes—many of which centered specifically on relations with industry.

While key leaders of the CVI were favorable to industry and wanted to build bridges to it, others, especially within WHO, were hostile and wary of getting involved with industry beyond the minimum necessary. Even more harmful was the fact that the legal structure of WHO made it impossible to provide a place where industry could function as an equal partner with the public sector. The CVI, governed and constrained by WHO legal rules, was powerless to give industry the seat at the table that both felt necessary.

Nevertheless, the CVI was successful in creating links between the public and private sectors in many ways. Despite the organization's basic structural problems, the CVI created a space in which the more innovative individuals within WHO and UNICEF could work to inform and educate the public sector about the economics of its own vaccine system. The innovative work of Batson, Milstien, and Evans laid a foundation for cooperation with industry by convincing the major UN agencies that they had to deal realistically with the economic constraints and realities of the marketplace. Without that realization, no common ground with the private sector could exist or constructive conversation with it be possible. Industry was continually frustrated by what it considered the naiveté of public health officials concerning the basic facts of life and death for the private sector.

After the CVI standing committee was absorbed into the meeting of interested parties, and the initiative was de facto absorbed by WHO under the leadership of Lee—executive director of both WHO-GPV and the CVI—relations with industry surprisingly became better. The reason for this was that Widdus, the CVI coordinator and de facto leader of the CVI, became the champion of closer public-private relations. Widdus helped make industry aware of how useful a vehicle for cooperation the CVI could be—if it were not hamstrung by lack of money, weak agency support, WHO legal rules, confusion over what it did, who led it, and what its mission was.

Industry was so impressed by the CVI's potential and so frustrated by its actual situation that it was motivated to try to radically change the system. This put industry in an awkward position. First, it did not want to be seen as taking over the CVI; second, it was inspired by what the CVI could be, but severely disappointed by what it was. In wanting to reform it—or replace it with another entity—industry did not want to appear critical of either Widdus or the CVI secretariat; though in fact, in pushing to achieve the change, it had to highlight the weaknesses of the existing initiative. Some outside observers were puzzled over how angry many people were at the termination of the CVI, given the high level of criticism those same people expressed during its lifetime. The answer was that the CVI many people mourned was the CVI that should have been, not the CVI that actually existed.

For the private sector to successfully cooperate with the public sector it is necessary for the latter to understand and accept the basic legitimacy of private enterprise and the profit motive that drives it. That is very hard for many public health officials to do when children are sick and dying from lack of money to buy vaccines. Many in the public sector still harbor the dream that government itself can do vaccine product development. Since vaccines are a public good, they should also be a public product. In an ideal world that probably would be best.

However, government vaccine institutes in the developed as well as developing world have been plagued by inefficiency and plant obsolescence. Governments have found it very hard to provide in a consistent manner and over long periods of time the high budget allocations that vaccine production, let alone product development, requires. It costs hundreds of millions of dollars to bring a vaccine from proof-of-principle through the development process. When there have been budget crunches or calls for tax reduction—and when haven't there been?—the financial needs of vaccine institutes have gotten very low priority.

Governments also tend to surround both hiring of staff and purchasing of supplies with elaborate bureaucratic requirements that make it difficult to obtain or retain the services of the best people and products. When money has been earned by vaccine institutes, governments usually haven't been willing to invest that income in upgrading their equipment or modernizing their plants, without which they cannot maintain good manufacturing practices—the gold standard of the vaccine industry. The experience of Dr. George Siber at the Massachusetts Public Health Biologic Laboratories—one of the last public vaccine institutes in the United States—is both paradigmatic and disheartening. He tried unsuccessfully for years to get the institute semi-privatized so that it could combine the flexibility in hiring and spending of the private sector without losing its commitment to public service. He failed bitterly and left public service for the private sector.

The public sector must also recognize the limitations that scientific, market, and economic realities place upon what the private sector can do. Nothing alienates industry more than requests from public officials that show an ignorance of the fundamental economic or production realties that business labors under. Industry's general frustration with what it considers public sector impracticality is laid out clearly by Michel Greco, director-general of Aventis-Pasteur:

> In the past WHO has developed vaccine strategies without thinking if it was feasible, [even] if the vaccine was [actually] available. I have been stunned at times to hear proposals fielded at Geneva—[with] just one person [successfully] pushing it . . . [because] when people are not well informed about the proposals, people can be persuaded. They don't understand what it implies. [For example] "sugar-glass" [used] as a coating for vaccines—in principle it makes them stable. It would be great for WHO distribution of vaccines—rid them of the [need for] the cold chain. . . . . [A WHO official] talk[ed] of sugar glass and did not present any data to show feasibility, cost, etc. He just said: 'do it.'

Even though the SAGE "diluted" the recommendation and suggested more study of it, the whole situation shows "how easy it is to lose credibility."[95] According to Greco, WHO's desire to solve a pressing problem may take precedence over dealing with the harsh realities:

> In the same manner, WHO pushes for vaccine monitors to put on vials to show it is still valid . . . I told them that we support it but it is not a substitute for a proper cold chain! . . . WHO is faced with the fact that the 1970–80 cold chain is becoming old, and proper investments are not being made. Rebuilding it is becoming an awesome challenge and we fear that monitors and sugar glass are seen as substitutes for the cold chain and that is not the case.[96]

In a similar vein, Walter Vandersmissen, director for governmental affairs, and Jean Stephenne, CEO of SmithKline, have bitterly complained that the public sector has no concept about production schedules and plant capacity limitations:

> *Six months ago we were called to UNICEF and WHO—they wanted to quadruple doses [of a vaccine] in one year and they wanted it right away! What naiveté. If we don't do it they are resentful and claim we aren't cooperative. [The] Mercer [report] said you need multiyear contracts—but they still are not in place. [Instead,] they look for lowest price. Their attitude has not changed.*[97]

Dr. Thomas Vernon of Merck, who before joining industry was a career public official—serving as both commissioner of health and state epidemiologist of Colorado—always felt he "knew R&D backwards and forwards." But when he went into the private sector he realized that he hadn't the foggiest idea of what development actually entailed—clearly not a problem unique to officials in Colorado.[98]

If the public sector has to reach out to industry and try to see the world through its eyes, industry needs to meet it half way as well. It must modify its market orientation enough to admit that it produces a public good as well as a profitable item. If there are no industry leaders visionary enough to balance public and private concerns, then bridges cannot be built.

The vaccine industry has always had a dual nature. Originally most vaccine manufacturers were public concerns, and those that were private were nevertheless aware that they made life-saving serums. The vaccine industry has never been purely a profit-making business. If you wanted to maximize return, vaccines were not the way to do it—not in the past, and not in the present. The private vaccine industry's need to juggle profit and service always has been a hard balance to maintain.

In recent years, with vaccine firms being absorbed by large pharmaceutical companies and public vaccine institutes being privatized, maintaining the equilibrium has been even harder to do. The raging stock market, which increasingly judges all business solely by the bottom line, is intensifying the pressure on the few remaining vaccine companies to ignore social issues entirely. The pressure is greatest in the United States, but it is mounting in Europe as well.[99] As Walter Vandersmissen of SmithKline has put it:

> *We want to stay in the Third World market. It gives us an image and we don't lose money. But it is more difficult because we compete in the company for*

resources. Bottom line issues are coming more to the front. Shareholders are now more and more anonymous—[increasingly] pension funds! In the past you could appeal to shareholders in a way that fund managers can't be. Since vaccines are so small [a part of big pharmaceutical companies] it can't have much effect on the [larger] bottom line, but to get money for plant expansion you are in direct competition with other [more profitable] drug products.[100]

Nevertheless, industry continues to produce people like Jacques-Francois Martin and Charles Merieux (founder of the Merieux Institute)[101] who embody the "profit plus social morality" that is the legacy of vaccine manufacturing. It is vital that the public sector reach out to them and make alliances while the window of opportunity still exists. Market forces notwithstanding, alliances are still made or broken by the existence of individuals willing to stretch across the public-private divide.

Notes

1. The first third of the paper is based on my *The politics of international health: The Children's Vaccine Initiative and the struggle to develop vaccines for the third world,* (Albany: State University of New York Press, 1998). Except for direct quotations, footnotes will not be provided. The last two-thirds of the paper is new material and documentation is supplied.

2. Interview with Jacques-Francois Martin, October 1999. Martin's dedication to saving the children of the Third World and moderating industry's profit seeking is based on his commitment to a socially active version of Catholicism.

3. J. W. Lee captures the situation very succinctly in a speech to the MIP in June 1999. The speech also captures Lee's own ambivalent feelings about the CVI that he technically headed: "Many of the activities in the CVI strategic plan have been carried out also by [WHO-]GPV [Global Program on Vaccines]. Increasingly our partners find it difficult to see the differences between WHO and CVI. Therefore, they find it increasingly difficult to support financially GPV and CVI at the same time. It resulted in the decrease of CVI's core funding for its secretariat function. . . . Some believe CVI will be most useful in a culture [i.e., outside of WHO] where it can freely dream about finding hundreds of millions [of] dollars if not billions to help introduce new vaccines. Some [i.e., Lee] believe that these ambition[s are] . . . an example of [a] false persistent belief not substantiated by sensory evidence, in other words, [a] delusion" (speech presented at CVI meeting of interested parties, June 12, 1998).

4. Evans quoted in CVI Forum: News From the Children's Vaccine Initiative 2 (October 1992).

5. Ibid.

6. Meeting of the task force on situation analysis, Copenhagen, September 21–22, 1992. By this time the Batson-Evans Grid was the core instrument used by the task force.

7. Amie Batson, Terrel Hill, and David Halliday, "Sustaining Immunization and Assuring Vaccines for the World's Children: A Strategy for UNICEF," October 5, 1994.

8. These factors were vital because "GNP per capita provides a measure of the country's relative wealth to buy vaccines. . . . Total population indicates whether a country has a sufficient market size to justify local production of vaccines. . . . GNP combines these two factors and provides a measure both of the country's 'voice' in the international market place and its ability to rely on an internal infrastructure or markets" ("Vaccine Supply and Quality—Global Program for Vaccines and Immunization, Draft Strategic Plan, 1995," draft presented for discussion by SAGE, June 11, 1995).

9. Interview with Thomas Vernon, executive director, medical, scientific and public health affairs, Merck Vaccine Division, January 2000.

10. Report of the Fifth Meeting of the Children's Vaccine Initiative Consultative Group (Sao Paulo, Brazil, 25–26 October 1995, CVI/GEN 96.06).

11. Ibid.

12. See "Report of the Meeting of Interested Parties for the Children's Vaccine Initiative Consultative Group" (Geneva, June 27, 1996 , CVI/GEN 96.7), where Widdus's pleas for more unrestricted money to fund the core CVI activities is strongly resisted and the vital "open forum" of the consultative group is cut back from a yearly meeting to a biannual meeting. Also see in the same minutes a summary of the comments by Ann Kern of Australia who reported on the meeting of the task force on strategic planning. She said, "There had been no questioning of the value of vaccines, the need to secure additional funds to meet rising costs, or the need for a broad-based coalition. However, there had been considerable debate on the role of the CVI and its added value. Both areas were difficult to define" (7).

13. Personal communication from Steve Landry to author after the Dakar meeting.

14. The ideal of the "end-to-end mission" and the importance of vaccine product development was certainly much in evidence in the rather impressive The CVI Strategic Plan: Managing Opportunity and Change: A Vision of Vaccination for the 21st Century (Geneva, 1998). However, as impressive as this plan is, significant confusion exists between the great plans and projects discussed and the role of the CVI as the CVI. While the plan is for CVI and her partners (and CVI is not an "implementer" the way her partners are), it still makes one ask the very question the plan should have answered: What exactly is the role of the CVI in all this?

That confusion is compounded by fact that achievements are claimed for the CVI that are clearly not the result of CVI-inspired work (e.g., taking credit for what partners have done which was not effected by anything the CVI did). Since some key work done by CVI partners was strongly CVI-influenced, the CVI's credibility is undermined by indiscriminately mixing the two categories. See the Fourth Annex for some egregious cases of this.

15. Comment by Regina Rabinovich, February 1999, at the National Vaccine Program's interagency meeting to advise the U.S. Secretary of Health on the best American response to the proposed reformation of the Children's Vaccine Initiative.

16. "Report of the Fifth Meeting of the Children's Vaccine Initiative Consultative Group" (Sao Paulo, Brazil, October 25–26, 1995, CVI/GEN 96.06), 35.

17. Comment by John LaMontagne, in "Report of the Meeting of Interested Parties for the Children's Vaccine Initiative Consultative Group," 7.

18. For most of those concerned with the introduction of existing new vaccines into the developing world, the goal was to cut the time for children of the poor to be protected. Once that was done, then as even newer vaccines were developed they could also be introduced speedily. Not everyone saw it that way. The problems of vaccine introduction were seen by some powerful groups as justification for not developing new vaccines at all. Thus, "concern" for vaccine introduction could hide very real areas of conflict. The 1996 MIP minutes describes how "Dr. Orttar C. Christiansen (Norway), questioned the usefulness of research into the development of new, more expensive vaccines, given that national immunization programs are having trouble introducing existing, recommended vaccines such as hepatitis B and yellow fever. Dr. Pia Rockhold (Denmark) supported Dr. Christiansen's statement and wondered why there was so much discussion on the development of new vaccines, rather than on increasing coverage of existing vaccines." It is unlikely that either the Danish or Norwegian foreign aid people were a potential constituency for Widdus and the CVI ("Report of the Meeting of Interested Parties for the Children's Vaccine Initiative Consultative Group," 7).

19. See "The Children's Vaccine Initiative/Rockefeller Foundation Conference on the Global Supply of New Vaccines" (Bellagio, February 3–7, 1997, 10), where Jacques-Francois Martin, the vaccine industry leader most committed to helping the children of the Third World, "emphasized that until existing vaccines such as hepatitis B and Hib vaccines were used in developing countries, there was little relevance in discussion of the alleged 'failure' of industry to develop vaccines for developing country needs."

20. Document CPV-CVI.98/WP.14, CVI files.

21. Widdus stated in an October 1999 interview that the "SAGE document was written by me, Jay Wenger, Mark Miller, and a little of Mark Kane, [with] ideas from CVI [that gave a] comprehensive look at what needs to be done to accelerate new vaccines."

22. Personal communication from Scott Wittet to author. The report was later taken off the web at Roy Widdus's request.

23. Scientific Advisory Group of Experts (SAGE), "What Actions Will Accelerate the Introduction of New Vaccines?" (Geneva, June 9–11, 1998, GPV-CVI.98/WP. 14), 4.

24. Ibid., 5.

25. Ibid., 8.

26. Ibid., 12.

27. Ibid, 13.

28. "Report of the Meeting of the Interested Parties for the Children's Vaccine Initiative" (June 17, 1997, CVI/GEN/98.02), 3.

29. "The Children's Vaccine Initiative-Rockefeller Foundation Conference on the Global Supply of New Vaccines," 2–3.

30. Interview with Jacques-Francois Martin, October 1999. In a February 2000 interview, Michel Greco, director-general of Aventis Pasteur, described the complex roots of the attitude toward tiered pricing in Europe: "Tiered pricing: there is a tradition in Europe to serve the poor countries but [it is] linked to the colonial past—not primarily humanitarian, but links remain and affects the present approach. It is a mix of tradition—they all [European vaccine companies] evolved out of public companies (national institutes etc.) —partly tradition and ethics but also good business. Some fail to realize that it is good business. We sell 80 percent of our volume to the Third World. . . . That 80 percent equals [only] 20 percent of sales and even less of profit. It looks like [it is] not very profitable, but it has allowed us to build manufacturing facilities and skills that help us with developed markets."

31. But even for the Europeans companies, the danger of a reaction against tiered prices in the developed world is real. In a February 2000 joint interview Walter Vandersmissen, director for governmental affairs, and Jean Stephenne, CEO of SmithKline said, "There is a fear that people in Europe will say why are vaccines so cheap in India. . . . I fear backlash to tiered pricing. We don't want to be punished for cheap vaccines for the Third World. The cost of HIV drugs is a problem. I am afraid it will spread to pharmaceuticals generally and then hit us in vaccines. . . . It is a real danger."

32. Interview with Jacques-Francois Martin, October 1999.

33. "The Children's Vaccine Initiative-Rockefeller Foundation Conference on the Global Supply of New Vaccines," 3.

34. Interview with Roy Widdus, September 1999.

35. Ibid.

36. As hard as it is for many in the public sector to accept what Widdus was emphasizing, some aspects of the position may be even harder to absorb. According to

Vandersmissen and Stephenne, with "traditional vaccines more volume lowered the price because there was over-capacity. [But] for new products it is not a given and it is a different paradigm. Volume by itself is not enough. The power of volume is just not that powerful. For the poorest of the poor, you will get closer to the rock bottom prices," but for intermediate countries, despite volume, the price should, in fact, rise slightly over what they are now paying. The willingness of UNICEF to accept a reasonable rise over current prices for HB and Hib vaccines would demonstrate that the public sector truly accepts the economic realities necessary to make cheap vaccines available to the poorest of the poor.

37. For details of the CVI's "Hib agenda" see "The Hib Vaccine and Edible Vaccines," CVI Forum 12 (August 1996): 2–9.

38. Interview with Jay Wenger, WHO, February 8, 2000.

39. Ibid.

40. In addition, the infusion of large amounts of money for vaccines from the Gates Foundation and the Children's Vaccine Program spotlighted the Hib vaccine specifically, which made its prospects vastly better than they had been before.

41. Interview with Jay Wenger, WHO, February 8, 2000.

42. Discussion with Roy Widdus, 1997.

43. "Report on the Fifth Meeting of the Children's Vaccine Initiative Consultative Group" (Sao Paulo, Brazil, 25–26 October, 1995, CVI/GEN/96.06), 23.

44. Interview with Harvey Bale Jr., IFPMA, February 2000.

45. Memo from M. Miller-Luy to working group, November 21, 1998, "Further Working Group Activities: Getting to Grips with the Real Questions." This memo was actually written by Roy Widdus.

46. Interview with Jacques-Francois Martin, October 1999.

47. As Harvey Bale Jr. put it: "There was concern about the CVI [as well as WHO]. The greatest concern by industry was [J. W.] Lee's lack of concern and aggressiveness, and [thus] power devolving down to Roy [Widdus]. [But] Lee and Roy [together] could not convince government to finance vaccines. That is why they [industry] were not comfortable with the CVI. I don't think it was a focus on Widdus but lack of dynamism of the whole CVI, [all the way] up to Lee" (interview, February 2000).

48. Interview with Jacques-Francois Martin, October 1999.

49. Ibid.

50. Ibid.

51. "Immunization Strategies: A Vision by Industry," October 1997, 2–3.

52. Interview with Jacques-Francois Martin, October 1999.

53. Ibid.

54. Interview with Richard Feachem, December 1999. An important part of Feachem's solution was to bring Amie Batson to the Bank to work on the immunization question.

55. Ibid.

56. Interview with Seth Berkley, November 1999.

57. Interview with Jacques-Francois Martin, October 1999. Feachem had a major ally in this in the person of Gustav Nossal, chairman of the SAGE. Nossal was a close friend of Wolfensohn, and soon after Wolfensohn had become head of the Bank, Nossal had contacted him to speak about the problem of vaccines and the need for the Bank to become a stronger partner. Feachem knew and approved of Nossal's intervention since it supported his own message (interview with Richard Feachem, December 1999). It is not clear, however, exactly what parts of Nossal's message supported Feachem's view. While Nossal certainly championed a greater involvement of the World Bank in immunization, he did not go to Wolfensohn simply carrying his own views. He engaged in consultation with WHO-GPV before going, and carried, at least to some extent, the WHO "wish list" for help from the Bank. One has to assume that Nossal's position was considerably more WHO-friendly than Jacques-Francois Martin's, or the position that Feachem himself ultimately developed.

58. "Vaccine Development and Delivery: Partnership for the 21st Century" (Bellagio, 1999), the background paper produced by the working group for participants at the Bellagio meeting.

59. Letter from Richard Feachem, no date, with the title "Meeting Summary: Vaccine Development and Delivery: Leadership for the 21st Century, 18 March, 1998, Washington, D.C."

60. Barry Bloom, dean of the Harvard School of Public Health School, pointed out in an e-mail to Muraskin (January 2, 2000) that "a soft loan is [in fact] a grant or gift." This is because the low interest rate and long-term payback are equivalent to not having to repay 80 percent of the loan. That is very important. However, many countries find that the 20 percent that they still owe makes a Bank loan far less attractive than an outright grant. Thus, a "soft loan" is not truly equal to a grant in the eyes of most poor countries.

61. Interview with Richard Feachem, March 9, 2000.

62. Some of her closest advisors were longtime WHO officials. Of special importance was Tore Godal.

63. Interview with Jonas Store, February 2000.

64. Ibid.

65. Interview with Richard Feachem, March 9, 2000.

66. Ibid.

67. Richard Feachem, "Meeting Summary" letter. The letter clearly contains ideas that occurred after the meeting and thus is actually more than just a summary of the meeting but an update of the meeting as well.

68. Feachem, "Meeting Summary" letter. According to Martin, at the end of the meeting there was no clear decision about what to do, "but each organization had nominated representatives to be part of the process. The working group idea came after two months of thought, not at the meeting itself. The Bank presented the working group as an outcome of the meeting, but it is not actually true" (interview with Jacques-Francois Martin, October 1999). The letter, which is not dated, certainly makes it appear that the working group was decided upon at the meeting.

69. The full implications of this mandate only developed over time. Initially the working group did not plan a great number of meetings, flung widely over the world. However, Tim Evans of the Rockefeller Foundation was very concerned that the views of Third World people were under-represented and he suggested a more concerted effort to involve them. Other interested parties, such as European bilateral donors, pushed in the same direction.

70. Feachem, "Meeting Summary" letter, "Draft Terms of Reference: Working Group on Preparation for Vaccine Meeting."

71. Ibid.

72. Interview with Tim Evans, Rockefeller Foundation, March 13, 2000.

73. Ibid.

74. Interview with Tim Evans, Rockefeller Foundation, March 13, 2000.

75. Ibid. In an e-mail dated December 18, 1999 the working group sent UNICEF (David Alnwick), the World Bank (David de Ferrenti and Helen Saxenian), Rockefeller (Tim Evans), WHO (Michael Scholtz), and the International Federation of Pharmaceutical Manufacturers Associations (Harvey Bale) a "Progress Report from the Working Group on the Global Coalition for Vaccine Development and Immunization." The paper was to serve as background for a meeting on January 5. The members of the working group would meet with their superiors to discuss how their labors were going. The report said the vehicle for the revitalized alliance "will not be dramatically different from CVI but will address the most important problems." Clearly, Evans and the others were aware of this before the official report was sent to them in mid-December.

76. Interview with Tim Evans, Rockefeller Foundation, March 13, 2000.

77. Ibid. In a July 24, 1998 letter to Michael Sholtz of WHO, David de Ferranti—vice president, head of Human Development Network at the World Bank, and

Feachem's boss—said that Feachem would become a senior adviser for Health, Nutrition, and Population as of September 1, 1998.

78. Interview with Tim Evans, Rockefeller Foundation, March 13, 2000. The United States Government Accounting Office (GAO), basing its comments on 1999 UNICEF data, had this to say: "Immunization funding decreased from about $182 million (57 percent of health expenditures) in 1990 to about $51.5 million (25 percent of health expenditures) in 1998. In addition, a growing percentage of immunization funds was spent on vaccine procurement . . . to support the polio eradication effort. . . . As a result, support for other immunization services, such as maintaining national vaccine delivery systems, has declined" ("Vaccine Availability," GAO/NSAID-00-4, 19). The decline of UNICEF's efforts started while James Grant—the charismatic leader of UNICEF and immunization champion—was still alive, and was accelerated under his successor. UNICEF had previously done "everything" to help support immunizations on the country level. They had bought equipment for the cold chain, done advocacy on all levels, built up massive enthusiasm, organized national immunization days, and got the top political leadership involved. As a result, "people in-country think UNICEF when they think vaccines, and they expect [it to take an] active role" (conversation with Judith Justice, March 3, 2000). That increasingly was not the case due to the large-scale cutbacks and change of policy toward vaccines at UNICEF, New York.

79. Interview with Tim Evans, Rockefeller Foundation, March 13, 2000. The Rockefeller Foundation itself was undergoing a major reassessment concerning its role in health. After a period of withdrawal from its traditional active role concerning international health problems it had decided to recommit itself, and to give more of its resources to it.

80. Interview with Tim Evans, Rockefeller Foundation, March 13, 2000.

81. Chris Lovelace is actually Feachem's replacement; Evans doesn't mention him at this point.

82. Interview with Tim Evans, Rockefeller Foundation, March 13, 2000. The belief on the part of the working group's superiors that there was nothing new (or acceptable) coming out of the working group was confirmed for them by a letter they received on December 18, 1999 from Amie Batson (World Bank), Mike Levine (special consultant, Rockefeller Foundation), Jacques Francois Martin, (special consultant, Industry), Bjorn Melgaard (WHO), Suomi Sakai (UNICEF) to David Alnwick (UNICEF), Tim Evans (Rockefeller Foundation), David de Ferranti (World Bank), Michael Scholtz (WHO), and Jonas Store (WHO). In that letter the working group said, "the Global Coalition for Vaccines and Immunization (GCVI) [the tentative name for the new alliance] . . . will not be dramatically different from CVI."

83. Jacques-Francois Martin was linked by telephone from France and Richard Feachem from San Francisco, while Michael Scholtz, Bjorn Melgaard, and Michel Zaffran were in Geneva.

84. Interview with Tim Evans, Rockefeller Foundation, March 13, 2000.

85. "Vaccines and Immunization: Video Conference of 5 January 1999 Summary of discussion," document found in CVI files.

86. Interviews with Jonas Store (executive director, senior policy adviser to the director-general of WHO), Michael Scholtz (executive director, health technology and pharmaceuticals, WHO), Bjorn Melgaard (director of vaccines and other biologics, WHO, and interim head of the CVI until its termination), February 2000. Most outside observers saw WHO's position as an example of traditional turf protection: hostility to the World Bank and to the idea of a stronger CVI. Store sees it very differently:

> She [Brundtland] wanted to link up with other organizations. She felt immunization was the place where WHO should exercise leadership. The new leadership [of WHO] was elected for change. . . .Brundtland was aware of the politics—which are changing all the time—and could deal with it. We saw in Washington [World Bank meeting] . . . that WHO had been gradually sidelined in areas of vaccination in the 1990s. . . . We saw the World Bank with more important role. . . . The tone in WHO was almost [to] blame . . . the World Bank [for being involved]. Brundtland said you can't talk like that—you can't say: stay out of our area because it is our mandate. There is more than enough for all of us. The World Bank gives more money for vaccines and that is good. Then we have to work it out. . . . We didn't want to give vaccination to someone else. That would be abdication.

87. Interview with Jonas Store, February 2000.

88. According to Michel Greco of Aventis Pasteur, at least part of the reason the letter was more mild than what the companies were feeling was that "we didn't want to 'corner' the World Bank which had differences with others like WHO. An overly strong letter might have destroyed the process altogether. That was key. . . . So the letter was specifically an attempt not to put Wolfensohn in a difficult spot" (interview, February 2000).

89. Interview with Harvey Bale Jr., IFPMA, February 2000.

90. Comment by Odette Morin Carpentier, director of regulatory and scientific affairs of the IFPMA, who sat in on the interview with Bale.

91. Letter addressed to Carol Bellamy, executive director of UNICEF, Gro Harlem Brundtland, director-general of WHO, James D. Wolfensohn, president of the World Bank, dated March 31, 1999, from Jean-Jacques Bertrand, chairman and CEO, Pasteur Merieux Connaught, R. Gordon Douglas Jr., M.D., president, Merck Vaccines, Kevin Reilly, president, Wyeth Vaccines and Nutrition, and Jean Stephenne, president and general manager, SmithKline Beecham Biologics.

92. Letter to Brundtland, WHO, March 30, 1999, from William J. Rutner, chairman, Chiron: "We left Bellagio concerned that this salutary undertaking had been

compromised by what seems to be artificial constraints on its function. . . . The WHO representative at the meeting voiced opposition to a coalition staff of any size external to the agencies [though he modified this to accept a small one]. We believe such a restriction on function and appropriate staff size will meet neither the immunization needs of children . . . nor the real potential of a coalition. . . . It is our strong hope that the WHO position was not fully represented at Bellagio."

93. Interview with Jonas Store and Bjorn Melgaard, February 2000.

94. The perception that the whole community had come close to falling apart and that there was a marked change in attitude on the part of all, but especially WHO, was very widespread. Most attributed the change to the "fear" that the violent reaction against Bellagio produced at WHO. This is denied by Store, who says that WHO always planned to cooperate with its partners, and once the question of a separate, independent, bureaucratic entity had been settled, it proceeded to do what it had planned all along.

95. Interview with Michel Greco, February 2000.

96. Ibid.

97. Interview with Walter Vandersmissen, director for governmental affairs, and Jean Stephenne, CEO, SmithKline, February 2000.

98. Interview with Thomas Vernon, January 2000.

99. Interviews with Tom Vernon, Michel Greco, Walter Vandersmissen, and Jean Stephenne, Harvey Bale Jr., January–February, 2000.

100. Interview with Walter Vandersmissen, February 2000.

101. In an interview Michel Greco, director-general of Aventis-Pasteur, says of the situation, "Europeans are moving closer and closer to Americans—and that may not be all good. We are becoming more realistic about the bottom line but [we] still retain that sense of mission or what you want to call it. And we believe it is possible. At Pasteur-Merieux [name before it was changed to Aventis-Pasteur] Charles Merieux is the soul of us. He is 93 and still taking major initiatives from his wheel chair. We are not just in the business to sell vaccines, he said. . . . Sometimes it is more words than substance, but we try. Pressure from the stock market makes it harder."

7

The World Health Organization and Global Public-Private Health Partnerships: In Search of 'Good' Global Health Governance

Kent Buse and Gill Walt

THE PAST DECADE HAS WITNESSED DRAMATIC CHANGES in international cooperation through the United Nations and its organizations. Two interrelated trends stand out. First, as a function of globalization—defined as the accelerated diffusion of capital, traded goods, people, ideas, etc. across increasingly porous national boundaries—it is progressively more evident that a variety of challenges cannot be met efficiently at the national level, but require additional collective international, if not global, approaches (Kaul et al., 1999). Moreover, the ascendancy of organized capital over the power of the nation-state adds impetus to the need for intergovernmental cooperation. It has been argued that "short of a backlash against globalization, states will have little choice but to pool their sovereignty to exercise public power in a global environment now mostly shaped by private actors" (Reinicke & Witte, 1999). Consequently, globalization has highlighted the need for strengthened international cooperation and has resulted in significant discussion of reform within existing multilateral institutions, as well as the establishment of new ones with distinctive characteristics—for example, a World Trade Organization lying outside of the UN system that can exercise unprecedented and binding authority over its member states.

A second significant trend in international cooperation within the United Nations involves a shift from vertical representation to horizontal participation (Walt, 2000). Vertical representation describes a hierarchical, bureaucratic relationship between the state and its representation in the international organizations that make up the UN. Representation through this process provides, at least in theory, both a form of democracy and accountability (i.e., citizens represented through member states, and member states represented in decision-making

169

bodies, with decision-making bodies responsible to member states). Horizontal participation is more typical of the network society, in which states and non-state organizations, including the UN and private for-profit organizations, form less hierarchical and less bureaucratic interorganizational relationships. Global public-private partnerships (GPPPs) provide a form of interorganizational networking.

While there is, as yet, relatively little experience in determining how well these horizontal public-private partnerships work, it is clear that, in addition to their many potential benefits, they also pose a variety of potential challenges and threats in relation to international cooperation in health. The purpose of the United Nations, at the point of its establishment, was to further peaceful and cooperative relations among states. As one of its specialized agencies, the World Health Organization's role was to coordinate activities in health against a very broad constitutional mandate that saw health as a fundamental right and WHO's main objective as "the attainment by all peoples of the highest possible level of health" (WHO, 1946). An international civil service was established to provide support to countries and actions to advance this mandate. While the UN and WHO have always been constrained in their ability to achieve these lofty goals, and although we acknowledge significant weaknesses in many UN organizations, we nevertheless argue that the UN plays critical functions with respect to global health, among other things. Our concern is that horizontal participation, as evidenced in the growth of public-private partnerships at the global level, will further fragment international cooperation in health and undermine UN aims for cooperation and equity among states.

Our chapter begins with a short discussion of the meaning of partnership. We then describe the context in which public-private partnerships have emerged, drawing particular attention to the shift from "international" to "global" governance in the health as well as other sectors. Thereafter, we enumerate the interests that private and public actors pursue in relation to partnership, as these carry important consequences for the impact of GPPPs for international cooperation in health. We review the critical functions performed by the UN in relation to health and argue that these are made possible by a number of facilitating attributes which characterize UN organizations such as WHO. The manner in which partnerships with the for-profit sector may impinge, both positively and negatively, upon these facilitating attributes is explored. The chapter concludes that more care needs to be exercised in relation to preserving these important functions and attributes as partnerships proliferate. Although our primary interest is with health partnerships and, consequently, WHO, we make an attempt to situate our discussion in a broader context and include examples that involve other UN organizations.

Defining Partnerships

Elsewhere we have described how the conceptual understanding of partnership has evolved over the past few decades (Buse & Walt, 2000a). In relation to development cooperation, the term was most frequently employed to describe aspirational relationships between official donor agencies and recipient ministerial bodies in developing countries. Today, a profusion of interpretations surround the term. We submit that the notion of partnership has become a cognitive device that groups similar things and thereby permits recognition and communication. However, when subjected to scrutiny, it becomes apparent that the notion of partnership is imbued with very different characteristics in different contexts. Although partnering (and the term *partnership*) clearly implies a tendency toward collaboration, it is also used to describe a wide range of relationships and activities. Consequently, there is the risk that the term often obscures more than it reveals. To assess the impact of partnerships on international cooperation for health and to judge under which circumstances partnerships are likely to be suitable and effective or what rules of engagement should guide partners' activities, we need greater specificity with respect to our object of analysis.

For this discussion, we employ a narrow and specific definition of a global public-private partnership for health. Health GPPPs are collaborative relationships that transcend national boundaries and bring together at least three parties—among them a corporation and/or industry association and an intergovernmental organization—so as to achieve a shared health-creating goal on the basis of a mutually agreed and explicitly defined division of labor (adapted from Buse & Walt, 2000a). While other parties, such as civil society organizations and private foundations, are often also critical partners in GPPPs, here our unit of analysis comprises for-profit and intergovernmental organizations.

Context

Globalization provides the defining contextual shift marking the widespread emergence of global public-private partnership. As noted above, international cooperation is affected in two major ways by increased global integration. First, globalization circumscribes some functional sovereignty of the nation-state and thereby reinforces recognition of the need for multilateral cooperation for solutions to common problems (Kaul et al., 1999). Second, globalization, particularly through advances in communication technologies, facilitates horizontal and network-oriented approaches to governance (Reinicke, 1998). Consequently, multilateral cooperation has increasingly and purposefully looked toward the potential for public-private collaboration. For example, in his 1999 address to the annual meeting of the World Economic Forum, UN Secretary-General Kofi Annan reflected that "the United Nations once dealt only with governments. By now we know that peace and prosperity cannot be achieved without partnerships involving governments, international organizations, the business community, and civil society" (Annan, 1999). Reflecting Annan's observations on the UN and relating these to the concept of governance, Mark Malloch Brown, administrator of the United Nations Development Program (UNDP), wrote in the foreword to the 1999 Human Development Report:

> We are seeing the emergence of a new, much less formal structure of global governance, where governments and partners in civil society, the private sector, and others are forming functional coalitions across geographic borders and traditional political lines to move public policy in ways that meet the aspirations of a global citizenry. . . . These coalitions use the convening power and the consensus-building, standard-setting, and implementing roles of the United Nations, the Bretton Woods institutions, and international organizations, but their key strength is that they are bigger than any of us and give new expression to the UN Charter "We, the peoples." (UNDP, 1999)

In so far as global governance involves the formal and informal "institutions and organizations through which the rules and norms governing world order are (or are not) made and sustained" (Held et al., 1999), Malloch Brown is correct in viewing partnership not solely as a reflection of globalization, but as a response to its processes as well. This is particularly the case where new principles, norms, and standards are elaborated within the framework of partnerships.

The emergence of GPPPs can be traced to a number of additional dynamics that marked the 1990s. First, the 1990s were characterized by an *ideological shift* from 'freeing' to 'modifying' the market. While many claim that "the age of medicine as a pure public service is over" (*The Economist*, 1998), most advocates of free markets have moderated their position to acknowledge a role for the public agencies, particularly in the health sector where markets are often not efficient and make equity difficult to achieve (Mills, 1997). This ideological shift is not based solely on economic philosophy but also on changes to the prevailing sociopolitical orthodoxy—as noted above, increasingly a variety of stakeholders, including private sector representatives, are believed to have a legitimate say in public policymaking (Giddens, 1998).

Another contextual shift that fuelled the rise of GPPPs involved the growing *disillusion with the UN* and its organizations. Concerns about the effectiveness of the UN, including increasing evidence of overlapping mandates and interagency competition, led directly towards establishing partnerships to deal with specific and limited issues. Partnerships that are housed outside of the UN bureaucracy are viewed as a way of getting things done, and where industry is involved, getting things done efficiently. In relation to the Medicines for Malaria Venture (a public-private drug research partnership), for example, it was agreed that "the organization should run as a not-for-profit-business and be based on operational paradigms of industry, not the public sector" (Ridley et al., 1999). It has been suggested that the UN may see the benefits of industry partnership as 'relegitimizing' the UN and thereby enabling it to regain a more central position in global policymaking. For example, the Corporate Europe Observatory argues that "working with the International Chamber of Commerce diversifies the UN's image, which in some countries, including the United States, is not ideal" (CEO, 1998).

Negative perceptions of UN effectiveness, among other things, have provided *financial impetus for partnerships* in that donors have imposed a policy of zero real growth in UN budgets and shifted toward supplementary (i.e., voluntary and ear-marked) funding. These funding trends have made GPPPs attractive (and perhaps necessary) to the UN. Resources provided by the private sector "are more than welcome; they are necessary" (Beigbeder, 1996). Beyond the commercial sector, important new sources of funding for UN partnerships are those from the new philanthropists (i.e., Bill Gates, George Sorros, and Ted Turner).

The re-emergence in some quarters of a broader approach to public health (McKinlay & Marceau, 2000) may have also provided more fertile ground for GPPPs. Increasing recognition of the multifactorial determinants of health furthered the view that the *health agenda is so large that no single sector or organization can tackle it alone*. Emerging health problems required a range of responses beyond the capacity of the public or private sectors working alone, and therefore bridges needed to be built between sectors (Harrison & Lederberg, 1997).

The last point relates to a new appreciation and explicit understanding of how the actions of one sector affect the ability of the other sector to achieve its goals and how partnership can result in win-win interactions among private and public actors. There was, for example, an "honest recognition by the public sector" of the "unique, unrivalled monopoly" of the pharmaceutical industry in drug and vaccine development: "They own the ball. If you want to play, you must play with them" (Lucas, personal communication, July 13, 1999). Batson (1998) demonstrated how the ability of the public sector to achieve universal immunization coverage is "inextricably linked" with the decisions and behavior of the vaccine-pharmaceutical industry and, conversely, how the behavior of industry with respect to research and development (R&D) into new vaccines is conditioned by the signals sent by the major public sector players. Batson argues, for example, that UNICEF's centralized procurement (based on lowest-bid purchasing policies) of developing countries' vaccines for the Expanded Program on Immunization ensured low prices but also sent signals that the public sector was not interested in encouraging pharmaceutical companies to invest in R&D for new vaccines which might benefit poor countries. More recently, one condition set by five major research pharmaceutical companies, as they forged a partnership with a number of UN organizations on access to AIDS medications, was that the public sector organizations commit themselves to strengthened intellectual property protection as a recognition of the significant investment these companies had made in product R&D (Gellman, 2000).

Changing markets and technology have heightened this appreciation of interdependence. In particular, new developments in biotechnology are making drug and vaccine discovery and development increasingly expensive, as are changes in the sphere of intellectual property rights. Concomitantly, extensive consolidation of the pharmaceutical industry has led to greater competition within companies, thus increasing the opportunity costs associated with investment in tropical diseases. These changes have led some health advocates to begin to explore ways in which public and private decision makers could work together to overcome market failures so as to develop and make available health promoting goods at a cost developing countries could afford, while minimizing the risk and guaranteeing a return to the private sector. Economic tools that reduce the costs of R&D, called 'push' factors, and those that address the lack of effective markets, termed 'pull' factors, are at the center of many health GPPPs (e.g., the International AIDS Vaccine Initiative, the Global Alliance for TB Drug Development, the Malaria Vaccine Initiative, etc.).

Changes in business-UN relations, as expressed by the formation of GPPPs, may also reflect the impact of globalization on the *structure of the global economy* (and within various industries) and on ways of doing business. In particular, three possibly interrelated elements stand out. First, as noted above, transnational corporations have become the lynchpins of the world economy; the globalization of production has entrenched the power of organized corporate capital vis-à-vis state power (Held et al., 1999). This has undoubtedly emboldened corporations to demand a voice in intergovernmental decision-making, for example in the WTO and WHO. Second, increasing concentration empowers individual megacompanies in relation to both state and intergovernmental organizations, but also increases the possibilities for industry-wide association and organization (Myteka & Delappierre, 1999). Consequently, we have seen a rise in self-organization and private-sector-influenced regulation at the global level (Cutler et al., 1999). Third, there have been changes in the form of business organization. It has been argued that globalization is fuelling corporate alliances (and may, indeed be replacing mergers). It is speculated, for example, that whereas "the average large company, which had no alliances a decade ago, now has in excess of 30" (*Business Week,* 1999). These are love affairs, rather than marriages: competitors in one market can collaborate in others, and it is natural that the commercial world extends this form of organization to its relations with governmental entities.

Finally, the trend towards global public-private partnerships may be related to the change in public attitudes and the growing response of the private sector to concerns and vocal demands for *corporate responsibility and accountability.* Corporations themselves have realized their need to take into account broader responsibilities to society (Control Risks Group, 1997). This recognition has been stimulated by the strength of consumer, environmentalist, and other civil society group actions in industrialized countries, which have challenged international companies' policies in a number of spheres and won considerable concessions (Wapner, 1995). GPPPs offer the possibility to improve corporate image. One company executive explained that public pressure was of highest consideration in terms of why his company sought partnerships with the public health sector (Auty, 1999). The positive experience of Merck's donation of Mectizan (ivermectin) to onchocerciasis control programs in a number of endemic countries played an extremely important role in stimulating further 'pharmaco-philanthropy' (Wehrein, 1999).

Partner Interests in Global Public-Private Partnerships Differ

The specific interests that each party to a particular partnership pursues, the extent to which the party seeks to realize those interests through the partnership, as well as its relative influence within the partnership arrangement will have some bearing on the effectiveness and outcomes of the partnership activity, but may equally play some transformative role within each partner organization. Here we enumerate some of the interests pursued by the private for-profit sector and United Nations (and WHO) through partnership generally before analyzing how the pursuit of these interests may alter characteristics of the UN. In the ensuing discussion, we have made generalizations about both the UN and the private sector. In practice, neither sector is comprised of homogeneous entities (nor indeed are GPPPs). There is a great diversity in size, competence, and efficiency among UN and for-profit organizations. Some divisions of UN bodies have been charged with malpractice, while firms are differentiated, among other things, by their willingness to comply with the rule of law and their interest in philanthropy and partnership. Moreover, private firms are also not solely driven by short-term economic imperatives to maximize profits. They may singly or collectively construct a variety of organizational arrangements that structure their own and others' behavior with a view to longer-term interests, and GPPPs provide one vehicle for so doing.

Private Interests in Global Public-Private Partnerships
Incorporating industry interests in global governance

> *We want neither to be the secret girlfriend of the WTO nor should the ICC have to enter the World Trade Organization through the servant's entrance.*
> Helmut Maucher (1997), ICC President

As the processes of globalization intensified during the 1990s, industry came to recognize the potential benefits of alliances with the United Nations. For example, according to Maria Cattaui, secretary general of International Chamber of Commerce (ICC), "Business believes that the rules of the game for the market economy, previously laid down almost exclusively by national governments, must be applied globally if they are to be effective. For that global framework of rules, business looks to the United Nations and its agencies" (Cattaui, 1998a). Maucher (1998) supports this position, arguing that "in this process of modernization and globalization of rules, ICC is making a positive contribution, both as an advisor and through its own standard setting. . . . Broader efforts should now follow in order to foster rules-based freedom for business, with the WTO assuming a key role." While the ICC conceded the need for additional authority for intergovernmental organizations, this was "with the proviso that they must pay closer attention to the contribution of business." The ICC was, however, concerned that the "power of world business" has been "poorly . . . organized on the international level to make its voice heard" (quoted in CE0, 1998). Consequently, the ICC established, in its words, a "systematic dialogue with the United Nations" in an effort to redress this perceived threat to its interests (Cattaui, 1998b).

Industry has embarked upon a multi-pronged strategy to influence UN decision making. For example, in June 1997 the executive director of the World Business Council on Sustainable Development (WBCSD) cohosted a high-level public-private sector meeting with the president of the UN General Assembly to "examine steps toward establishing terms of reference for business sector participation in the policy setting process of the UN and partnering in the uses of UN development assistance funds" (Korten, 1997).[1] The meeting concluded that "a framework" for corporate involvement in UN decision making be worked out under the auspices of the UN Commission on Sustainable Development (Korten, 1997). The ICC also conceived the Geneva Business Partnership. Established in September 1998, the Partnership enabled 450 business leaders to meet with representatives of international organizations so as to determine "how to establish global rules for an ordered liberalism" (CEO, 1998). One outcome of the industry effort is a joint UN-ICC statement on common interests which includes a call to "intensify the search for partnerships" (United Nations, 1998). Interaction among the commercial and public sectors, while neither new nor ipso facto 'partnership,' reflects the increased intensity, extent, and purpose of growing private-sector interests in public-sector decision making.

GPPPs and emerging market penetration

Corporate success will be increasingly dependent on harnessing these new markets and production opportunities.
UNDP, 1998

Globalization is perhaps most advanced in the economic sphere. Nonetheless, according to the World Bank, more people live in poverty than ever before. The United Nations portrays poverty as a "downside of globalization" but also suggests that poverty is both a threat and an opportunity to industry interests. It is a threat in the sense that mass poverty could lead to destabilization, thereby jeopardizing the smooth functioning of the market, and an opportunity in terms of the poor being a potential market-in-waiting. Companies such as Dupont, Unilever and Johnson and Johnson are experimenting with rural poor markets as they see most growth potential at the bottom of the pyramid (Slavin, 2001). Market creation is the explicit goal of a number of UN-industry partnerships. For example, through the Global Sustainable Development Facility (GSDF), leading corporations and UNDP aimed to include two billion new people in the global market economy by the year 2020 (UNDP, 1998). The GSDF was to be established as a separate legal entity outside the UN system that would be "primarily governed by participating corporations and will benefit from the advice and support of the UNDP through a special relationship" (UNDP, 1998). The GSDF was addressed, among other things, to "developing products and services adapted to the emerging markets of the poor" (UNDP, 1998). Despite early interest and participation of numerous corporations, UNDP aborted the initiative due to the controversy that it provoked (New, 2000).

Thus public-private partnerships are sometimes proposed as priming-the-pump of economic globalization in those areas where the market is not well enmeshed in the global economy, but also as an opportunity for individual firms to penetrate specific markets. As the president of the medical systems unit of Becton Dickinson & Co. has remarked, "Of course we want to help eradicate neonatal tetanus, but we also want to stimulate the use of non-reusable injection devices, and to build relationships with ministries of health that might buy other products from us as their economies develop" (Deutsch, 1999).

GPPPs and corporate citizenship

Kofi Annan has warned that because "globalization is under intense pressure . . . and business is in the line of fire . . . business must be seen to be committed to global corporate citizenship" (Annan, 1999). Emerging public-private relationships often move beyond the simple philanthropy (gift giving) of the past and can be differentiated by a range of motivations including corporate responsibility (obligation-oriented), corporate citizenship (rights and responsibilities) and, as noted above, strategic gain (Waddell, 1999). Collaboration is in part due to the fact that the commercial sector has been increasingly challenged to show greater social responsibility, to invest in the well being of populations, to adhere to global labor and environmental standards, and to invest in research and development that benefits the poorest. Debate surrounding the WTO Agreement on Trade-Related Aspects of Intellectual Property Rights (TRIPS) is illustrative of the manner in which GPPPs provide industry an opportunity to demonstrate its corporate citizenship. Concerns have been raised that implementation of the TRIPS Agreement will increase the costs and, thereby, limit access to essential drugs in developing countries (pursuant to strengthened patent protection on process and product and controls on the manufacturing and export/import of generic drugs) (Velasquez & Boulet, 1999). Industry acknowledges that access to medicines in poorer countries is an issue but suggests that the "long-term donation programs instituted by pharmaceutical companies for such debilitating diseases as trachoma, filariasis and river blindness" (i.e., high profile GPPPs) provide a means to redress the access problem (Bale, 1999). Similarly, UN-industry partnerships are also seen as a solution to contentious issues arising out of the implementation of TRIPS, such as compulsory licensing (i.e., licenses issued by governments on public health grounds, authorizing third parties to manufacture a patented product without the consent of the patent holder). Some GPPPs have been promoted on the grounds of offering an alternative to compulsory licenses to protect the poor. For example, the Bristol-Myers Squib's partnership with UNAIDS and a variety of actors in southern Africa, known as 'Bridging the Gap,' has been cited as one way forward in lieu of compulsory licensing (*Chicago Tribune*, 1999). Furthermore, as mentioned above, a number of pharmaceutical companies have entered into a partnership to lower their prices for AIDS drugs for developing countries in an effort both to forestall the granting of compulsory licenses and to react to negative publicity (Gellman, 2000).

United Nations interests in global public-private partnerships

The interests that the United Nations and its organizations pursue through participation in GPPPs have already been alluded to. First, there is the financial imperative. Budgets throughout the system have been frozen and/or reduced. Partnership with the private sector enables the UN system to leverage its own resources and advice and to access new resources that enable it to fulfill its mandate. This carries weighty implications for the power and influence that the UN organizations bring to various partnership arrangements. Second, the UN has increasingly accepted the prevailing orthodoxy that suggests that partnership is the way to overcome market and government failure. It therefore has an interest in experimenting with partnership strategies and mechanisms that might overcome these failures to produce global public goods. Finally, in recognition of the rise of corporate power and influence, partnership allows the UN to maintain a voice in arrangements of global governance.

WHO's enthusiasm for partnership mirrors that of the UN. Nonetheless, WHO's approach is distinct because of its explicit focus on health—the specific health goals pursued by the organization as well as the underlying ethical values that support its mission (Buse, 2001). WHO tends to enter into partnerships which have well-defined and specific health outcomes such as those that are disease or risk-factor oriented. Through partnership with the commercial sector, WHO seeks (in addition to the broad motivations described above) to achieve a range of objectives that include:

- To encourage industry to adopt and abide by the universal health principles established in Health For All
- To facilitate universal delivery and access to existing essential drugs and health services
- To accelerate research and development of vaccines, diagnostics, and drugs for neglected diseases
- To prevent premature mortality, morbidity, and disability
- To encourage industry to develop 'healthier' products in ways that are less harmful to workers and the environment
- To integrate health in all sectors for sustainable development
- To absorb and acquire knowledge and expertise from the private sector
- To enhance the organization's image among constituencies hostile to the UN

Functions and Attributes of the United Nations— What Implications Partnership?

The preceding discussion suggests that public and private actors pursue a variety of interests through partnership, and that these may affect the particular objectives of any individual partnership. In that the partnering process may be transformative, it is arguable that the pursuit of the aforementioned interests may influence the work of either sector. Such influence may be positive or negative. Partnering, for example, may imbue the UN with entrepreneurial talent and business culture which some might argue may thereby improve its efficiency. Similarly, the business community may adopt norms and values espoused by the UN in relation to workers' rights or occupational health, for example. Alternatively, less beneficial outcomes from partnering might obtain. The values and norms of the UN might be captured or diluted, and its decision-making structures subject to commercial considerations. Business may become mired in public-sector bureaucratic procedures.

Although it is still unclear exactly how public-private partnerships between the United Nations and the for-profit sector will influence the work of the UN, this section explores some of the potential changes in relation to public health. The section is organized around a framework that proposes that multilateral organizations such as WHO play four critical functions with respect to global health, enabled, to varying degrees, by a variety of facilitating attributes. The manner in which partnership impinges upon these attributes constitutes the substance of this section (summarized in table 7.1). In presenting this idealized model of the functions of WHO, we are not suggesting that the organization has fulfilled them consistently in an effective and efficient manner. We fully acknowledge that the UN in general and WHO in particular have a variety of shortcomings that have inhibited them from fulfilling these functions (Godlee, 1994; Walt, 1996). However, we believe that every effort should be made to enable the UN to fulfill its potential and feel that attempts at reform of the organization of the past decade have been similarly motivated by such concern. We are also concerned that without due attention, global public-private partnerships may further compound the organization's difficulties.

GPPPs and normative frameworks

The United Nations' so-called Charter Model aims to organize world affairs according to the principle, among others, that nation-states are bound to a series of 'universal' norms and values (Cassese, 1986). The UN plays a prominent role in providing a platform for the discussion, negotiation, and promotion of these norms and values.

This role, however, is not without tension. Norms and values are culturally based and regularly contested. For example, in societies characterized by goals of universality and equity, based on principles of risk pooling and resource redistribution, citizens have different expectations of the state than do those in societies driven by individualism and markets, with collective response often limited to instances of market failure. Perhaps because of these underlying differences in norms and values, differences also exist in the perception of the legitimacy of close connections between the corporate world and the public sector. In European societies organized along principles of solidarity, for example, there has been greater separation and less interaction between public and private sectors

Table 7.1: Functions and attributes of the World Health Organization and how these might change through partnerships with the private sector

CRITICAL AND UNIQUE FUNCTIONS	ENABLING ATTRIBUTES	POSITIVE INFLUENCE OF PARTNERSHIP	NEGATIVE INFLUENCE OF PARTNERSHIP
WHO acts as the world's health conscience (e.g., human rights and equity), providing a moral framework and agenda for health.	Moral authority deriving from near universal membership. Constitution specifies concern for health of all peoples and special attention to needs of poor.	Partnerships may provide resources that enable WHO to promote its moral framework more forcefully. Partnerships may encourage for-profit entities to support WHO mission and values.	Function and attributes potentially undermined through value diffusion by more powerful private-sector interests.
Establishing global norms and standards	Legitimacy deriving from universality (particularly representation of poor countries and population groups), specialization, expert technical networks, and associated attributes of impartiality and neutrality.	Private sector may be more willing to abide by standards and norms elaborated through multilateral means if it has a voice in articulating them through its participation in partnerships.	Function potentially eroded if normative activities are shifted to GPPP expert committees where particularistic private interests may prevail.
Promotion and protection of the global commons (including creation of transnational public goods such as R&D capacity, information dissemination, and control of transnational externalities such as environmental risks, spread of pathogens, trade in illegal substances).	Mobilizing collective state action and resources through convening power and consensus building.	Enhanced for particular goods through access to additional resources from non-state actors. Potential to bring new resources into the control process. Potential to involve those private actors whose activities have the greatest impact on transnational externalities.	Depends on how private partner's interests are impacted by the creation of any good or control of any bad. Where conflicts of interest arise, private partners may seek to subordinate social and health standards to profit objectives thereby thwarting WHO objectives. May also entail shift to industry self-regulation.
Supportive cooperation at country level (particularly for unfashionable activities such as training and health systems support).	Reliant on members dues and bilateral (and other) donations to fulfill its mandate.	Potential to raise additional resources and engage additional partners to support health sector development in countries in greatest need.	EBF funding for country level activities may be reduced as 'profitable' activities hived off to GPPPs while difficult activities left with WHO. May lead to intercountry inequity as GPPPs focus on countries.

than in the United States. Thus the scope and extent of corporate philanthropy has differed. In Europe corporate philanthropy has a long tradition, but it has been low profile and relatively limited. In the United States corporate philanthropy has had a strong institutional presence and made significant investments in community and international development efforts.

Public and private sectors, similar to societies, social groups, and individuals, bring a number of different values to partnerships. At the one end of the continuum are the values of the UN: "Our main stock in trade . . . is to promote values: the universal values of equality, tolerance, freedom, and justice that are found in the UN Charter" (Annan, 1999). Also at this end of the continuum is WHO, with its concern for the health of the marginalized and dispossessed, and its claim to be the world's health conscience. WHO's values flow from its constitutional mandate, while its claims to promoting universally held values derive from its wide membership (the majority of nation-states).

At the other end of the continuum are the 'bottom line' values and interests to maximize profits so as to increase shareholder value that are reflected in company policies, although such values are increasingly framed within explicit goals of social responsibility. For example, the Royal Dutch Shell Group sees their role "not just as commercial operators, but as investors in communities, in people, in societies around the world." Irrespective of one's interpretation of such rhetoric, two caveats are in order. First, as stated above, the corporate sector is diverse, and among the socially responsible business entities are those whose activities have been highly criticized for pursuing profits by aggressive marketing or poor labor practices. Second, despite encouraging signs of enhanced corporate social responsibility, the primary responsibility of any commercial enterprise remains a fiduciary one to its owners.

There has been, therefore, great debate over whether or not—despite shared partnership goals—private and public interests are mutually compatible. Several mechanisms have been identified through which profit maximization may undermine the goal of better health (Hancock, 1998). Within partnerships, the question arises as to whether or not private sector values will ultimately dominate as the UN and industry move closer towards jointly defining their goals through GPPPs—and as the values of the weaker partner are captured by the more powerful. It is possible that WHO's emphasis on and advocacy for the marginalized and the poor will be displaced as resource-rich partnerships dictate organizational priorities and strategies. It has been suggested, for example, that

WHO's involvement in the Global Alliance for Vaccines and Immunizations (GAVI) has derailed the organization's commitment to equity in relation to the goal of universal vaccination with traditional vaccines as it joins with its partners in bringing 'new' vaccines to the relatively less hard to reach (Hardon, 2001). Similarly, it was argued that recent WHO-convened deliberations on breast-feeding were subject to censorship due, it is asserted, to considerations of the sensibilities of WHO's new commercial constituencies (Ferryman, 2000).

Alternatively, is it possible to ensure that core public and private identities and values are preserved as partnerships limit themselves to specific win-win situations? This will depend first on the selection of private partners. Hancock urges "sober second thoughts" regarding the suitability of the pharmaceutical industry as a partner for WHO, at least in terms of health promotion, because of "perceived or actual conflict of interests" (1998). Second, it will depend on the rules of engagement. In practice, given the financial imperatives that sometimes motivate UN organizations to enter into partnerships with the private sector (i.e., the stagnation of funding referred to above), they may find it difficult to refuse corporate offers that do not comply with internal guidelines.

Optimistically, many believe that increased interaction through partnership will be transformative in a more positive manner. In particular, that partnership will promote more socially responsible business entities and practices, which actively promote and uphold the values and norms enshrined within the UN Charter and subsequent conventions. And that some of the strategic, outcome-oriented methods of the private sector might be absorbed into the UN.

Establishing global norms and standards

The United Nations plays an important role in the area of developing normative standards governing activities in all spheres of social life—from shipping lanes to postal services. In the health sector, WHO has a mandate to develop standards (and international treaty law) in five areas: quarantine requirements; nomenclatures in respect to diseases, etc.; standards for diagnostics procedures; standards for safety, purity, and potencies of medications; and advertising, marketing, and labeling of health related goods. A series of attributes enable WHO to assume this role in global norm and standard setting, including relative legitimacy, technical competence and authority, impartiality, and neutrality. These attributes, which are in some ways interlinked, derive from and rest upon the governing arrangements of WHO. Partnerships with the commercial sector may entail reform of these arrangements and therefore raise questions of how to preserve these crucial attributes upon which global norms and standards are developed, particularly those which sustain or promote the ethical values described above. In relation to independent norm and standard setting within WHO, critics charge that partnership may subject WHO to commercial influences. It is argued, for example, that its impartiality was jeopardized during the elaboration of the Guidelines for the Management of Hypertension as a result of the influence of a firm that stood to benefit from them (Woodman, 1999).

Legitimacy concerns the extent to which authority is considered valid by those affected by it. Legitimacy confers upon its holder a recognized right to establish norms and standards. It is fair to argue that most UN organizations derive some of their legitimacy from near universal membership in their governing bodies. For example, the World Health Assembly is currently attended by 191 member states, all of which have equal voting rights irrespective of size of financial contribution. In contrast, representation in global public-private partnerships is both narrower and more eclectic. No health GPPP can claim near universal membership of nation states (which would make it unwieldy in any event), but, more importantly, few partnerships include low-income country representation, not all of them include WHO on their governing boards and technical committees, and in some cases it would appear that the private sector representation is ad hoc and based on personal contacts.

In recognition of the limitations of representative legitimacy, the legitimacy of many GPPPs will depend largely on the expert committees that are established to advise them. Whereas the specialized agencies of the UN, such as WHO, rely on extensive networks of technical experts and have established means for selecting and operating expert groups, there are concerns that GPPP expert groups may be chosen from exclusive epistemic communities, may (due to funding) suffer from a lack of independence, and may have circumscribed powers (Buse & Walt, 2000b).[2] Although many analysts have drawn attention to the extent to which international agenda setting and formulation of policy is controlled by transnational policy elites (Haas, 1992), the implications of the increasing prominence of the private sector in policy networks on global standard setting has yet to receive much attention (Cutler et al., 1999). Sell's (1999) detailed account of the role of twelve CEOs of US firms in drafting the WTO TRIPS Agreement provides an exception.

Partnerships also raise difficult questions in relation to competence and appropriateness. WHO has a constitutional mandate to coordinate international efforts in relation to health. This has always been a difficult task, one which will be made more difficult as the sector is further fragmented through the advent of numerous and sometimes competing partnerships and initiatives. By 2001, there were, for example, several partnerships focusing on malaria, on vaccinations, and on anti-retroviral drugs for HIV/AIDS. The strong emphasis on infectious diseases attracted attention and financial resources, putting other health issues into shadow and undermining any role WHO might have played in forging a coherent global agenda. Moreover, as global responsibility for specific health issues is transferred from WHO programs to GPPPs, there is some danger that WHO will fail to continue to establish expert groups on these issues so as not to duplicate the technical committees established under the aegis of the partnerships (whose membership is usually vetted by the corporate sponsors). This raises the specter of the erosion of WHO's normative function. Where the private sector assumes a greater voice through partnership in WHO technical discussions, will global standards and norms not begin to more closely reflect private interests, thereby jeopardizing their credibility? For example, if a malaria vaccine is developed under the sponsorship of the Medicines for Malaria Venture partnership, there may be a risk that process and product standards concerning any vaccines developed will be unnecessarily high, thus discriminating against low- and middle-income countries.

The global health commons

As noted in the introduction, the determinants of health as well as the means to address them are increasingly subject to transnational forces. It can, therefore, be argued that the imperative for nation-state collaboration to address problems of the global health commons is more compelling than ever. The promotion of global public goods (i.e., those which are nonexcludable, nonrival, and exhibit significant positive externalities), such as research and development on health, the generation and dissemination of knowledge, norms and regulatory standards, and the control of negative international externalities such as transborder spillover of environmental risks, drug resistance, etc., are therefore gaining increased attention. A central role for the United Nations has been proposed in relation to the protection and promotion of the global commons (Kaul et al., 1999). This role derives from its ability to convene a broad array of actors, develop consensus, and mobilize resources.

A number of GPPPs have been established to address problems of the global health commons (such as the Stop TB Initiative). Consequently, it can be argued that the addition of private resources through GPPPs further enables collective international action on critical public health issues. Private resources may be provided to partnerships directly which aim to promote global public goods, or partnerships may encourage private behavior that minimizes negative transnational externalities or promotes positive transborder spillovers. The challenge remains, however, to establish systems for priority setting that are fair and just with respect to which public goods to produce and which externalities to control. At present this is decided in a somewhat ad hoc and opportunistic manner.

Supportive cooperation at the country level

In a world marked by increasing inequalities, the United Nations also plays a role of protecting the health of vulnerable populations and providing development support (e.g., capacity development) in low-income countries. While WHO shares this role with a host of other agencies, its aid need not be conditional upon political and economic objectives (as is often the case with bilateral aid) and can therefore be allocated according to objective measures of need— although this is patently not always the case (Michaud & Murray, 1994). The WHO is able to play this role as a function of the dues it receives from its members and it can allocate these resources according to nonpartisan criteria as a function of its relatively 'apolitical' nature. Public-private partnerships can enable the UN to further its work in poor countries and populations as demonstrated by the success of the African Program for Onchocerciasis Control to deliver drugs to the poorest Africans in the most remote settings.

On the negative side, those countries that do not benefit from partnerships might feel abandoned by the global community. And partnerships may increase inequities within societies: for example, the World Alliance for Community Health, which includes Rio Tinto, Placer Dome and other multinational corporations, aided by WHO, is helping companies develop a "business plan" for health, "to improve health of firms as well as ordinary people." While potentially bringing better quality primary health services to workers and their families, such efforts may undermine universal health systems (*The Economist*, 1999). Worse yet, if activities that are in vogue are hived off to special partnerships, there is the potential that bilateral funds that might have been allocated to the UN may be redirected to GPPPs, thereby further imperiling the financial situation of the organizations, as well as undermining (or devaluing) government efforts, and possibly increasing inequity among countries.

There is also the danger that GPPPs focus on relatively narrow problems and solutions (drugs for malaria and TB, vaccines for HIV/AIDS) and pay insufficient attention to the strengthening of health service delivery systems, which are crucial if new proposals are to work. For example, Hardon (2001) has raised the concern that the Global Alliance on Vaccines and Immunization (GAVI) is focusing largely on the introduction of new vaccines to countries, while little attention and few funds have been allocated to making fragile health systems more effective. In such a situation, helping sustain health systems through training and support might be left to organizations such as WHO.

In summary, table 7.1 suggests that there are potential pros and cons of partnerships in relation to WHO. While partnerships may reinforce some of WHO's functions, the potential threats enumerated above in relation to the organization's mandate, the manner in which global norms and standards are established, and which global public goods and countries receive WHO support, suggest that some caution should be exercised in the partnering process. WHO performs very specific functions based on particular values, institutional characteristics, and decision-making processes. Uncritical support for poorly designed partnership initiatives may undermine WHO's functions and further fragment intergovernmental health cooperation. The extent to which a partnership may impinge upon the work of WHO will depend not only on the nature of the problems and resources available to address it, but also, to a great extent, on the institutional arrangements by which it is governed. These include the selection of partners, the composition of the governing bodies, balance of power among private and public parties, the mechanisms by which decisions are made, and the systems established to ensure accountability and transparency.

Partnerships and Governance

Governance can be defined as "the process whereby an organization or society steers itself" (Rosenau, 1995). Broadly speaking, governance comprises the systems of rules, norms, processes, and institutions through which power and decision making are exercised. Good governance is thought to be based upon: (1) representative legitimacy; (2) accountability; (3) competency and appropriateness; and (4) respect for due process (World Bank, 1994).

A number of challenges to good governance confront the UN as it enters into partnerships with the private, for-profit sector. For example, in relation to representative legitimacy, it would appear that GPPPs provide the commercial sector and purposely selected (predominantly northern) scientists with improved access to decision making within the UN, which is not matched for recipient countries, not-for-profit agencies, southern scientists, and other marginalized groups. This carries significant risks and will have to be handled with caution: "Opening up participation to a broader group of non-state actors and NGOs . . . there is a risk that institutions will simply increase access to representatives of US-based and European-based groups and further skew institutional participation and accountability away from the broader, more universal set of members" (Woods, 1999, p. 57).

Accountability, which is broadly concerned with being held responsible for one's actions, poses similar challenges. Public and private sectors have well-established mechanisms of accountability. In the private sector, management is accountable to the company's shareholders. In the public sector, administrative structures report to political structures, which are accountable to the ruled through the contestability of political power. We argued above that accountability within the UN rested upon representation of member states in its governing bodies. However, accountability within public-private partnerships may be less straightforward, partly because of the distance between the global partners and the beneficiaries and the length of time for any impact to be felt. Moreover, actually holding a partner accountable presents difficult challenges, as they are autonomous entities. Presently, systems of sanctions do not appear to have developed to apply to negligent partners. In a number of GPPPs, accountability appears to be predominantly oriented towards the commercial sponsors—e.g., the Mectizan Donation Program (Frost & Reich, 1998)—whereas in others, the management group reports to a governing body whose members report back to their respective organizations—e.g., the International Trachoma Initiative (J. Cook, personal communication, May 20, 1999).

In relation to competence and appropriateness, we have described how partnerships may shift the locus of technical groups outside of the remit of the UN organizations and how, through this process, global norms and standards may tend to more closely reflect private interests. We may also witness a brain-drain from WHO to 'competing' partnership institutions, which could affect the organization's capacity and technical authority. Due process, or the extent to which institutional regulations are observed, has yet to receive much attention in relation to the governance of GPPPs. Although WHO has developed provisional guidelines and a process for vetting partner companies, introduced conflict of interest forms, and established other internal procedures, these have provoked controversy—even among members of its executive board (WHO, 2001). While transparency of decision making to the public will be essential, conflicts of interest may well arise, with information controlled or censored. At present, although many high profile partnerships host a website and produce annual reports, these contain surprisingly little information on the arrangements through which the partnerships are governed.

Conclusions

Globalization necessitates novel arrangements for health governance in which international organizations and nation-states, as well as global and local private, for-profit, and civil society organizations work together. GPPPs provide one such mechanism—and an apparently popular one. While GPPPs have great positive potential they also raise a number of challenges in relation to the United Nations system, especially regarding the potential for further fragmentation of international health cooperation. UN organizations are well aware of some of these potential problems. Although positive towards GPPPs, UNICEF's present executive director has warned, "it is dangerous to assume that the goals of the private sector are somehow synonymous with those of the United Nations, because they most emphatically are not" (Bellamy, 1999). WHO's provisional guidelines on involvement with the commercial sector reflect this and other concerns, particularly those dealing with real and perceived conflicts of interest (WHO, 1999). As these guidelines fall short on a number of counts (Buse, 2001), there are grounds for a wider debate on a regulatory framework that can differentiate between acceptable and unacceptable GPPPs by ensuring that the former meet specific minimum conditions. Accrediting GPPPs may allay concerns of critics while benefiting private sponsors of partnerships as well.

Falk (1999) reminds us that "there is little, or no, normative agency associated with this emergent world order: it is virtually designer-free, a partial dystopia that is being formed spontaneously, and in the process endangering some of the achievements of early phases of statist world order." Greater thought needs to be given to how the present patchwork of alliances and partnerships in health move towards a system of 'good global governance' without losing their energy and creativity. How far is it realistic to work towards *a global health governance network* that would build on existing organizations, common values, and agreed regimes (Kickbusch & Buse, 2000)? Although we are in a period of exploration and experimentation, it is not too late to ensure that, within the patchwork, the critical functions and attributes of the World Health Organization elaborated in this chapter remain intact. More research and debate on how to safeguard these functions, establish criteria for acceptable partnerships, and design a legitimate oversight body will undoubtedly prove more challenging than bringing public and private actors together to act on neglected health concerns, but it will ultimately prove equally rewarding.

Notes

1. The WBCSD is a council of transnational corporations established to represent the interests of global corporations at the UN Conference on Environment and Development in Rio in 1992.
2. For example, the Technical Advisory Group of the International Trachoma Initiative was not consulted on the choice of recipient countries.

References

Annan, K. (1999, June 8). United Nations Secretary-General address to the United States Chamber of Commerce [Press release]. Washington, DC.

Auty, R. (1999, June 8). Remarks made at parallel session number 7.1 at the Third Global Forum for Health Research, Geneva.

Bale, H. (1999, April 24). The globalization of the fight against disease [Advertisement sponsored by Pfizer written by the director general of the International Federation of Pharmaceutical Manufactures Associations]. *The Economist*, p. 26.

Batson, A. (1998). Win-win interactions between the public and private sectors. *Nature Medicine Vaccine Supplement*, 4 (5), 487–491.

Beigbeder, Y. (1996, June 24–26). Another role for an NGO: Financing a WHO program—Rotary International and the eradication of poliomyelitis. Paper presented to 1996 ACUNS Ninth Annual Meeting, Turin, Italy, p. 8.

Bellamy, C. (1999). Public, private and civil society. Statement of UNICEF Executive Director to Harvard International Development Conference on 'Sharing responsibilities: public, private and civil society.' Cambridge, Mass, 16 April 1999. Available from: *http://www.unicef.org/exspeeches /99esps.htm*

BMS (1999, May 6). Bristol-Myers Squibb commits $100 million for HIV/AIDS research and community outreach in five African countries [Press release UN SG/SM/7022]. Washington, DC: Author.

Buse, K. & Walt, G. (2000a). Global public-private partnerships: Part 1—A new development in health? *Bulletin of the World Health Organization, 78*(4), 549–561.

Buse, K. & Walt G (2000b). Global public-private partnerships: Part II—What are the issues for global governance? *Bulletin of the World Health Organization, 78*(5), 699–709.

Buse, K. (2001). Partnering for better health? Ensuring health gains through improved governance: A strategy for WHO. *Bulletin of the World Health Organization*, forthcoming.

In praise of business alliances. (1999, October 25). *Business Week*, p. 106

Cassese, A. (1986). *International law in a divided world.* Oxford: Clarendon Press.

Cattaui, M. S. (1998a, August 3). Business and the UN: Common ground. *ICC Business World.*

Cattaui, M. S. (1998b, February 6). Business partnership forged on global economy [Press release]. Paris: ICC.

CEO (1998). The Geneva business dialogue. Business, WTO and UN: Joining hands to deregulate the global economy? [Online]. Available from: *www.globalpolicy.org/socecon/trncs/maucher.htm*

Editorial. (1999, June 15). *Chicago Tribune.*

Control Risks Group (1997). No hiding place: Business and the politics of pressure. Unpublished paper.

Cutler, A. C., Haufler, V., & Porter, T. (1999). Private authority and international affairs. In A. C. Cutler, V. Haufler, & T. Porter (Eds.), *Private authority and international affairs* (pp. 3–28). New York: SUNY.

Deutsch, D. H. (1999, December 10). Unlikely allies with the United Nations; for big companies, a strategic partnership opens doors in developing countries. *The New York Times*, p. C1.

Falk, R. (1999). *Predatory globalization: A critique.* Cambridge, U.K.: Polity Press.

Ferryman, A. (2000). WHO accused of stifling debate about infant feeding. *British Medical Journal, 320*, 1362.

Frost, L. & Reich, M. (1998). *Mectizan Donation Program: Origins, experiences, and relationships with coordinating bodies for onchocerciasis control.* Boston: Department of Population and International Health, Harvard School of Public Health.

Gellman, B. (2000, December 28). A turning point that left millions behind. *The Washington Post*, p. A1.

Giddens, A. (1998). *The third way: The renewal of social democracy*. Cambridge: Polity Press.

Godlee, F. (1994). The World Health Organization: WHO in crisis. *British Medical Journal, 309*, 1424–1428.

Haas, P. M. (1992). Epistemic communities and international policy coordinates. *International Organization, 46*, 1–35.

Hancock, T. (1998). Caveat partner: Reflections on partnership with the private sector. *Health Promotion International, 13*(3), 193.

Hardon, A. (2001). Immunization for all? A critical look at the first GAVI partners meeting. *HAI-Lights, 6*(1). Available from: *http://www.haiweb.org/highlights/mar2001*

Harrison, P. & Lederberg, J. (1997). *Orphans and incentives: Developing technologies to address emerging infections*. Washington, DC: Institute of Medicine, National Academy Press.

Held, D., McGuire, A., Goldbatt, D., & Perraton, J. (1999). *Global transformations: Politics, economics and culture*. Stanford: Stanford University Press.

Kaul, I., Grunberg, I., & Stern, M. A. (1999). *Global public goods: International cooperation in the twenty-first century*. Oxford: Oxford University Press.

Kickbusch, I. & Buse, K. (2000). Global influences and global responses: International health at the turn of the twenty-first century. In M. Merson, R. E. Black, & A. J. Mills (Eds.). *International Health*. Gaithersberg: Aspen.

Korten, D. (1997, July). The United Nations and the corporate agenda [Online]. Available from: *http://www.igc.org/globalpolicy/reform/korten.htm*.

Maucher, H. O. (1998, September 24). The Geneva business declaration. Geneva: ICC.

Maucher, H. O. (1997, December 6). Ruling by consent [Guest column]. *The Financial Times*, FT Exporter, p. 2.

McKinlay, J. B. & Marceau L. D. (2000). To boldly go . . . *American Journal of Public Health, 90*(1): 25–33.

Michaud, C. & Murray, C. J. L. (1994). External assistance to the health sector in developing countries: A detailed analysis, 1972–1990. *Bulletin of the World Health Organization, 72*(4), 639–651.

Mills, A. (1997). Leopard or chameleon? The changing character of international health economics. *Tropical Medicine and International Health, 2*(10), 963–977.

Mytelka, L. K. & Delapierre, M. (1999). Strategic partnerships, networked oligopolies and the state. In A. C. Cutler, V. Haufler, T. Porter (Eds.). *Private Authority and International Affairs* (pp. 129–149). New York: SUNY.

New, W. (2000, June 1). Special report: NGOs wary of UN corporate links. *UN Wire Business Weekly* [Online serial]. Available from: *http:// www.unfoundation.org/*

Reinicke, W. H. (1998). *Global public policy: Governing with government?* Washington, DC: Brookings Institution Press.

Reinicke, W. H. & Witte, J. M. (2001). Interdependence, globalization and sovereignty: The role of non-binding international legal accords. In D. H. Shelton (Ed.), *Commitment and compliance: The role of non-binding norms in the international legal system* (forthcoming). Oxford: Oxford University Press.

Repositioning the WHO (1998, May 9). *The Economist.*

Ridley, R., Gutteridge, W. E., & Currat, L. J. (1999, June 8–11). *New Medicines for Malaria Venture: A case study of the establishment of a public sector- private sector partnership.* Paper presented at the Third Global Forum for Health Research, Geneva.

Rosenau, J. N. (1995). Governance in the twenty-first century. *Global Governance, 1*(1), 13–43.

Sell, S. K . (1999). Multinational corporations as agents of change: The globalization of intellectual property rights. In A. C. Cutler, V. Haufler, & T. Porter (Eds.), *Private authority and international affairs* (pp. 169–197). New York: SUNY.

Slavin, T. (2001, April 5–11). The poor are consumers too. *Guardian Weekly*, p. 27.

United Nations (1998, February 9). Joint statement on common interests by UN secretary-general and International Chamber of Commerce [Press Release SG/2043]. New York: Author.

UNDP (1999). *Human development report.* Foreword. New York: Author.

UNDP (1998, July). *The global sustainable development facility.* Internal document. New York: Author.

Velasquez, G. & Boulet, P. (1999). Essential drugs in the new international economic environment. *Bulletin of the WHO, 77* (3), 288–291.

Waddell, S. (1999). The evolving strategic benefits for business in collaboration with nonprofits in civil society: a strategic resources, capabilities and competencies perspective. Providence, R.I.: Organizational Futures. Unpublished.

Walt, G. (1996). International organizations in health: The problem of leadership. Paper presented at Pocantico Retreat, Feb 1–3 1996. Rockefeller Foundation, Social Science Research Council, Harvard School of Public Health.

Walt, G. (2000). Global cooperation in international public health. In M. Merson, R. E. Black, & A. J. Mills (Eds.), *International Health*. Gaithersberg: Aspen.

Wapner, P. (1995). Politics beyond the state: Environmental activism and world civic politics. *World Politics, 47*, 311–340.

Wehrein, P. (1999, Summer). Pharmaco-philanthropy. *Harvard Public Health Review,* 32–39.

WHO (1999, July). *WHO guidelines on interaction with commercial enterprises* [Preliminary version]. Geneva: Author.

WHO (1946). Constitution of the World Health Organization. Geneva: Author.

WHO (2001, January 22). Minutes of the twelfth meeting of the WHO's executive board. Document EB 107/SR/12.

Woodman, R. (1999). Open letter disputes WHO hypertension guidelines. *British Medical Journal, 318*, 893.

Woods, N. (1999). Good governance in international organizations. *Global Governance, 5*, 39–61.

World Bank (1994). Governance: The World Bank's experience. Washington, DC: Author.

Contributors

James E. Austin is McLean Professor of Business Administration and chair of the Initiative on Social Enterprise at Harvard Business School. Professor Austin's current research concentrates on collaboration among nonprofits, businesses, and government.

Diana Barrett is Senior Lecturer in the area Social Enterprise at the Harvard Business School. She received both her M.B.A. and doctorate from Harvard Business School. Her research interests are in the area of corporate involvement in social sector activities.

A. G. Breitenstein is currently a doctoral candidate at the Harvard School of Public Health. Ms. Breitenstein's research focuses on the role of process and engagement in ethical discourse.

Kent Buse is Assistant Professor of International Health in the Department of Epidemiology and Public Health at Yale University School of Medicine. He is presently involved in a comparative analysis of the policies, guidelines, and implementation procedures of the World Bank, UNICEF, UNFPA, UNAIDS and WHO in relation to their interaction with the commercial sector.

Laura Frost is a doctoral student in the Department of Population and International Health at the Harvard School of Public Health, and is an Irish Health Research Board Health Services Research Fellow at University College Cork, Ireland. Her research focuses on international health policy, including a study of the international campaign to eliminate trachoma and an examination of breastfeeding promotion in Ireland.

Tomoko Fujisaki is a representative for Management Sciences for Health, Inc., in Japan. Her current research focuses on health commodity management in developing countries, Japanese international development assistance in the health sector, and the role of nonprofit organizations in international cooperation.

Adetokunbo O. Lucas is Adjunct Professor of International Health, Harvard School of Public Health, and was formerly a professor in the Department of Preventive and Social Medicine of the University of Ibadan, Nigeria. His research has focused on clinical and epidemiological features of parasitic and tropical diseases and the promotion of health research. He currently chairs the Global Forum for Health Research, a new entity that was established to promote international health research.

Sheila M. McCarthy is a research associate at the Harvard Business School. Ms. McCarthy is currently collaborating with Professor Diana Barrett on research related to business leadership in the social sector.

William Muraskin is Professor in the Department of Urban Studies, Queens College, City University of New York. Professor Muraskin is currently working under a grant from the Rockefeller Foundation to study the origin and development of the Bill and Melinda Gates Children's Vaccine Program, the Global Alliance for Vaccines and Immunization (GAVI), and the Vaccine Fund.

Michael R. Reich is the Taro Takemi Professor of International Health Policy at the Harvard School of Public Health, and director of the Harvard Center for Population and Development Studies. He received his doctorate in political science and has research interests in the politics of health and development policy, with particular attention to pharmaceuticals.

Marc J. Roberts is Professor of Political Economy and Health Policy at the Harvard School of Public Health. Educated originally as an economist, he has served as a consultant to and trainer for health care organizations and governments around the world on issues of organizational change and health care reform.

Clement S. Roberts is a lawyer with the San Francisco law firm of Kecker and Van Ness. He has taught moral and political philosophy at both the undergraduate and graduate levels.

Gill Walt is Professor of International Health Policy at the London School of Hygiene and Tropical Medicine. Her current research focuses on policy transfer between international and national jurisdictions, especially in relation to tuberculosis and sexually transmitted diseases, and on the growth and implications for international health policy of global public-private partnerships.

Index

R

Resource mobilization, 4, 186
Rights and responsibilities, 4, 68, 178
Rockefeller Foundation, 2, 7, 91, 115, 131–155
Roll Back Malaria, 7, 150

S

SAFE strategy, 30, 43, 52
Schistosomiasis, 9, 20, 80, 129
Schumpter, Joseph, 71
SmithKline Beecham, 30, 88, 138, 143, 153
Social capital, 12, 81
Social worlds theory, 87, 90
Sovereignty, 171
Steere Jr., William, 49
Stop TB Initiative, 186
Strategic alliances, 41, 47, 54
Strategic integration, 42, 56

T

Task Force for Child Survival and Development, 10, 33, 90
Tetracycline, 30, 44
Tiered pricing for vaccines, 132
Trachoma, 30, 42
    Expert Committee (TEC), 57
    Morocco Pilot control program, 45
    SAFE strategy, 30, 43, 52
Trade-Related Aspects of Intellectual Property Rights (TRIPS), 178–179
Transparency, 15
    accountability and, 3, 188

Tropical Disease Research Program (TDR), 8, 19, 98
    diseases included, 20
    experience with public-private partnerships, 24, 98
    Joint Coordinating Board, 22
    lessons learned, 36
    new products created, 24, 27
    research and development effort, 20, 22
Tropical diseases, 8
    investment in, 174
Trust, 11, 102
    between partners, 47, 108
Trypanosomiasis, 7, 20, 26
Tuberculosis, 15, 21, 80, 129, 174

U

United Nations (UN), 169–191
    accountability of partnerships, 14
    financial impetus to join partnerships, 173
    interests in private-sector partnerships, 175, 179
    outcomes of partnering, 180
    public-private partnerships and, 3, 170, 183
United Nations Development Programme (UNDP), 8, 19, 91, 115, 140, 172, 178

V

Vaccine(s)
    as capital investments, 143
    as public goods, 156